Of Time
and Judicial Behavior

Of Time
and Judicial Behavior

United States Supreme Court
Agenda-Setting and Decision-Making,
1888–1997

Drew Noble Lanier

Selinsgrove: Susquehanna University Press
London: Associated University Presses

Associated University Presses
2010 Eastpark Boulevard
Cranbury, NJ 08512

Associated University Presses
Unit 304, The Chandlery
50 Westminster Bridge Road, London SE1 7QY, England

Associated University Presses
P.O. Box 338, Port Credit
Mississauga, Ontario
Canada L5G 4L8

The paper used in this publication meets the requirements of the American National Standard for Permanence of Paper for Printed Library Materials Z39.48-1984.

Library of Congress Cataloging-in-Publication Data

Lanier, Drew Noble, 1962–
   Of time and judicial behavior : United States Supreme Court
agenda-setting and decision-making, 1888–1997 / Drew Noble Lanier.
      p. cm.
   Includes bibliographical references and index.
   ISBN 1-57591-067-5 (alk. paper)
   1. United States. Supreme Court—History. 2. Judicial process—United
States—History. 3. Constitutional history—United States. I. Title.
KF8742.L364 2003
347.73'26'09—dc21

                                                                    2002155202

PRINTED IN THE UNITED STATES OF AMERICA

For Allison,
who teaches me about Love every day

Contents

Illustrations

Tables

Acknowledgments

There have been many people whose help made the completion of this book possible. First, the love, support, kindness, and generosity of my parents, J. E. and Jeannine Lanier, were key to my completing this work and my education in general. Their love for knowledge and learning provided me the motivation to earn education's highest degree. My father's analytical way in particular provided me an environment in which to sharpen my own cognitive skills. These have been greatly helpful in the completion of this study.

Second, the unbelievable patience, high standards, good nature, and humor of my mentor, Dr. C. Neal Tate, have carried me through the ordeal of completing this study. He prodded me when I was simply not working up to the level that he, thankfully, knew that I could do. He has made a tough road a little bit easier. I certainly hope that I can learn from his example as a scholar, teacher, and supervisor of future graduate students.

Third, the kindness, warmth, intelligence, and generosity of Dr. Frank Feigert have helped me immeasurably during the nearly five years that this work has taken to complete, especially during a particularly bleak time of my life. His love of politics inspired me as a teacher and as a scholar. His genuine friendship (if a professor ever can be a graduate student's friend) is heartily appreciated and has made this study easier to complete.

Fourth, this study could not have been completed without the work of three of my colleagues: Sandra L. Wood, Linda Camp Keith, and Ayo Ogundele. Each of them helped code the bulk of the data on which the analyses done in this work are based. Without their diligence, the data most likely would not have been collected. I extend my dearest thanks to them for their efforts and their approval for me to use the data that we collected. They, of course, bear no responsibility for any of the analyses conducted in the study.

Fifth, the data utilized in this work were made available in part by the Inter-university Consortium for Political and Social Research. The data for

United States Supreme Court Judicial Database, 1953–1997 Terms were originally collected by Harold J. Spaeth. Neither the collector of the original data nor the Consortium bears any responsibility for the analyses or interpretations presented here.

And most importantly, my wife, Allison, has been an unending source of support and kindness, even when I really did not deserve either.

Of Time
and Judicial Behavior

1

The Decision-Making and Agenda-Setting of the United States Supreme Court, 1888–1997

Purpose, Outline, and Importance of the Book

THE MOST IMPORTANT WORK ON THE UNITED STATES SUPREME COURT THAT scholars have done in the subfield of judicial politics has been limited to analyses of the Courts composed after the end of the Second World War. This study investigates the earlier Courts much more systematically than they have been studied to date, and it analyzes the shape of and influences on their agenda-setting mechanism and decision-making. It thereby provides a base against which the findings for the post-1945 Court can be compared and a more comprehensive analysis for explaining and predicting the general political behavior of the Court and its members.

In particular, building on the works of Richard Pacelle and Gerhard Casper and Richard Posner, this study investigates the change in the issues that the Court considers, and their relative share of its decision-making agenda, beginning in 1888 and extending through 1997.[1] Analytical emphasis is placed on the pre-1945 period, since it has been less thoroughly studied than the post-1945 years. The study also examines the liberalism of the Court's decisions and its determinants across major issue areas, providing a more complete picture of the agenda-setting and decisional trends of the Court across the same period. Hence, this study provides a bridge to link the studies of the post-1945 Court with a more comprehensive and systematic study of the Court's agenda-setting and decision-making in prior years, thus providing an analysis of over a century of Supreme Court behavior.

17

THE UNITED STATES SUPREME COURT AND ITS DECISION-MAKING AND AGENDA-SETTING

The United States Supreme Court and Politics

The United States Supreme Court has captured judicial politics scholars' attention for many years, beginning most notably with C. Herman Pritchett's *Roosevelt Court*.[2] Pritchett's work formally inaugurated judicial politics as a subfield. It systematically analyzes for the first time the personal influences on the justices' decision-making, thereby indicating the political nature of the Court's role within the American system of governance. Later, Glendon Schubert's *Judicial Mind* and *Judicial Mind Revisited* analyze the attitudes and ideologies of the Supreme Court justices from the Vinson Court through the Warren Court so as to understand more clearly the psychological basis of their decision-making.[3] More recent work extends this notion of attitudinal influences beyond the Warren Court to include the Burger and Rehnquist Courts.[4]

A second aspect of the behavior of the Supreme Court that has received scholarly attention is its agenda-setting process. By issuing rulings, the Court proclaims the issues that it will resolve, thereby greatly affecting the contour of American politics. Pacelle examines this aspect of the Court's behavior from the time of Franklin D. Roosevelt to that of Ronald Reagan.[5] However, no other scholars have sought to extend Pacelle's analysis to periods prior to the Roosevelt Court. Indeed, Charles R. Epp laments "[b]ecause systematic data on the Court's agenda are available only after 1932, [analyses of the Court's agenda composition] miss important changes before that year."[6] Such inquires are important because the Court is a countermajoritarian institution beyond direct control of the electorate and, thus, its workings and the influences affecting its members' behavior should be carefully examined.[7]

The Supreme Court's Agenda-Setting Process

By examining the composition of the Court's agenda, we can more clearly understand its priorities across time. Casper and Posner take a long-term perspective on the Court's agenda.[8] They advance a theory of the caseload change of the Supreme Court and criticize Paul A. Freund's argument[9] that asserts that the number of cases that the Court hears will be positively associated with the size of the nation's population and the growth of the economy.[10] As those two factors increase, the number of cases on the Court's docket will increase, Freund argues.

Casper and Posner, on the other hand, assert that first, the primary behavior underlying legal disputes will affect the frequency of those disputes.[11] As the number of labor strikes or government contracts increase, for example, so will the number of cases filed in the Court dealing with them. Second, the relative costs of litigation affect the incidence of cases. Not surprisingly, the higher the costs, the fewer cases filed. Third, the uncertainty of the law can cause cases to be filed, since the parties are unsure of the state of the law. Uncertainty can increase "the difficulty of arriving at a mutually attractive settlement by complicating the prediction of the outcome of litigation."[12] Fourth, the stakes that the parties have in the case can determine the number of cases filed. These stakes can "magnify any differences between the parties with respect to the settlement terms, relative to the costs of litigation."[13] If a party has a very large financial or personal stake in the outcome of his or her case, then he or she may be less willing to settle the matter and, thus, more likely to pursue Supreme Court review. Fifth, the amount of previous litigation can decrease the frequency of cases filed because previous rulings serve as precedents for cases filed later.[14] Hence, Casper and Posner argue that Freund's theory of a monotonic increase in the workload of the Court due to an increase in the broad social trends of population and economic growth is simply inaccurate. A multivariate function, therefore, more accurately describes the increase or decrease in the Court's docket over time.

Analyzing the Court's caseload during the period after the Civil War, the authors find that it was increasing largely due to acts of Congress enlarging the Court's jurisdiction. First, the Act of March 3, 1875 gave the federal courts for the first time general federal-question jurisdiction.[15] Second, in 1889, Congress authorized the Court to review criminal defendants' convictions in capital cases. In 1891, Congress extended this right of review to all cases of "infamous crimes," which included all cases in which the accused could be sentenced to prison.[16] Moreover, the Court itself contributed to its ever-growing docket by reversing state court decisions that had invalidated contracts that previous state decisions had authorized.[17]

By 1890, the number of cases seeking space on the Court's limited docket was 1800. This massive burden led the Congress to establish the Federal Circuit Courts of Appeals in the Act of March 3, 1891.[18] Until then, the Court had largely served as an appellate court for the state courts. However, the creation of the circuit courts was only a stopgap measure because of the increased demands on the Court's resources due to challenges to burgeoning federal legislation around 1900. Also, the Court decisions striking down as unconstitutional social and economic legislation of the day led to an ever-larger docket.[19]

After the creation of the Circuit Courts in 1891, the Court's discretionary jurisdiction began to expand with several acts of Congress, notably the

Judiciary Act of 1925.[20] The Judges' Bill, as the 1925 act became known, gave the Court for the first time the power to grant certiorari only in cases that the justices deemed to be worthy of the Court's review.[21] The primary purpose of the act was to limit the Court's ever-growing docket. It did so, with the result that by 1930 discretionary decisions comprised 85 percent of the Court's total jurisdiction, thereby giving the Court a powerful tool to whittle down the items claiming space on its limited docket and allow it to concentrate on cases involving constitutional questions.[22]

In empirically analyzing the Court's docket from 1956 to 1973, Casper and Posner find that what has driven a large part of the growth in the Court's workload responsibilities is the number of criminal cases. "In 1956, 48 percent of the docket was criminal; by 1973 the figure was 62 percent."[23] The growth of the criminal docket itself is due in part to a large increase in the number of federal criminal cases, itself increasing by 345 percent.[24] These cases alone account for 54 percent of the docket's growth over the period studied. Also, a very important factor in the growth of the criminal portion of the Court's docket was the Criminal Justice Act of 1964. It provided that persons convicted of federal crimes could seek appellate review at public expense. In the eight years following the act's passage, the number of federal criminal appeals grew by 314 percent.[25]

However, the growth in the number of state criminal appeals outpaced even the phenomenal growth of the federal criminal docket. Casper and Posner attribute this change in the composition of the Court's workload to, at least in part, the jurisprudence of the Warren Court, which expanded the fundamental rights of the Constitution that are applied to the states through the Due Process Clause of the Fourteenth Amendment.[26]

On the civil side of the Court's docket, Casper and Posner find that it has increased by 61 percent during the time of their study.[27] A significant portion of the overall growth of the Court's docket is due to an increasing number of constitutional cases filed. From 1956 to 1973, there was an increase of 188 percent in the number of constitutional cases as compared to nonconstitutional cases.[28] If both the criminal and the civil dockets are examined, the authors find that the number of constitutional cases doubled during the roughly twenty years of the study. As of 1973, constitutional cases comprised about two-thirds of the Court's overall docket.[29]

A major factor driving the substantial increase in the civil docket until 1973 is the Court's expansive interpretation of the Equal Protection Clause and Congress's enactment of civil rights statutes. Casper and Posner, thus, assert that when there is a confluence of an increase in the activities underlying litigation and an expansion of personal rights, the Court's docket will increase as a result, so as to allow the Court to resolve the conflicts that the legal hierarchy and the larger society itself cannot resolve.[30] Hence, the authors reject Freund's theory as too simplistic and argue that what has primarily affected the size and composition of the Court's docket is changes in the law.[31]

Notably, Casper and Posner conduct their analyses of the Court's workload over time. By doing so, they are able to discern the particular effects of influential factors. For example, they are able to trace the effect of the Criminal Justice Act of 1964 on the composition of the Court's docket. Their findings thus lead other scholars to build more generalizable models of the Court's agenda-setting process.

The leading example of such a theory-based analysis of the Supreme Court's agenda is that of Pacelle.[32] Pacelle systematically investigates the agenda-setting of the Supreme Court from the Roosevelt era to the Reagan era. Pacelle theorizes that its agenda is driven by three sets of factors: goals, rules, and situations.[33] The goals are those of the individual justices and their attitudes about what is proper public policy. The rules are the formal processes, procedures, and norms that underlie the judicial process. One such norm is that of role orientation.[34] The situations are the contextual conditions in which the Court is acting. The 1930s and FDR's New Deal provided a very favorable atmosphere in which the Court could expand its policymaking role, for example.[35]

These three elements, Pacelle argues, combined to influence the Stone Court (1941–46) in particular not to be an advocate of civil liberties.[36] First, the individual members of the Court themselves opposed the expansion of civil liberties. Although Hugo Black was a strong supporter of civil liberties, many of the remaining members (Harlan Stone, Owen Roberts, Stanley Reed, Felix Frankfurter, James Byrnes, Robert Jackson, and Harold Burton) were not strong advocates of such claims. Second, the dictates of the judicial role required that the Court hear those cases that caused conflict among the courts below; these cases raised issues of regulatory power rather than civil liberties. Third, an important situational factor that caused a decline in support for civil liberties claims was the outbreak of the Second World War and a naturally heightened suspicion of allowing increased liberty in such times. Pacelle argues these factors can help promote an issue on the Court's agenda as well.[37]

Pacelle conceptualizes the Court's agenda as being composed of two parts: the exigent and the volitional agendas.[38] As the names imply, the exigent agenda is composed of issues that require the Court's attention; for example, the Court must hear a case to resolve conflict among the courts below it. During the period from 1938 to 1952, in particular, economics cases comprised a large percentage of the Court's exigent agenda because of the institutional imperative to resolve issues necessary to ensure the smooth operation of the overall judicial administrative hierarchy. The volitional agenda, on the other hand, is composed of those cases that help to fulfill the policy goals of some or all of the Court's members.[39] For example, the volitional agenda was composed of civil liberties items during the latter part of the Warren Court because the justices themselves had rational, policy goals to advance, even though concerns of judicial administration or the dictates of the judicial role did not require such issues to be addressed.[40]

Because of the strictures of the American judicial process, and in particular the case or controversy requirement of Article III of the Constitution, the justices cannot advance their policy goals alone.[41] They must wait for a case to enter the judicial process before they can act. The justices must be concerned about stability and consistency in the law as well.[42] These elements of the judicial role tend to restrict the discretion that the justices possess to implement their policy views through the Court's agenda.

Pacelle suggests that they are greatly assisted in their endeavors by policy entrepreneurs (such as interest groups), who seek to advance a particular policy agenda themselves.[43] They do so through filing petitions for certiorari (cert.). The number of groups that file cert. petitions in a particular case implicitly indicates to the justices the importance of the case to the larger society. Such actions provide a cue to the justices that they should include that issue or case on the Court's agenda.[44] Thus, there is a rational basis underlying the Court's agenda-setting process, since the justices and the external policy entrepreneurs attempt to link similar issues with related policy pronouncements and thereby advance their respective policy goals.[45]

Once the case has been filed, the justices do not follow a lockstep process in their consideration of the case. They may demonstrate what Pacelle calls "issue fluidity," by expanding or contracting the issue involved in a case, depending on their particular policy goals.[46] Issue expansion involves opening agenda space to consider a theretofore unconsidered issue, a prime example of which is *Gideon v. Wainwright*.[47] Pacelle suggests that a new issue area is almost always a function of related policy areas; these are known as "policy windows."[48] Occasionally, different issues areas will result in a new policy area being initiated; these are known as "spillover effects."[49] For example, the government's power to regulate in economics cases and the increasing frequency of U.S. regulation under the rubric of federalism led to the emergence of cases dealing with related substantive areas of regulation, including such areas as labor relations, securities regulation, energy, and communications, while general regulation issues began to wane.[50] In time, labor relations cases led the Court to hear cases dealing with First Amendment questions; regulation cases led to concerns of due process being considered.[51] This is a process that Pacelle describes as "horizontal spillover." Hence, rather than creating novel issues out of wholly new cloth, the Court often combines previously considered issues into novel ones, the development of which depends on situational and conditional factors.[52]

The primary mechanism of inaugurating such policy change is through landmark decisions.[53] Agenda change is also affected by flux in the membership on the Court, since this influences the ideological mix of the justices.[54] Additionally, the cases that the justices select to hear, and the language and tone of the opinions, provide cues to litigants and lower courts concerning the direction that Supreme Court policy will likely take in the future. The Court's opinions, hence, lead policy entrepreneurs to file further cases, and the Court to hand down subsequent opinions, in a process that highlights the evolution of issues affecting American politics.[55] Thus, the dynamics of the Court's agenda-setting mechanism describe an iterative, incremental process involving organized litigant groups and the justices themselves attempting to engineer policy change within the constraints of the institutional norms and structures of the American judicial process.

Substantively, Pacelle finds that the Court's agenda has historically been composed of two main elements since the 1930s: civil liberties–civil rights and economics. Up until the 1960s, its agenda was dominated by economics cases, with very few civil liberties–civil rights issues being brought to the Court.[56] But by 1964, economic cases comprised only 20 percent of the cases that the Court heard. This trend has continued, with such cases constituting only 10 percent of the contemporary agenda.[57]

When the Court upheld the government's exercise of power in economic and regulation decisions, it opened a window to incorporate the protections of the Bill of Rights into the Fourteenth amendment. Slowly, the Court began to devote an increasing proportion of its agenda to questions of substantive individual liberties and rights rather than simply notions of due process, and, thus, a decreasing proportion of economics cases was observed.[58] In the civil liberties–civil rights domain, Pacelle argues that the Supreme Court became the primary policymaker and, in doing so, fundamentally transformed its role in the American political system and indeed the overall complexion of American politics.[59]

Robert G. McCloskey also provides an inspired examination of the history of the Supreme Court.[60] Pacelle's results confirm, in part, McCloskey's observations about the transformation of the issues that the Court has considered since it began and the existence of three distinct periods of Supreme Court jurisprudence: 1787 to 1865 (dealing with issues of nationalism); 1865 to 1954 (dealing with issues of economics); and 1954 to the present (dealing with issues of civil liberties and civil rights).

Determinants of Supreme Court Decision-Making

The majority of the contemporary studies investigating aspects of the Supreme Court's political behavior have focused on the period after the end of World

War II. These analyses may have been completed because of the ready availability of data, a concern with more contemporary matters, or simply a desire to study the most recent eras of the Court's behavior. While these inquiries are certainly important, they do not analyze the important trends of, and influences on, the Court's behavior in earlier periods, which may be entirely distinct in form and character from the post-1945 period.

STUDIES OF THE POST-1945 PERIOD

Based in part on the pioneering work of Pritchett, Schubert's *Judicial Mind* was perhaps the first major empirical study of the influence of the attitudes and ideologies on the behavior of the Supreme Court justices in the post-1945 period.[61] Schubert examined nonunanimous decisions that the Court handed down from the October term of 1946 to the end of the annual term in June 1963.[62] Using Harold Laswell's study as a foundation,[63] Schubert theorizes in his "psychometric model" that Supreme Court justices play political roles in the American system that allow them to displace their "private motives on public objects for which [they] then provide a rationalization in terms of public interest."[64] They seek to effectuate their own attitudes in terms of public policy by using their voting behavior as institutionally sanctioned vehicles in cases that come before the Court; they implement their political beliefs, therefore, through their decision-making. Because the justices' attitudes cannot themselves be directly observed, Schubert states that scholars must gain more knowledge about them through indirect methods: observation of the justices' discernible voting behavior.[65] If there are consistent regularities in the justices' manifest decision-making behavior, then, Schubert asserts, scholars can validly infer that these regularities are being produced by constrained and organized syndromes of psychological variables known as attitudes or values.[66] Schubert posits that each justice's large-scale social views could be represented by an ideal point along a liberal-conservative continuum that reflects the best approximation of the collection of the justice's own values or attitudes and, thus, the justices' view of an ideal policy. This ideal, or i point, was compared with a stimulus point, j, that reflected the most salient issues present in a particular case the Court was considering.[67] The distance between the justices' individual ideal points is hypothesized to be a function of their ideological differences relative to the substance of their underlying psychological dimension.[68] "Differences in ideology (which are differences in their attitudes toward particular issue aggregates) cause the justices to vote differently in decisions of the Court in which such issues are at stake. The votes of the Supreme Court justices are, therefore, articulations of ideological differences."[69] Hence, Schubert theorizes that the justices' ideologies affect their voting behavior.

Therefore, some thirty years prior to Jeffrey A. Segal and Harold J. Spaeth's publication, Schubert blazed a trail in judicial politics research that still is being followed by scholars positing an attitudinal model of decision-making.

If an ideal point was farther along one of three dimensions than was the corresponding stimulus point, then the justice's attitudes on that particular issue would be scored positive and its manifestation, his or her vote, would reflect a relatively liberal ideology. Similarly, if the justice's ideal point was not as far along the continuum as was the stimulus point, then the vote, the empirical manifestation of his or her attitudes, were scored negative, reflecting a relatively conservative ideology.[70] By investigating the distance between the justices' individual ideal points estimated from their votes, this methodology allows Schubert to rank the justices based upon their relative support for the issue represented in the stimulus point.[71]

Schubert discovers that there were two major dimensions underlying the decision-making of the justices. He labels these dimensions the "C" scale, measuring the justices' support for civil liberties claims,[72] and the "E" scale, measuring support for governmental regulation of the economy and for the interests of the economically underprivileged against those of the economically well-off.[73] He finds these two dimensions to be consistent and stable across issues and justices.[74] He concludes that these dimensions, therefore, represent a manifestation of the latent attitudinal structure of the justices themselves that provide a window on their ideologies and, hence, their comparable liberalism.[75] By virtue of this rather complex methodology, Schubert succeeds in indirectly measuring a fundamental influence on the behavior of the Court members and discovers a powerful explanation for their voting. Rather than simply asserting that the facts of the case and the law are exclusively influential, as legalistic explanations had asserted, Schubert demonstrates that the justices' attitudes and ideologies are indeed important factors in their decision-making.

Moreover, Schubert finds that the justices' scores are consistently aligned on these two scales. This finding suggests two important hypotheses: (1) the justices' voting behavior has a latent structure, in which the attitudes underlying the C and the E scales have a constrained and consistent relationship; and, (2) the subsets of the justices are the manifestation of fundamental attitudinal types in such a latent structure.[76] "There is indeed a universe of psychological content that might be called liberalism, but that it is not sufficiently homogenous to permit us to speak of an attitude of liberalism even though we might well speak of an ideology of liberalism."[77] Therefore, Schubert theorizes that the fundamental factor explaining the variance in Supreme Court decision-making is the differing content of the justices' ideologies rather than their discrete attitudes about particular issues of public policy. Their scores on the political and economic liberalism scales are, thus, functions of this fundamental psychological construct.

However, Schubert's methodology of factor analyzing the decisions, creating axes from the underlying scales and then manually rotating them is problematic because there was (at the time of Schubert's original study) no commonly accepted standard for the correlation between the axes or the manner in which they were rotated. This lack of a standard is problematic because the relationship between the axes and the justices' relative position on them demonstrate the scales' validity and, in turn, that of Schubert's conclusions based on the Court members' cumulative scale rankings.[78] In *The Judicial Mind Revisited*, Schubert extends the period analyzed through the end of the Warren Court (1969); he essentially confirms his earlier study's findings concerning the two major scales (the C scale and the E scale) underlying Supreme Court decision-making.

A recent influential attempt to demonstrate attitudinal influences on the post-1945 Court's decision-making more clearly is Segal and Spaeth's study.[79] Segal and Spaeth argue that justices' votes are largely influenced by their own attitudes towards public policy questions. The attitudinal model is contrasted with the legal model, which asserts that the justices decide cases by simply examining the facts, dispassionately applying the law to them, and coming to a ruling.[80] Segal and Spaeth allege that the justices' public support of the legal model is simply designed to obfuscate their efforts to write their policy views into the law.

Segal and Spaeth provide several measures to demonstrate the validity of their model. Segal and Spaeth use computed scores of the justices' ideologies to predict their voting behavior. The methodology, developed by Segal and Albert D. Cover, involves content analysis of newspaper editorials written about the justices between the time that they were appointed and their confirmation to the Court.[81] The authors read the editorials and assigned a score ranging from most conservative (-1) to most liberal (1).[82] Segal and Spaeth correlate these scores with the justices' voting behavior and find a rather strong correlation.[83] They also specify a multivariate model that includes the facts of the case the justices decided and their ideological scores. They find that the influence of the justices' attitudes is significant.[84] Further, there is a "marked difference separat[ing] the liberally inclined from the other justices."[85] Therefore, the attitudinal model is explanatory of Supreme Court behavior, Segal and Spaeth argue, because if the legal model were truly explanatory, the justices (having been exposed to the same set of facts) would have all voted the same way consistently over time.

However, Segal and Spaeth's findings may not be entirely explanatory of overall Supreme Court voting behavior. Segal, Lee Epstein, Charles M.

Cameron, and Spaeth attempt to extend the methodology that Segal and Spaeth employ back in time, and find that the relationship between the measure of the justices' attitudes and their voting behavior is less impressive for the justices who served during the Roosevelt and Truman eras than for those in more contemporary periods.[86] Moreover, Epstein and Carol Mershon find that the use of Segal and Cover scores, as a measure of the justices' attitudes, in studies predicting votes in issue areas other than civil liberties–civil rights is problematic and therefore caution scholars not to use that protocol for measuring the justices' ideologies in predicting votes in issue areas other than civil liberties–civil rights, the area for which Segal and Cover originally developed the scoring metric.[87]

C. Neal Tate and Tate and Roger Handberg provide an alternative protocol for assessing justices' attitudes.[88] They do so through the use of personal attribute models. Personal attribute theory suggests that one's personal attributes (e.g., party identification, regional origins, prior professional experience) greatly affect and shape's one worldview, thereby influencing one's attitudes.[89] Because attitudes are so difficult to measure directly, Tate and Tate and Handberg employ attributes as surrogates for attitudes themselves because these data are much more readily available and manipulable than the attitudinal data themselves.

Tate finds a strong association between a justice's social attributes and his voting in civil liberties and economics decisions.[90] This author's model of civil liberties decision-making, for example, includes the justices' prior prosecutorial experience. He theorizes that if a justice had such a prior career, then he would be more likely to vote in the conservative direction in civil liberties–civil rights decisions (that is, against the claim of civil liberties) because such experience is associated with a greater likelihood of favoring the government's interests.[91] Overall, Tate's models explain 61 and 82 percent of the variance of the dependent variable for the economics cases and civil liberties–civil rights cases, respectively.[92]

However, S. Sidney Ulmer challenges Tate's analysis as being time bound. Ulmer split his sample of the justices' votes into pre- and post-1930 subsamples and finds that personal attribute models, regressed onto support for the government, performed well for the post-1930 sample, but much less so for the earlier period.[93] Yet Ulmer's methodology is lacking in several respects. First, his study does not replicate Tate's model because Ulmer used an entirely different dependent variable than that of Tate. Second, Ulmer's models only include three variables: father as a state officer, father as a state officer interacting with time, and party identification. Ulmer's model, thus, may be underspecified, and his results do not encourage the reader to have confidence in them.

While the bulk of the literature deals exclusively with the post–World War II Supreme Court, only a few studies investigate the pre-1945 period systematically. Tate and Handberg respond to Ulmer's assertion that personal attribute models are time bound by replicating Tate's analysis for the period 1916 to 1988. They specify separate models for the justices' individual decision-making in economics and civil liberties–civil rights cases.[94] Party identification and the appointing president's policy intentions are significant in both types of decision-making. Also, a measure of the justices' rural origins is significantly associated with their voting behavior, while regional origin is associated with economics voting only. As a measure of the career experience, Tate and Handberg find that an index of judicial experience is associated with the justices' civil liberties–civil rights decisional behavior and that a combined index of prosecutorial and judicial service is related to both types of decision-making. Thus, these authors find that personal attributes are strongly associated with, and explain a great deal of, the variance of the Court's voting behavior.[95]

A methodologically rigorous study that analyzes the pre-1945 Supreme Court decision-making at the aggregate level is that of Stacia L. Haynie and Tate. These authors examine the liberalism of the Court as expressed in the justices' votes in nonunanimous economics and civil rights and liberties cases from 1916 to 1988, a period including two world wars, the Great Depression, the Cold War, the oil crisis, and Watergate. The Court over this period includes forty-six justices, from Edward White to Anthony Kennedy.[96] The individual-level influences include the mean levels of the justices' partisanship, the appointing presidents' policy intentions, the justices' regional and agricultural origins, and a measure of the justices' prosecutorial and judicial experience.[97] The environmental influences are modeled as interventions and include crucial historical events that may affect the liberal outcomes of the Court (e.g., the Great Depression). Similarly, the authors hypothesize that the World Wars created an incentive for the Court to curtail civil rights and liberties.[98]

In their civil liberties–civil rights model, the authors find that only the parameter measuring the rate of decay of the impact of World War II is significant.[99] This finding suggests that one term year's liberalism is significantly and positively related to the following term year's liberalism. Therefore, there is a time dynamic to the Court's civil liberties–civil rights liberalism. They also find that the Great Depression is associated with the Court's becoming more liberal in economics decisions.[100]

Similarly, Handberg investigates the decision-making of the Supreme Court during the period from 1916 to 1921. Basing his study on Schubert's psychometric model, Handberg analyzes 261 nonunanimous decisions, three-quarters of which were economics or E-scale cases.[101] He constructs quasi-scales for both the E and C dimensions, and he finds, similar to Schubert's results for later periods, that the two-dimensional space fits the data quite well during this period of Supreme Court decision-making.[102] Thus, the Court's decision-making prior to 1945 can be analyzed along two attitudinal scales, reflecting the justices' views of economic and civil liberties–civil rights questions.

There have been only a handful of studies examining the Court's behavior prior to 1946. Donald C. Leavitt investigates the attitudinal influences on the policy preferences of the White Court (1910–20).[103] Handberg examines the White Court from 1916 to 1921, and finds a two-dimensional attitudinal structure underlying the justices' decision-making.[104] Mary R. Mattingly studies the influences on the voting behavior of the Hughes Court, spanning twelve years.[105] Peter George Renstrom studies the attitudinal influences of the five-year period of the Stone Court.[106] Pritchett examines the growing voting division and ideological polarization on the Court during the tenures of Charles Evans Hughes (1930–41) and Harlan Fiske Stone (1941–46).[107]

CHAPTER SUMMARY

The bulk of the literature in the subfield of judicial politics has been to this point limited to studying the Supreme Courts composed after 1945. This study provides a systematic analysis of the behavior of the United States Supreme Court from 1888 to 1997. It investigates the influences on the Court's decision-making behavior, and it thereby provides both the longest wide-ranging perspective on the Court's behavior now present in judicial politics research and a base against which the findings concerning the post–World War II Court can be compared.

Pacelle and Casper and Posner author the two major empirical works on the Court's agenda. Casper and Posner find that the Court's workload is a function of several variables. In particular, they assert that jurisdictional changes first enlarged and then (in 1925 in particular) decreased the workload of the Court. The Judiciary Act of 1925 gave the Court for the first time substantial powers of discretionary jurisdiction, thus allowing it to reduce its ever-growing docket. Moreover, Casper and Posner find that statutes have influenced the types of issues that the Court decided. Finally, Casper and Posner find that the Court itself contributed to its burgeoning docket by its expansive interpretation of the Due Process and Equal Protection Clauses.[108]

Pacelle more systematically analyzes the changes in the Court's agenda from the time of Franklin Roosevelt to that of Ronald Reagan. He theorizes that three elements influence the composition of the Court's agenda: the goals of the justices, the rules structuring the American judicial process, and situational factors. He finds that these three factors influenced the Court to include on its agenda a large percentage of economics cases up until the 1950s. Thereafter, economics issues began to decline to make way for decisions dealing with civil liberties and rights,[109] confirming the observations of McCloskey.[110]

Building his work in part on that of Pritchett,[111] Schubert finds that a major influence on the justices' voting behavior is their attitudes. In his psychometric model, he is able to array the justices along scales measuring support for claims of economic regulation and civil liberties and civil rights. In so doing, he demonstrates a fundamental concept underlying Supreme Court decision-making.[112] The theory of attitudinal influences on the Supreme Court has since been applied to the Courts beyond the Warren Court by other scholars.[113] These authors also demonstrate the underlying psychological component to the Court's voting behavior. However, their measure of ideology has been shown to be less impressive during the period of Franklin Roosevelt and prior periods.[114] Tate and Tate and Handberg, in particular, employ personal attribute models as another measure of ideology that does not encounter these methodological obstacles.[115]

The next chapter discusses the historical events and personalities of the Supreme Court beginning with Fuller Court in 1888 and extending through 1945. This review provides the reader some context into which the latter analyses may be placed and, thus, better understood.

2

Historical Setting of the United States Supreme Court, 1888–1946

The Court in Historical Perspective

To provide some context to the analyses conducted in this study, this chapter reviews the historical setting in which the Court operated and the vast macropolitical changes that occurred beyond the walls of the "Marble Temple" from 1888 to 1946.[1] Within that period, there were five different chief justices who led the Court, and indeed the nation itself, through twists and turns in jurisprudence that accompanied large-scale changes in society and politics. They are Melville W. Fuller (1888–1910), Edward D. White (1910–21), William Howard Taft (1921–30), Charles Evans Hughes (1930–41), and Harlan Fiske Stone (1941–46).[2]

During the 1880s and up until the late 1930s, the Court's economic decisions allegedly reflected the laissez-faire perspective that then prevailed in the country.[3] Thereafter, the Court consistently began to support social welfare liberalism. Swindler summarizes the sociological challenges on-going from the late 1880s to the late 1930s:

> The passing of the frontier, the rise of an interstate industrialism, the shift from a rural to an urban distribution of population, the breakdown of nineteenth-century capitalism and the efforts to construct in its stead a twentieth-century capitalism, the breakthrough in science and technology, the change in the society of nations brought about global wars and the militant dialectic of totalitarianism—the constitutional posture of the American people had to be readjusted in response to each of these.[4]

Being the final arbiter of jurisprudence for the United States legal system, the Supreme Court thus faced enormous challenges as it attempted to resolve the issues that it faced during this transformative period. The effects of this changing milieu are manifested in the Court's decisions. These are more systematically discussed in chapters 3 and 4.

THE FULLER COURT (1888–1910)

During Melville Fuller's tenure as chief justice, the Court's membership nearly completely changed. When he arrived at the Court in 1888, Fuller joined Samuel F. Miller, Stephen J. Field, Joseph P. Bradley, John Marshall Harlan I, Stanley Matthews, Horace Gray, Samuel Blatchford, and Lucius Q. C. Lamar.

Brief Biographical Sketches of the Fuller Court Justices

Melville Fuller was born in Maine. His father was a prominent attorney, as was his uncle; his grandfathers were distinguished judges. Fuller attended Harvard Law School and became an attorney in 1855. In 1856, he moved to Illinois and became involved in politics, joining the state Democratic party. He served two years in the state legislature, where he opposed many of President Lincoln's policies, including the Emancipation Proclamation.[5] He then began to build a private practice devoted to real estate and corporate law. Fuller espoused a strict constructionist view, advocating a limited role of government in economic activity. President Cleveland nominated him in 1888 to replace Chief Justice Morrison Waite, who had died. Fuller's political views were conservative, supporting the doctrine of laissez-faire and the limited scope of federal power.[6]

The most senior justice on the Fuller Court was Samuel F. Miller. Justice Miller was born in Kentucky, but left the South because of his opposition to slavery.[7] He grew up on a farm and farmed himself after earning a medical degree in 1838. Having later earned a law degree as well, he was in private practice when President Lincoln appointed him to the Court in 1862.[8] He had previously served as a justice of the peace. By all accounts, he was "scholarly, skillful and creative."[9] During his time on the Court, Miller voted to support both the national government's taxing power and its power to regulate interstate commerce and (being an abolitionist) vigorously supported individual liberties.[10] However, he did write the majority opinion in the narrowly decided *Slaughterhouse Cases*,[11] holding that the Fourteenth Amendment did not prevent state governments from regulating economic activity.

The third justice to serve on the Fuller Court was Stephen J. Field. Field read the law in his brother's law office and was admitted to the New York bar soon thereafter.[12] He moved to California in 1849, served as chief magistrate for a newly founded town, and then entered private practice. In 1857, he was elected to the California Supreme Court and became its Chief Justice in 1861. Field befriended railroad magnate Leland Stanford, who recommended Field to President Lincoln; Lincoln nominated Field to the Court in 1863. During his entire tenure on the Court, Field was an ardent conservative and proponent of laissez-faire economic theory. He resigned from the Court in 1897.[13]

Joseph P. Bradley was the fourth justice to serve on the Fuller Court. Bradley read law in an attorney's office, like many of those who would later become Supreme Court justices.[14] He practiced law with a noted railroad lawyer and eventually entered politics, joined the Republican party, and supported Lincoln's candidacy in 1860. Because of his political involvement, Bradley's name came to the attention of President Grant, who nominated him to the Court in 1870. Generally, Bradley voted to support the expansion and exercise of federal power while he was on the Court.[15] Even though he had been a railroad lawyer, Bradley often voted to support governmental regulation of economic interests. He died in 1892.[16]

John Marshall Harlan I was also a member of the Fuller Court. His grandson (John Marshall Harlan II) would later serve on the Court. Justice Harlan's father was a prominent lawyer, Whig Congressman, and Kentucky Secretary of State.[17] The first Justice Harlan was born in Kentucky, read law in his father's law office, and became an attorney in 1853.[18] He entered private practice and eventually became a county judge. When the Civil War broke out, Harlan was a vigorous supporter of the Union. In 1864, he was elected Kentucky attorney general. Being a loyal Democrat, Harlan opposed Lincoln's renomination in 1864, Lincoln's Emancipation Proclamation, and the proposed Thirteenth Amendment to the Constitution. Once the war ended, however, Harlan aligned himself with the policy positions of the Republican party and became an ardent civil libertarian. As a result of his party involvement, President Hayes nominated Harlan to replace Justice Davis, who had resigned in 1877. Once on the Court, Harlan was a strong supporter of judicial restraint, leaving to the legislature questions of the formation of public policy and voting to support the Interstate Commerce Act and the Sherman Antitrust Act.[19] Harlan is perhaps best known for his ringing dissent in *Plessy v. Ferguson* (1896), stating that "'[o]ur Constitution is color blind, and neither knows nor tolerates classes among its citizens.'"[20]

Stanley Matthews was the next member of the Fuller Court. Justice Matthews was born in Lexington, Kentucky in 1824. His father was a mathematics professor, who moved the family to Cincinnati in 1832.[21] Matthews read the law in Cincinnati and then entered private practice. Matthews, who was active in the abolitionist movement in the area, became a judge on the Court of Common Pleas in 1851; he also served two years in the state senate. In 1858, President Buchanan appointed him United States attorney for the Southern District of Ohio. After a stint in the Union Army, Matthews served as Superior Court judge in Cincinnati for two years, after which he returned to private practice, representing railroad interests. He also became active in Republican state politics, helping an old school chum, Rutherford B. Hayes, become president. Matthews eventually became a U.S. senator from Ohio. Hayes nominated Matthews in 1881, but the Senate blocked the nomination. President Garfield resubmitted Matthews's nomination, and Matthews was quickly confirmed due in part to Garfield's influence. However, once on the Court, Matthews did not distinguish himself. He was generally a conservative in economic and civil rights matters.[22]

Horace Gray was the seventh person to serve on the Fuller Court. Gray was born into a prominent Boston family, known for its involvement in shipping and commerce. He graduated from Harvard Law School in 1849 and shortly thereafter entered private practice.[23] Gray became a member of the Republican party in 1855 and was a strong supporter of the Union. In 1864, he joined the Massachusetts Supreme Court and served as its chief justice beginning in 1873. His decisions on that tribunal betrayed a perspective supportive of property rights. President Arthur nominated him to the Court in 1881. Even though Gray was an economic conservative, he was an ardent nationalist, voting to support the federal government's control over currency.[24] Gray resigned from the Court in 1902.

Samuel Blatchford, born to a prominent Manhattan attorney's family, read the law in the New York governor's office and earned admission to the bar in 1842.[25] In 1867, he was appointed to the federal bench in the Southern District of New York. In 1872, he joined the United States Court of Appeals for the Second Circuit. President Arthur nominated him to the Court in 1882. Blatchford was generally moderate in his economic policy preferences, but somewhat more liberal in decisions involving questions of civil liberties.[26]

Lucius Q. C. Lamar was the last justice on the first natural court during Fuller's tenure. Lamar was born in Georgia in 1825. He read the law and entered private practice in Georgia in 1847.[27] Through his law practice, Lamar was able to cultivate great respect, and he was elected to the Georgia legislature in 1853. In 1856, Lamar won election to Congress, representing Mississippi. Having been a plantation- and slave-owner, he was an ardent opponent of civil rights. When Lincoln won the presidency in 1860, Lamar himself authored the ordinance for Mississippi to leave the Union in January of 1861. After the war, he returned to private law practice; he was reelected to Congress in 1872, becoming a prominent spokesman for states' rights.[28] In 1876, he was elected to the Senate, and in 1884, President Cleveland appointed him secretary of the interior. Three years later, Cleveland elevated him to the Court. Once on the Court, Lamar was predictably a conservative in economics and civil liberties–civil rights decisions, supporting a limited reach of the protections of the Fourteenth Amendment. However, he did occasionally vote to uphold state regulation when the public interest required it.[29]

Within the first five years of the Fuller Court, four new members—David J. Brewer, Henry B. Brown, George Shiras, Jr., and Howell E. Jackson—joined the Court.[30] Justice Brewer was born in 1837 to missionary parents.[31] Brewer read law in his uncle's law office and earned admission to the bar in 1858, after which he moved to Kansas. In 1865 he was elected county attorney; in 1870 he was elected to the Kansas Supreme Court, where he was known as a judicial conservative. After his service on that court, Brewer was appointed to the Federal Court of Appeals for the Eighth Circuit, where he defended private property and espoused a laissez-faire perspective. In 1890, President Harrison nominated Brewer to the Court. Brewer joined his uncle, Justice Field, on the Court, and together they represented a strongly conservative duo. Once on the Court, he continued his conservative tendencies, often finding himself the lone dissenter as the Progressive era developed.[32] He died suddenly in 1910.[33]

Henry Billings Brown also served on the Fuller Court. Brown, who was born in 1836 in Massachusetts, attended Yale and Harvard law schools, read the law, and eventually earned admission to the Michigan Bar. He opened a law office, specialized in admiralty, and joined the Michigan Republican party. Brown served as a federal marshal and assistant United States attorney for the Eastern District of Michigan.[34] He also served as a county judge for Wayne County.[35] When President Harrison nominated Brown for the Court in 1890, Brown was serving as United States district judge in Michigan, a post he had held for eight years.[36] Once on the Court, Brown often aligned himself with fellow conservative Justices Peckham, Brewer, and Fuller, although he did write the majority opinion in a decision in which the Court upheld a law prescribing the maximum numbers of hours that a miner could work. However, Brown is perhaps best known for his majority opinion in *Plessy v. Ferguson*.[37]

The third new justice to be appointed during the first five years of the Fuller Court was George Shiras. Shiras was born in 1832 in Pittsburgh to a wealthy brewer and his wife, and was brought up on the family farm outside of town. He eventually attended Yale Law School and read law in a Pittsburgh attorney's office, passing the state bar in 1855.[38] Like many of his future colleagues on the bench, he entered private practice and joined the Republican party.[39] Shiras's clients included railroad, banking, oil, coal, and iron and steel concerns, some of which industrialist Andrew Carnegie headed. He refused an appointment to the Senate that the state legislature offered him, and he did not serve in any political or judicial office before coming to the Court. President Harrison nominated Shiras to the Court in 1892.[40] On the Court, Shiras's decision-making was consistently conservative, being more flexible than his more ardently conservative colleagues such as Chief Justice Fuller and Justices Field, Brewer, or Peckham.[41]

The last of the new appointments to the Fuller Court during its first five years was Howell E. Jackson. Jackson was born in 1832 in Tennessee to a physician's family. He attended law school at the University of Virginia and Cumberland University, gaining admission to the Tennessee bar in 1856.[42] Jackson entered private practice and accepted an administrative position in the Confederate government when the Civil War broke out. After the war, he joined the Democratic party and was appointed to the Provisional Court of Arbitration in Tennessee. In 1880, he was elected to the Tennessee legislature, and one year later he was elected to the Senate.[43] In 1886, President Cleveland nominated him to the Sixth Circuit Court of Appeals, where he served for six years until President Harrison nominated him to the Court. Jackson was on the Court only about two years due to recurring tuberculosis. When he did participate, however, he was a consistent conservative.[44] Jackson is perhaps best known for his lone dissent in *Pollock v. Farmers' Loan and Trust Co.*[45]

During the next seventeen years, as justices died or retired, ten new justices were appointed. At the end of Fuller's tenure as chief justice, the only remaining members from Fuller's first natural court were John Marshall Harlan I and Brewer.[46] Thus, the Court's membership was in flux throughout Fuller's chief justiceship.

One of the justices to be appointed during the latter part of the Fuller Court was Edward D. White, who would later serve as chief justice. White, born in 1845, was the son of a prominent Louisiana lawyer, politician, judge, congressman, and governor. His father also owned a large sugar plantation. White received Jesuit-sponsored instruction in his early education and attended Georgetown College before the Civil War began, when he joined the Confederate army.[47] After the war, White read the law, attended the University of Louisiana School of Law, and passed the bar in 1868. He entered private practice and deeply involved himself in Democratic politics. He was elected to the state senate in 1874 and gained a post on the state Supreme Court in 1879. After serving on that court for two years, White returned to private practice, becoming a prominent member of the New Orleans community. In 1891, White was appointed to the Senate, where he was largely a loyal Cleveland Democrat.[48] In 1894, President Cleveland nominated him to the Court. Overall, White was conservative, supporting limited governmental power since he was an ardent defender of

Southern interests. However, White would occasionally vote to uphold regulations that he believed benefited the public interest.[49]

Two particularly influential appointments affected the tenor of the Fuller Court's decisions: Rufus W. Peckham in 1895 and Oliver Wendell Holmes, Jr. in 1902.[50] Peckham was born in 1838 in Albany, New York. His father was a prominent attorney, who served on the New York Supreme Court (the trial court in New York state) and the Court of Appeals (the highest judicial authority in the state).[51] Peckham read the law and earned admission to the bar in 1859. He began private practice and became a district attorney in 1869.[52] In 1872, he returned to private practice in Albany, where he became actively involved in Democratic politics, being a steadfast opponent of New York's Tammany Hall. He was counsel to such tycoons as "Cornelius Vanderbilt, John D. Rockefeller, . . . and Pierpont Morgan."[53] Like his father, he served on the state's Supreme Court and the Court of Appeals. While on the latter tribunal, Peckham espoused a conservative economic perspective, protecting private property from governmental regulation.[54] "[H]is avowed political philosophy was very much Clevandesque Democratic: anti-Populist, antipaternalistic in government, economically and socially conservative. In fact, Peckham embraced a social Darwinist approach that went considerably beyond that of his nominator. . . ."[55]

Once on the Court, Peckham was predictably a proponent of the doctrine of liberty of contract.[56] This concept formed the foundation of Fuller Court jurisprudence in economics cases. Schwartz best summarizes this view: the Fuller Court "furnished the legal tools to further the period's galloping industrialism and ensure that public power would give free play to the unrestrained capitalism of the era."[57]

Joseph McKenna joined the Fuller Court in 1898. He was born in Pennsylvania in 1843.[58] McKenna's father was an Irish immigrant; he worked as a baker and then migrated with his family to a small town in California. Justice McKenna became an orphan at age fifteen, forcing him to work in a bakery to help support his family.[59] McKenna read law in California and passed the bar in 1865. He became more actively involved in politics than he was in his own law practice. After joining the Republican party in the 1860s, he was elected district attorney of Solano County. In 1875, he joined the state assembly and in 1884, he was elected to Congress, becoming friends with then–House Ways and Means Committee Chairman William McKinley. In 1892, President Benjamin Harrison nominated him to the Ninth Circuit Court of Appeals. When McKinley was elected president, he nominated McKenna to the post of U.S. attorney general. Only one year later, the President nominated him to the Court when Justice Field resigned. "As a result of his judicial inexperience and the lack of a solid legal background, McKenna never developed any consistent judicial philosophy, and his decisions often conflicted with each other in cases involving similar legal principles."[60] Sometimes, he would vote to uphold governmental regulation (for example, dissenting when the majority struck down a child labor law), and sometimes he would vote to strike down attempts to regulate economic activity.[61]

Perhaps the best-known member of the Fuller Court was the justice from Beacon Hill: Oliver Wendell Holmes, Jr. Holmes's father was a prominent physician in Boston and "the acknowledged leader of a noted group of Massachusetts literati known as the Boston Brahmins."[62] His mother was the daughter of a Massachusetts Supreme Court justice. Holmes attended Harvard University and then enlisted to fight in the Union Army. He then returned to Harvard Law School and earned a law degree, being admitted to the bar in 1867. He was a prodigious scholar, publishing, among other works, his classic study *The Common Law* in 1881. In 1883, Holmes was appointed to the Massachusetts Supreme Court, serving there for twenty years and becoming its chief justice in 1899. On that court, Holmes developed a reputation for liberalism in his voting behavior.[63] Holmes was not involved directly in Progressive politics, but he did befriend many Progressives, such as Louis Brandeis, with whom he would later serve on the Court.[64]

In 1902, Theodore Roosevelt chose Oliver Wendell Holmes to succeed Justice Gray. Although the Court was markedly conservative during the majority of Holmes's tenure, his greatest contribution to the development of the law was through his dissents, which the Court would later cite as support for more progressive decisions.[65] Although there was a chilling effect on the promulgation of social legislation because of the Court's conservative decisions, Holmes's idea of judicial restraint, expressed in dissent, began to lay the groundwork for the eventual change in the Court's jurisprudence to support regulatory laws and the coming welfare state.[66] His voting was generally supportive of the Progressive tradition, supporting the Sherman Anti-Trust Act, among other legislation. He also is known for his relatively strong support of civil liberties, developing the idea of a marketplace of ideas in deciding free speech cases. He served on the Court until 1932.[67]

William R. Day was also a member of the Fuller Court. Day was born in 1849 in Ohio. His father was a prominent attorney and served as chief justice of the Ohio Supreme Court, and his family included many lawyers and judges. Day attended the University of Michigan as an undergraduate and its law school, although he did not complete his legal studies there. After he left law school, he read the law and earned admission to the Ohio bar in 1872.[68] He entered private practice and began to represent large corporations. He befriended another local attorney, William McKinley. Day joined the Republican party and became involved in local politics. In 1886, Day was elected to the Court of Common Pleas, but served only six months because of the poor salary. He was, however, continually active in politics, helping his long-time friend McKinley become Ohio governor and, in 1896, president. In 1898, McKinley appointed him secretary of state; in 1899, McKinley appointed him to the Sixth Circuit Court of Appeals. On that court, he became friends with two future colleagues: William Howard Taft and Horace Lurton. President Roosevelt nominated him to the Supreme Court in 1903. Day became a relatively strong liberal, supporting the use of federal and state power in the regulation of economic and social concerns. He resigned from the Court in May 1923 due to poor health.[69]

William H. Moody joined the Fuller Court in 1906. Moody was born in Massachusetts in 1853. After growing up on the family farm, Moody attended Harvard University as an undergraduate and Harvard Law School for one semester. Thereafter, he read the law and passed the bar in 1878.[70] He opened his own practice and began to handle corporate law cases. He was soon involved in Republican politics and became district attorney for eastern Massachusetts in 1890, serving as the prosecutor in the infamous Lizzie Borden case.[71] Because of his involvement in the Republican party, he developed a friendship with a rising star, Theodore Roosevelt. In 1895, Moody was elected to Congress, where he served until 1902 when his friend, President Roosevelt, nominated him to be secretary of the Navy. In 1904, Roosevelt appointed him U.S. attorney general, where he brought several suits against corporations charging them with violating antitrust laws, in line with Roosevelt's Progressive policies. In 1906, Roosevelt again looked to his friend and nominated Moody to the Supreme Court. Although he wrote relatively few decisions, Moody demonstrated a clearly liberal policy perspective. He resigned from the Court in November 1910.[72]

Horace H. Lurton is the final justice to have served on the Fuller Court. Lurton's father was a physician who moved the family to Tennessee. Justice Lurton enlisted in the Confederate Army when the Civil War broke out.[73] After the war, he entered Cumberland Law School, graduating in 1867. He earned admission to the Tennessee bar in the same year, and then entered into private practice. In 1886, he was elected to the Tennessee Supreme Court and became its chief justice in 1893. In 1893, President Cleveland nominated him to the Sixth Circuit Court of Appeals, where he remained until 1910. While on the Court of Appeals, Lurton befriended William Howard Taft and William Day. On that court, Moody clearly demonstrated his conservative policy preferences.[74] In 1909, President Taft, Lurton's longtime friend, appointed him to the Court. Once on the Court, however, he showed a liberal perspective, voting to uphold the Sherman Anti-Trust Act and numerous other statutes designed to enlarge the federal government's regulatory powers.[75] He died shortly after the end of the 1913 term year.

Substance of the Fuller Court's Decisions

The Fuller Court bridges two centuries, and it witnessed vast social, technological, and legal changes, reflected in its decisions. The Court had "one foot in the Gilded Age and another in the Progressive Era."[76] The Fuller Court had ample opportunity to affect economic regulation, since its agenda was composed mostly of economics decisions.[77] Overall, the Fuller Court endorsed in its economics rulings the doctrine of substantive due process.[78] That concept provides the courts with the authority to review the substance of legislation and not simply the procedures that the law mandates, illustrating the prevailing relationship between government and business.[79] The Court also extended the protections from state regulatory power of the Fourteenth Amendment to businesses. Hence, the Court began to review the wisdom of the economic theory underlying challenged legislation.[80]

The Court's laissez-faire notions not only shackled the efforts of the states to regulate business activity but also the efforts of the Congress to regulate interstate commerce.[81] For example, in *United States v. E. C. Knight Co.*,[82] the Court held that the Sherman Anti-Trust Act did not make illegal manufacturing monopolies because the Court did not consider manufacturing to be "commerce" and, therefore, it was not within Congress's power to regulate under the Interstate Commerce Clause on which the Sherman Act was predicated, thus making the act invalid.[83] Further, in *Pollock v. Farmers' Loan and Trust Co.*,[84] the Court struck down the Income Tax Act of 1894 as unconstitutional because the tax was a direct one on the people, rather than being apportioned among the states as the Constitution requires. "The case was used as the vehicle for a broadside attack upon governmental interference with private property."[85]

The Fuller Court's interpretation of the commerce clause complemented the laissez-faire conception of the proper role of government that prevailed in the political and economic theory of the day, culminating in *Lochner v. New York*.[86] *Lochner* struck down a New York law regulating the maximum number of hours that bakery workers could work daily. The New York legislature had passed the law with the intent to provide some protection to the workers, who were mostly immigrants, from their employers' demands to work in dangerous and unhealthy conditions. While this decision may seem rather innocuous to contemporary observers, in effect it affirmed the idea that the government cannot restrict two parties' freedom to contract, regardless of the fairness of the underlying bargain.[87] This decision marked the high point of the Court's laissez-faire jurisprudence, which continued up until the famous switch that the Court orchestrated in the face of growing national opposition to its repeated striking down of New Deal legislation. Because of the highly regressive nature of the ruling, the *Lochner* decision has been compared to *Dred Scott v. Sanford* (1857).[88]

The Fuller Court was equally hostile to the interests of organized labor. In *In Re Debs*,[89] the Court upheld the contempt conviction of labor organizer Eugene V. Debs, who had led a Pullman railway strike in direct contradiction to a federal injunction against doing so.[90] In 1908, the Court also struck down a law that invalidated "yellow-dog" contracts and interpreted the Sherman Anti-Trust Act to forbid secondary boycotts.[91] Hence, the Court generally held a narrow view of the rights that employees had as against their employers.

However, the Court was not entirely deaf to the pleas of workers. In *Muller v. Oregon*, the Court upheld an Oregon law setting the maximum number of hours that women were allowed to work in laundries.[92] The Court's decision was largely based upon the brief of Louis Brandeis, who would later join the Court (in 1916). He cited sociological and historical data supporting his client's claim of the deleterious effects of long work hours on women and their children.[93] The Brandeis brief, as it would become known, for the first time brought to the Court's attention such questions.

In addition to the issues of economics and labor relations, the Fuller Court issued several important decisions in the area of civil liberties–civil rights, foreshadowing the predominance that such cases would later exert on the Court's agenda.[94] Perhaps the Court's most famous decision is one that some observers suggest was one of the its worst: *Plessy v. Ferguson*, which affirmed the doctrine of separate but equal as constitutional.[95] Schwartz observes that the Fuller Court was "a reflection of the less tolerant society in which it sat" and, thus, it "could hardly hope to lift itself above the ingrained prejudices of its day."[96] However, "[i]n lonely if prophetic dissent, Justice Harlan warned that this decision would 'in time, prove to be quite as pernicious as the decision made by this tribunal in the *Dred Scott* case.'"[97]

However, the Court was not entirely deferential to governmental power. In 1892, the Court held that the Fifth Amendment required that one could be forced to testify against himself only if the government agreed to not use that evidence against him in any way.[98] Thus, while the Fuller Court's economics, civil liberties–civil rights, and labor relations decisions were mostly conservative, some of them were liberal.

THE WHITE COURT (1910–21)

The White Court comprises eleven years of the Court's history. Overall, its decisions were moderately influenced by the reforms of the Progressive era:

it upheld laws governing employer liability, wage and hour laws, and workmens' compensation.[99] Leavitt divides the Court into two subperiods for analytical purposes: 1910–15, and 1916–21. He notes that in the former period the Court had eleven different justices; Chief Justice Edward White, Justices Oliver Wendell Holmes, William Rufus Day, Joseph McKenna, Charles Evans Hughes, Willis Van Devanter, and Joseph Rucker Lamar served during the entire period.[100] Mahlon Pitney replaced John Marshall Harlan I in March of 1912, and James C. McReynolds replaced Horace Lurton in October of 1914.[101]

Brief Biographical Sketches of the White Court Justices

Only those justices who joined the Court during White's tenure are discussed in this section since those justices who had served on the Fuller Court, and who continued to serve on the White Court, are discussed above. The justices who were new appointments to the White Court were Charles Evans Hughes, Willis Van Devanter, Joseph Lamar, Mahlon Pitney, James McReynolds, Louis D. Brandeis, and John H. Clarke.[102]

Leavitt reviews the justices' fathers' occupations to illustrate the influence of their socioeconomic backgrounds on their political values.[103] Charles Evans Hughes was the child of "a poor [Welsh] immigrant who became a clergyman with a[n annual] meager income" of $1,200 in 1866.[104] Hughes was a child prodigy who entered Brown University at fourteen and went on to earn a Phi Beta Kappa key. He eventually graduated with highest honors from Columbia University.[105] He soon began to practice law, earning the respect and admiration of his colleagues and often taking cases of underdog clients. He worked as counsel for a New York state legislative committee, investigating the gas utility monopoly and later assisted in the investigation of the insurance industry. He was elected governor of New York as a reform candidate in 1906.[106] William Howard Taft thought that Hughes was a political rival and nominated him to the Court in 1910 to prevent Hughes from competing in the upcoming presidential election— much as President Eisenhower reputedly did with respect to Earl Warren's nomination. Once on the Court, Hughes was consistently liberal in his policy preferences, although he was more moderate than some of his brethren, such as Justice Brandeis. He supported state and national Progressive policies and protected the interests of labor and civil libertarians.[107]

Willis Van Devanter's father was a successful lawyer in Indiana. In his youth, Van Devanter moved to Wyoming, where he became friends with the Republican territorial governor and U.S. senator Francis Warren. Van Devanter served in several legislative offices and eventually became chief justice of the Wyoming Supreme Court.[108] He also served in the U.S. Department of Interior, specializing in public lands and Indian affairs, where he earned a reputation as a Progressive. His Progressivism influenced Teddy Roosevelt to nominate him to the Eighth Circuit Court of Appeals. However, while on that court, Van Devanter's voting behavior was consistently conservative, evidence of the ties that he previously had with powerful Western economic interests. Taft, seeking to appease elements of the Republican party, chose Van Devanter because of his conservatism and his Western geographic origins. Once on the Court, he continued his conservative perspective, becoming one of the vaunted Four Horsemen of the Apocalypse.[109]

Joseph Lamar came from a wealthy Southern family who fled the famous march to the sea of Union General William Tecumseh Sherman during the Civil War. As a result of witnessing the ravages of Civil War, Lamar became a strong civil libertarian, seeking to "preserve the rights of all by protecting the rights of each."[110] Lamar entered law practice and represented both corporations and individuals suing corporations. In economic matters, he was moderately conservative. He was elected to the Georgia legislature, serving from 1886 to 1889, and then went on to serve on the state Supreme Court from 1902 to 1905.[111] President Taft appointed him to the Court in 1910, where he was a strong supporter of civil liberties and civil rights.[112]

Mahlon Pitney's father was a distinguished lawyer and judge who co-founded a bank, having been the Vice Chancellor of New Jersey. Pitney himself was active in Republican state politics and served in Congress from 1895 to 1898. He served in the state senate and eventually became its president. Three years later he was elected to the state supreme court. While on that court, his decision-making was clearly opposed to civil liberties' claims and the interests of labor. However, he was moderately liberal in economic decisions and continued these voting trends when he joined the Supreme Court.[113]

Similarly, James C. McReynolds's family was from the upper social class; his father was a moderately wealthy surgeon who also owned a plantation.[114] McReynolds attended the University of Virginia Law School, graduating in 1884, and entered governmental service. In 1903, he began to serve as an assistant attorney general in the Theodore Roosevelt administration, initially being involved in the antitrust prosecution of tobacco companies. He also served in the Taft administration in the same position, but resigned twice from his post when the administration acted in ways in which McReynolds did not approve, finally turning his back on the Republican party entirely.[115] Eventually, McReynolds joined the Democratic party and supported Woodrow Wilson. Wilson appointed him Attorney General of the United States in 1913, where McReynolds continued his trust-busting work.[116] Wilson nominated him to the Court in 1914 with the hope that he

would continue his Progressivism. "History would prove him utterly wrong—
for McReynolds, continuing to manifest his violent temper and abrasive
nature on the bench, not only became a member of the anti–New Deal
Four Horsemen, he turned into their loudest, most cantankerous, sarcastic,
aggressive, intemperate, and reactionary representative."[117] McReynolds
was consistently conservative in both economic and civil liberties–civil rights
decision-making.[118]

In the later subperiod that Leavitt analyzes (1916–21), the White Court
saw only nine different justices. Louis Brandeis replaced Joseph Lamar in
1916. An emigré from Prague, Brandeis entered Harvard Law School,
graduating two years later. His father was a Jewish immigrant who became
wealthy as a grain merchant.[119] Brandeis eventually became a partner in a
prominent Boston law firm, representing corporate clients, which made
him a millionaire. He later began to represent underdog clients who were
suffering economic and political injustices. He argued *Muller v. Oregon* before the Fuller Court in 1908, and authored his famous Brandeis Brief in
which he included statistical data underlying the issue to be considered.[120]
He worked to prevent corporations from becoming too powerful, striving
for example to prevent two railroads from gaining a monopoly in New
England.[121] He also supported Progressive policies, assisting in their passage and implementation in Massachusetts. Brandeis was a key advisor to
the Wilson administration, helping to create the Federal Trade Commission and the Federal Reserve System, and continuing to provide counsel to
the administration after he joined the Court.[122] He was consistently liberal
in his policy preferences.[123]

The last justice to join the White Court was Justice John Clarke (in
1916), replacing Charles Evans Hughes (who resigned from the Court to
run for the presidency), while Holmes, Pitney, McReynolds, Day, Van
Devanter, and McKenna remained on the Court.[124] John Clarke's father
was an immigrant of Irish descent, who was involved in Democratic party
politics and later became a lawyer and prosecuting attorney.[125] Clarke held
Progressivist ideas, supporting various reform efforts and, being a former
newspaper publisher, was a strong supporter of civil liberties, particularly
the First Amendment.[126] Although Clarke's clients included corporations
and railroads, he did support labor's interests and was a moderate Progressive.[127] In 1914, President Wilson nominated Clarke to the federal bench.
Wilson was impressed by Clarke's Progressive voting record and appointed
him two years later to the Court. Clarke was more liberal on civil liberties
and civil rights questions than he was on questions of economics while he
was on the Court.[128]

When Brandeis and Clarke joined the Court, they became the strongest supporters of Progressivist ideals. They, Pitney, and Holmes formed a liberal wing on the Court.[129] Occasionally, Harlan and Hughes would vote with the liberal bloc. The Anti-Progressives were McReynolds, Lamar, Van Devanter, and White. Although McKenna had Progressive tendencies in the first period, he became anti-Progressive in the second period.[130]

Political Context of the White Court

During the period from 1910 to 1915, the majority of the cases that the Court heard involved laws passed during the Republican Taft administration, although in the last two years of this period the Court operated under the more Progressive Wilson administration.[131] Also during this time, the larger Progressive movement was still unified over the questions of trusts and interest group–friendly legislation.[132] Progressivism generally involves the support of governmental intervention to protect "interests of equality."[133]

From 1916 to 1921, the Court considered many acts and policies arising from Woodrow Wilson's second term.[134] Even if an act had been passed during a Republican administration, Wilson was able, as a Democrat, to interpret and implement them with his policy preferences in mind. Thus, Leavitt argues that the Democrats on the Court were aligned in favor of federal action; Republicans were opposed to such power.[135] Moreover, during the last half of the White Court, Democrat Woodrow Wilson became the leader of the Progressive movement, although he was not in the mold of Theodore Roosevelt or even William Howard Taft, who later supported and took credit for several Progressivist policies. Because of the conflict with the president, many of the Republican justices did not identify with Wilson or his policies, or even the national movement in general.[136]

Substance of the White Court's Decisions

Generally, the White Court had not become entirely deferential to legislatures. In *Hammer v. Dagenhart*,[137] for example, it invalidated a federal law that prohibited the placement of goods that children had manufactured into the stream of interstate commerce.[138] It reasoned that Congress had been trying to regulate manufacturing, which was beyond the reach of Congress's powers under the Interstate Commerce Clause.

Also, the Court breathed new life into the Sherman Anti-Trust Act by ruling that the act outlawed unreasonable restraints of trade, rather than *all* such restraints as it had previously held, thereby breaking up the Standard Oil trust.[139] It later upheld Congress's power, through the Interstate Commerce Commission, to prescribe rates even for railroads operating within only one state.[140] Hence, the Court was beginning to uphold larger exercises of governmental power, although it did so only by slim majorities.[141]

In the area of civil liberties–civil rights, the Court's decisions were more liberal than were those of the Fuller Court. The White Court ruled that the exclusionary rule applied to the federal government. It would not extend that rule to the states until 1961. It also struck down Oklahoma's grandfather clause as violative of the Fifteenth Amendment.[142]

However, during the years surrounding World War I, the Court's civil liberties and civil rights decisions appeared to be more conservative than those during other periods. In *Schenck v. United States*,[143] the Court upheld Charles Schenck's conviction for distributing leaflets that advocated resistance to the draft because his actions presented a "clear and present danger" to the security of the United States.[144] Further, the Court upheld the constitutionality of the Selective Service Act in 1918. Hence, the Court looked to concerns of national security and national welfare when announcing rulings involving issues of civil liberties in the period near World War I.

THE TAFT COURT (1921–30)

The Taft Court was composed of the following justices: William Howard Taft (chief justice), Joseph McKenna, William Day, Oliver Wendell Holmes, Willis Van Devanter, Mahlon Pitney, James C. McReynolds, Louis Brandeis, John Clarke, George Sutherland, Pierce Butler, Edward Sanford, and Harlan Fiske Stone. In addition to the Chief Justice himself, Justices Sutherland, Butler, Sanford, and Stone were new appointments to the Taft Court.[145]

Brief Biographical Sketches of the Taft Court Justices

As before, a brief review of the justices who joined the Court during the tenure of William Howard Taft is completed to provide context to the Court's decision-making during this period. Taft had served as president (1909–13), but truly coveted the position of chief justice. Taft began his political service in 1887 when Governor Foraker of Ohio appointed him to the Superior Court of Ohio. In 1892, he resigned the post of solicitor general to accept an appointment on the Sixth Circuit Court of Appeals, after which he served as the governor of the Philippine Islands.[146] In 1903, President Roosevelt nominated him to be secretary of war. Eventually, Taft was elected president of the United States, but he still longed to be chief justice.[147] Taft's lifelong dreams were fulfilled when President Harding nominated him to the Court when Chief Justice Edward White died in May of 1921. Once on the Court, Taft was consistently conservative, but he did manage to engineer significant reforms during his tenure, including the Judiciary Act of 1925.[148]

George Sutherland joined the Taft Court in October of 1922. Sutherland was from Utah and brought to the Court a significant amount of legal and judicial experience. He was an expert in constitutional law and a leading member of the state bar. He had served in the Congress and the state and U.S. senate. While in the U.S. Senate, he befriended Warren Harding and later served as a policy advisor to Harding when he became president. Once on the Court, Sutherland espoused a lucid conservative perspective, joining the coalition of McReynolds, Butler, and Van Devanter.[149] However, Sutherland did approve of some exercises of governmental power, especially those relating to foreign affairs.[150]

Pierce Butler was Harding's third appointment to the Court. Butler was a member of a large Irish Catholic family from Minnesota. Butler was a self-made millionaire who earned his wealth by representing several railroads. However, in 1910, he represented the federal government in several antitrust prosecutions.[151] He was a Cleveland Democrat and "no friend of liberals or progressives."[152] Once on the Court, Butler continued his ultraconservatism, being one of the Four Horsemen of the Apocalypse, although one of the less distinguished members of that voting coalition.[153]

Edward Sanford joined the Taft Court in 1923. Born in Tennessee in 1865 in one of the few Republican areas of the post–Civil War South, Sanford rose from an impoverished background to amass a fortune from the lumber and construction business. He involved himself in Republican politics and rose to prominence in that party. He eventually became an attorney and entered private practice. As a special assistant to Attorney General William H. Moody, Sanford, like McReynolds, earned a reputation as a trustbuster. In 1907, he was appointed as an assistant attorney general. Only a year later, President Roosevelt nominated him to the federal district court for Tennessee, a post that he held until 1923 when President Harding nominated him to the Court.[154]

The last justice to join the Taft Court was Harlan Fiske Stone. Stone was born in New Hampshire in 1872. He earned a law degree from Columbia University in 1898 and soon thereafter began to practice law at a prominent Wall Street firm. He also served as a law professor and dean at Columbia Law School.[155] In 1924, President Coolidge appointed him U.S. attorney general, and he began to reform the Justice Department. In 1925, the president nominated Stone to the Court.[156] Once on the Court, Stone was a strong advocate of the doctrine of judicial self-restraint.[157] Even though he was a nominal Republican, Stone often voted with Brandeis and Holmes, and his policy preferences were generally liberal throughout his tenure on the Court, although a current study suggests that Stone became somewhat more moderate when Roosevelt elevated him to the chief justice position.[158]

Substance of the Taft Court's Decisions

The Taft Court continued the trend that the White Court had initiated, approving some legislation designed to remedy the profound social and economic problems that the nation faced during the Great Depression. "William Howard Taft's term as Chief Justice spans the 'fabulous' nineteen twenties, an era of expansion, expense, and high finance. The gospel of goods—make the goods, sell the goods, get the goods—then dominated the American people. Industrial leaders inflamed by victory in war, encouraged by the political glory of Harding's triumphant election in 1920, were certain that under such a national administration progress must be unending."[159] Perhaps the most celebrated justice on the Taft Court who led the vanguard to approve such laws was Justice Louis D. Brandeis. "If 20th century law has enabled the society to move from laissez-faire to the welfare state, that has been true in large part because it has accepted Justice Brandeis' approach."[160]

However, the Taft Court ruled conservatively in a larger percentage of economic and labor relations decisions than did the White Court, striking down both federal and state laws. For example, in *Adkins v. Children's Hospital*,[161] the Court declared a law requiring a minimum wage for women to be unconstitutional, using the freedom of contract doctrine as its reasoning.[162] Its labor relations decisions, additionally, made it easier for management to invoke antitrust laws against labor unions.[163]

In the areas of civil liberties and civil rights, the Taft Court's decisions would have long-lasting effects. "The Court's role as balance wheel can give its work a paradoxical character. So it was in 1925 when the conservative Court ignited the spark that eventually would flare into the 'due process revolution' of the 1960s." For example, in *Gitlow v. New York*,[164] the Court stated that the Fourteenth Amendment protected individuals' rights against state action. This statement would form the basis for the Court's later striking down of state laws violative of the First Amendment beginning in the 1930s.[165]

However, the Court's liberalism then did not extend as far for civil rights issues. In *Corrigan v. Buckley*,[166] the Court held that the Fourteenth Amendment did not apply to private discrimination, upholding racial restrictive covenants applying to the sale of real estate to African Americans.[167] Yet the Court did strike down discriminatory state action by invalidating "white primaries."

The Taft Court, moreover, considered questions of separation of powers. In *Myers v. United States*, the Court held that the Congress did not have to consent to the president's removal of postmasters.[168] And, it approved "Congress's delegation of power to the president to adjust tariff rates in response to the competitive conditions."[169]

THE HUGHES COURT (1930–41)

The fourth chief justice court contained within the pre-1945 period under analysis herein is the Hughes Court. The political context in which the Hughes Court operated was largely determined by the Great Depression and the New Deal policies designed and implemented in response to the demands of the Depression. Mattingly suggests that what made the Hughes Court in part unique was the great exposure that accompanied the initial conservative nature of its decision-making, the inevitable clash with the President and the Congress, Franklin D. Roosevelt's subsequent Court-packing plan, and the abrupt turnabout in the Court's voting behavior to become more supportive of greater governmental power in many matters, principally economic regulation.[170]

Brief Biographical Sketches of the Hughes Court Justices

The justices who joined the Hughes Court were Owen J. Roberts, Benjamin N. Cardozo, Hugo L. Black, Stanley F. Reed, Felix Frankfurter, William O. Douglas, and Frank Murphy, in addition to the nomination of Charles Evans Hughes to be chief justice. Oliver Wendell Holmes, Willis Van Devanter, James C. McReynolds, Louis Brandeis, George Sutherland, Pierce Butler, Edward T. Sanford, and Harlan Fiske Stone continued to serve on the Court during at least part of Hughes's tenure.

Owen J. Roberts was born to a prominent Philadelphia family. He attended the University of Pennsylvania and its law school. After graduation, he entered private practice, representing corporate clients, including the Pennsylvania Railroad. For four years, he served as assistant district attorney in Philadelphia.[171] In 1918, he was appointed special deputy attorney general, prosecuting cases under the Espionage Act and the Teapot Dome oil scandals.[172] When President Hoover's nomination of John J. Parker failed, Hoover named Roberts to the Court in 1930.[173] Once on the Court, Roberts initially voted with the conservative bloc, but then began to become more liberal, allegedly switching his vote in the 1937 term to uphold a key piece of New Deal legislation.[174] After Justice McReynolds left the Court in 1941, however, Roberts became more conservative in his decision-making.[175]

The last Hoover appointment to the Court was that of Benjamin Cardozo, named to replace the aging Oliver Wendell Holmes. Cardozo was born in 1870 in New York City to a Jewish family. He attended Columbia University and its law school, although he did not graduate. He earned admission to the bar in 1891 and began to practice law.[176] In 1914, Cardozo ran against the dominant political machine, Tammany Hall, and was elected to New York's trial court. Soon thereafter, Cardozo was appointed to the New York Court of Appeals, on which he served for eighteen years. He also served as that court's chief justice, as did many other former Court members for their respective state courts of last resort. In addition, Cardozo was a scholar, publishing many classic legal works, including *The Nature of the Judicial Process*.[177] Hoover nominated him to the Court in 1930; once on the Court, Cardozo predictably joined the liberal wing of the Court (Brandeis and Stone), supporting major pieces of the New Deal program as well as broader protections of civil liberties.[178]

The first of the nine Roosevelt appointees was Senator Hugo L. Black. Black was born in 1886 in Alabama to a family headed by a Baptist merchant and farmer. Although he never finished high school, he graduated from the University of Alabama Law School in 1906.[179] He established a private practice, representing the United Mine Workers, among other clients. In 1914, Black, having been elected county solicitor, investigated the unwarranted use of force by the local police department. In 1918, he returned to private practice and began to specialize in labor law and personal injury cases. In 1923, he joined the Ku Klux Klan, but he later resigned and denounced that organization in order to make a bid for the United States Senate, which he won. While in the Senate, he was active in introducing liberal legislation, including one setting the length of a maximum workweek, which became the Fair Labor Standards Act. A strong supporter of New Deal programs and the Roosevelt administration, President Roosevelt nominated him to the Court in 1937.[180] Black held a literalist view of the Constitution, thus being quite liberal in matters of civil liberties and supporting the complete incorporation of the protections of the Bill of Rights against the actions of the states.[181] He authored the landmark majority opinion, for a unanimous Court, in *Gideon v. Wainwright*.[182] His decision-making was equally liberal in economic matters.[183]

The second justice to join the Hughes Court during the Roosevelt administration was Stanley Reed. Reed, whose father was a physician, was born in Kentucky in 1884. He attended Yale University, and the University of Virginia and Columbia law schools. Reed entered private practice in Kentucky and was elected to that state's general assembly for four years.[184] Reed served in the Hoover administration, acting as general counsel to a federal agency that made loans to Depression-era banks, businesses, and agricultural concerns.[185] Franklin Roosevelt appointed him solicitor general in 1935, and he argued many cases before the Supreme Court, including a successful argument on behalf of the constitutionality of the National Labor Relations Act, a key piece of labor legislation during the Roosevelt administration. The president nominated him to the Court in 1938, when Justice Sutherland died.[186] Although Reed did occasionally join the liberal bloc on the Court, he more consistently voted conservatively in economic and civil liberties–civil rights matters, fitting more "into the law-and-order mold."[187] Reed aligned himself with the conservative bloc of Justices Burton, Clark, and Minton in matters of civil liberties.[188]

Felix Frankfurter joined the Hughes Court in 1939 after Justice Cardozo died. Born in Vienna, he immigrated to the United States when he was twelve; his family lived in the squalor of New York's Lower East Side. He attended City College of New York and then Harvard Law School. After graduation, he began to practice law with a prominent New York attorney.[189] In 1914 Frankfurter took a teaching post at Harvard Law School, which afforded him the opportunity to argue many highly publicized cases, notably the defense of Nicola Sacco and Bartolomeo Vanzetti, who had been accused of treason. He was a founding member of the American Civil Liberties Union (ACLU) and active with the National Association for the Advancement of Colored People (NAACP). Frankfurter developed a friendship with Franklin Roosevelt, becoming his confidant and advisor.[190] Once on the Court, Frankfurter was quite conservative in civil liberties decisions, being nearly the most extreme member on such questions.[191] In state regulation and taxation decisions, however, he was much more liberal, although in other types of economics cases he voted consistently conservatively.[192] Overall, Frankfurter's voting behavior tends to be conservative, even though he himself espoused the notion of judicial self-restraint in judicial decision-making.[193]

William O. Douglas joined the Court in 1939. He was born in Minnesota in 1898 to an economically disadvantaged family. He attended Columbia Law School, graduating in 1925. Douglas entered private practice but quickly realized that he did not like representing corporate clients. He then accepted a position teaching law at Columbia.[194] Franklin Roosevelt nominated Douglas to the Securities and Exchange Commission in 1936, and he became its chair in the following year. Roosevelt nominated him in 1939 to the Court to replace Justice Brandeis.[195] Douglas was a moderate in questions of civil liberties, although his voting does have liberal tendencies. In economic decisions, however, Douglas was clearly liberal, second only to Justice Black.[196]

The last justice that Franklin Roosevelt nominated to the Hughes Court, and to the Court generally for that matter, was Frank Murphy. Murphy was born in 1890 in Michigan to an Irish Catholic family; his father was a country lawyer. He attended the University of Michigan as an undergraduate and a law student. After law school, Murphy worked as chief assistant attorney general in Michigan and, after three years, he became a criminal court judge.[197] Being a pro-labor Democrat, Murphy was elected Detroit mayor, serving three years until 1933. He held several additional political offices prior to joining the Court, including governor of Michigan and governor general of the Philippine Islands, where he implemented New Deal policies. In 1938, Roosevelt then named Murphy attorney general. In that position, Murphy prosecuted many political bosses, instituted antitrust prosecutions, and established the first civil liberties division in the Justice Department.[198] When Justice Butler died in 1939, Roosevelt appointed Murphy to the Court. Once on the Court, Murphy was part of the liberal wing of the Hughes Court, being more liberal on questions of civil liberties-civil rights than he was on economics matters; he thus joined the voting coalition of Douglas and Black on these questions.[199] For example, he filed a dissent in *Korematsu v. United States*.[200] Overall, he brought to the Court a strong pro-labor orientation and filled the so-called Catholic seat on the Court that Butler had occupied previously.[201]

Substance of the Hughes Court's Decisions

As the Court's administrative head, Charles Evans Hughes faced four colleagues (Willis Van Devanter, James C. McReynolds, George Sutherland, and Pierce Butler) who had voted with the *Adkins* majority to strike down a minimum wage law.[202] However, the Court's membership was soon to change. As indicated above, in 1932, Judge Benjamin Cardozo succeeded Oliver Wendell Holmes. Cardozo was a vital member of the liberal wing of the Court who resisted the Hughes Court's ardent conservatism.[203] Cardozo, like Holmes, eventually helped to move the law from the prevailing conception of the law as a disinterested referee to an effective instrument of social change.[204]

This change in the jurisprudence of the Hughes Court can be better understood if the Court is divided into two periods: 1930–37 and 1938–41. Pritchett finds that prior to 1936, the centrist bloc was not too distant from either the left or right voting coalitions.[205] In 1936, however, Hughes (and to lesser extent Roberts) aligned themselves with the liberal bloc, serving to create a majority of the liberal justices and to make the justices on the right a minority. Hughes's shift also made the voting coalitions more polar,[206] being associated with an increase in the rate of concurring opinions.[207]

In the earlier period of the Hughes Court, the Court's decisions were dominated by a string of cases in which the Court struck down many significant New Deal laws as well as state attempts to regulate business activity. These laws included the National Industrial Recovery Act (NIRA) and the Agricultural Adjustment Act.[208] Robert H. Jackson, then attorney general, a member of the New Deal coalition, and later a member of the Court, observes:

> The Court is almost never a really contemporary institution. The operation of life tenure in the judicial department, as against elections at short intervals of the Congress, usually keeps the average viewpoint of the two institutions a generation apart. The judiciary is thus the check of a preceding generation on the present one; a check of conservative legal philosophy upon a dynamic people, and nearly always the check of a rejected regime on the one in being.[209]

Thus, the Court serves to retard proposed public policy changes that the Congress and the president may try to legitimate. The Hughes Court, in particular, continued the laissez-faire perspective of previous Courts.

However, the Court did change course somewhat when it ruled in *Nebbia v. New York*[210] that *any* business could be subject to "reasonable regulation" rather than simply those that were "'affected with a public interest.'"[211] The Court extended this holding, in piecemeal fashion, to regulation of bread weights, sales of tickets, and the operation of employment agencies. It also approved a state law imposing a moratorium on mortgages, even in the face of a liberty of contract challenge, because the Court considered the law to be a reasonable response to the economic crisis of the Great Depression.[212]

In April 1937, the Court drastically altered its course; it began to consistently uphold New Deal legislation and approve a larger scope of governmental power. The Court clearly did so in *West Coast Hotel Co. v. Parrish*,[213] thereby overruling *Adkins* and similar decisions.[214] The Court, with Chief Justice Hughes writing the majority opinion, reasoned that the Fourteenth Amendment did not protect liberty of contract, but rather "liberty in a social organization which requires the protection of the law against the evils which menace the health, safety, morals, and welfare of the people," which the Washington law at issue protected.[215] Chief among other decisions upholding the New Deal, and the NIRA more specifically, was *NLRB v. Jones & Laughlin Steel Corp.*[216] The Court also went on to uphold the Social Security Act of 1935, the Federal Farm Bankruptcy Act, and provisions of the Railway Labor Act relating to collective bargaining.[217]

Bernard Schwartz suggests that the change in philosophy of the Court to one of more judicial pragmatism was due in large part to the changes in ideology that were taking place in the country as a whole.[218] This change in the Court's perspective was due to not only the justices' realization that the liberty of contract doctrine, on which *Adkins* was based, was simply inadequate in the face of the enormous demands of the Great Depression but also their realization that an unregulated market was unable to support even a modicum of social welfare.[219]

In the realms of civil liberties and civil rights, the Hughes Court allegedly continued the drift toward greater liberalism that the Taft Court had initiated. For example, in *Near v. Minnesota* (1931), the Court invalidated a state law punishing newspapers that criticized public officials because the law violated the protections of the press.[220] Additionally, it extended the Sixth Amendment right to counsel and Seventh Amendment right to a fair trial, through the Fourteenth Amendment, to defendants in state courts. However, the Court did hold that the Fourteenth Amendment did not bar the Texas Democratic Party's exclusion of African Americans from membership because no direct state action was involved.[221] It also ruled that the Due Process Clause of the Fourteenth Amendment protected only "fundamental" rights listed in the Bill of Rights, rather than all the guarantees contained therein.[222]

After the transformative year of 1937, the latter Hughes Court was drastically different than its predecessor, largely due to a drastic change in the Court's members. Justices no less than Senator Hugo Black, SEC chairman William O. Douglas, and Harvard law professor Felix Frankfurter joined the Court.[223] Over the following six years, Roosevelt would be able to nominate eight justices and select the Chief Justice. "The men he would place on the Court were young enough to be the sons of the men they succeeded, and the views of the Court would change accordingly."[224]

During the post-1937 years of the Hughes Court, the Court retreated from the hard-line concept of substantive due process that had colored many of its prior decisions. Moreover, it moved toward the conception that Holmes had proffered in the 1920s: adopting a test in which the law would pass constitutional muster if legislators could rationally have thought the law would reach its desired outcome. Under the post-1937 conception of judicial interpretation, the Court's job was not to judge the appropriateness of the economic theory that undergirded the law at hand.[225] This transformation reached its high-point when the Court upheld the Fair Labor Standards Act of 1938 in *United States v. Darby Lumber Co.*[226] The act made child labor illegal and prescribed a minimum wage for workers in interstate commerce and a maximum numbers of work-week hours.[227]

The revolution also extended to issues of civil liberties and civil rights. This turnabout was most clearly expressed in *United States v. Carolene Products*, in which the Court enunciated a two-tiered standard of review in constitutional cases.[228] If the law regulated economic activity, the Court would presume the law to be constitutional unless it was demonstrated otherwise.

If the law impinged upon civil liberties that the Bill of Rights protected, then the Court would be less willing to uphold the law's validity because such laws curtail the very political processes necessary to repeal repressive laws.[229] This was not the case for laws restricting economic activity, however.

Thus, decisions involving issues of civil liberties and civil rights began to consume more of the Court's agenda. For example, in *Lovell v. Griffin*,[230] the Court held that the guarantees of freedom of religion, contained within the First Amendment, prohibited a city from requiring Jehovah's Witnesses to be licensed before they could lawfully pass out religious tracts to residents of the city.[231] It also held in 1938, as a precursor to *Brown v. Board of Education*,[232] that the Constitution mandated that states provide equal opportunity to higher education for white and black residents. This standard was not satisfied by Mississippi's paying for a black student to attend law school in another state. However, the Court's support of civil liberties was supposedly curtailed when the war in Europe broke out. In 1940, the Court upheld a state law requiring public school students to recite the Pledge of Allegiance even though to do so conflicted with the students' religious beliefs.[233]

The Court also reconsidered issues of labor rights and federalism. The Court turned away from its anti-union bias of the past and, in *Hague v. CIO*, invalidated a city ordinance that prohibited union members from gathering and discussing issues of common concern because the law violated the First Amendment.[234] In addition, the Court ruled that federal and state officials' salaries were subject to state and federal taxes, respectively.[235]

Hence, during the Hughes Court, there had been a true revolution because the Court recognized the validity of increased governmental power that had long been dismissed as contrary to the needs of the marketplace. The period also witnessed a drastic transformation in the balance of power among the branches. As a result, after 1937 the Court became much more subdued than it had been in prior years.[236]

THE STONE COURT (1941–46)

The fifth and last chief justice court examined in detail in this study is the Stone Court. The justices who served on the Stone Court were almost completely nominees of Franklin Roosevelt, who appointed nine of the eleven members who served. Owen Roberts, a Hoover appointee, and Harold Burton, a Truman appointee, were the only exceptions.[237] To underscore the importance of Franklin Roosevelt's appointments to the Court from 1937 to 1947 (covering the period of the Hughes and the Stone Courts), C. Herman

Pritchett titles his book *The Roosevelt Court*, rather than identifying the Court by the chief justices who were its titular leaders during that time period as is customarily done. Through his appointment power, therefore, Franklin Roosevelt re-formed the Court and, thus, affected the tenor of its decision-making and policy-making preferences, especially with regard to economic regulation decisions.

In addition to Chief Justice Harlan Fiske Stone, ten associate justices served during the five-year period from 1941 to 1946. They are Hugo L. Black, William O. Douglas, Felix Frankfurter, Frank Murphy, Owen J. Roberts, Stanley Reed, James F. Byrnes, Robert H. Jackson, Harold H. Burton, and Wiley B. Rutledge.[238] Byrnes, Jackson, Rutledge, and Burton were newcomers to the Court.

Brief Biographical Sketches of the Stone Court Justices

James C. McReynolds retired from the Court during the 1941 term year, giving Roosevelt his sixth opportunity to impact the Court's decision-making. The president chose James F. Byrnes of South Carolina. Since his family was impoverished, Byrnes completed no formal education. He did manage to read the law, however, and earned admission to the bar in 1903. He served in the House of Representatives beginning in 1910, where he became acquainted with Franklin Roosevelt. He was elected to the Senate in 1931, supporting the Roosevelt administration, despite his personal objection to New Deal policies. He resigned from the Court in 1942 to become the Director of Economic Stabilization. Although Byrnes was strongly liberal in economics decisions, he was much less so in deciding questions of civil liberties claims. Indeed, after he left the Court, he was highly critical of the Warren Court's civil liberties voting, particularly its desegregation decisions.[239] Byrnes was elected South Carolina governor in 1950 on a platform of states' rights and separate-but-equal education.[240]

When Roosevelt nominated Stone to be chief justice, Roosevelt also nominated Robert H. Jackson to fill the vacancy that Stone left. Jackson, like Byrnes, read the law, rather than attending formal legal education.[241] Jackson entered private practice in New York, working as a corporate lawyer until he joined the Roosevelt administration as general counsel for the Bureau of Internal Revenue in 1934. He then went on to serve as assistant attorney general, solicitor general, and finally attorney general for several years prior to being elevated to the Court. His service as solicitor general allowed Jackson the opportunity to voice his support for New Deal policies. During the 1945 term year, Jackson did not participate in any decisions of the Court, acting as the chief United States prosecutor of the International Military Tribunal at Nuremberg.[242] Overall, Justice Jackson was moderately conservative in civil liberties cases and much closer to the right wing of the Court in economics matters.[243]

The last of the Roosevelt justices was Wiley Rutledge, who succeeded Justice Byrnes. Rutledge, whose father was a Baptist preacher, was born in 1894 in Kentucky. He graduated from the University of Colorado Law School in 1922, practiced law for a short period, and then took a position teaching law.[244] He also served four years on the District of Columbia Court of Appeals. Like many of the Roosevelt appointees, Rutledge was an ardent supporter of New Deal policies. On the Court, he was a member of the liberal bloc, advocating expanded civil liberties.[245] Overall, Rutledge was highly liberal in questions of civil liberties, but not as a strong supporter of those claims as was Justice Murphy.[246] He was relatively moderate in his economic policy preferences.[247]

The final member to join the Stone Court was Justice Harold Burton, appointed by President Truman just prior to the start of the 1945 term year to fill Justice Roberts's seat. Burton attended Harvard Law School and, after graduation, moved to Ohio and became mayor of Cleveland.[248] He then sought and won a seat in the Senate, an office which he occupied at the time that Truman appointed him to the high Court. Although he was a Republican, he was more of a moderate on many issues and did not bring to the Court a traditional Midwest conservative perspective, being more liberal on economics issues than he was on civil liberties questions.[249]

Renstrom calculates interagreement scores for the justices on the Stone Court and finds two distinct voting blocs. The liberal bloc members were Justices Black, Douglas, Murphy, and Rutledge. The conservative bloc included Jackson, Frankfurter, and Reed, with Burton being a marginal member of this voting coalition. Stone was often a member of this coalition after he was elevated to the chief justiceship. Byrnes's voting record positioned him between these two blocs. Roberts's voting was not strongly associated with either voting coalition, however.[250]

Substance of the Stone Court's Decisions

The occurrence of World War II may have significantly affected the Court's decision-making. The nation had just emerged from the Great Depression when the Stone Court began. It had, during the period from 1929 to 1939, decided questions of the expansion of governmental power during a national emergency and the limits that a constitutional structure places on governmental action. Having decided these types of questions, the Court was somewhat better prepared to meet the challenges that faced the national judiciary during the Second World War. The nation had weathered a previous world war only about twenty years earlier. The Stone Court was, thus, once again called upon to decide compelling questions of national policy, especially as they related to civil liberties in light of the compelling threat to national security that the war represented.

Renstrom states that the decision-making of the Stone Court was particularly substantively rich because it finely tuned the policy direction of the Court that had begun during the Hughes Court. It did so in such decisions as *NLRB v. Jones-Laughlin Steel Corp.*,[251] yet it did not become ardently activist even in light of the strong policy preferences of President Roosevelt and the Congress.[252] Rather, it simply lent its sanction to policies that other branches had legitimized, which broadened the powers of the federal government, especially as they related to regulation of business activity.[253]

Perhaps the most important rulings that the Court announced during Stone's tenure dealt with the U.S. government's war effort and, consequently, with issues of civil liberties. Chief among these was *Korematsu v. United States*,[254] upholding the government's decision to intern Americans of Japanese ancestry, for fear that they may be collaborating with Japan to sabotage American national security.[255] Yet, the Court reversed itself in *Murdock v. Pennsylvania*,[256] when it ruled that cities could not lawfully require people seeking to distribute religious literature to obtain licenses because that requirement unduly burdened the free exercise of religion.[257] It went on to strike down Texas's so-called white primary in 1944 because, the Court reasoned, the primary is a vitally important part of the electoral process that the Fourteenth Amendment protects.[258] The Stone Court also upheld the enactment of price controls in *Yakus v. United States*.[259] Hence, the decisions of the Stone Court generally deferred to claims of governmental power in economics decisions and began to support claims of civil liberties and civil rights more readily.

Chapter Summary

From the waning days of the nineteenth century to the period surrounding World War II, the decisions of the Supreme Court drastically changed, from those endorsing a laissez-faire economic philosophy (during the Fuller and White Courts particularly) to those deferring to reasonable laws that the legislature had passed. This change was due, in part, to the change in the prevailing economic theory, the enormous challenges of the Great Depression, the change in the Court's membership (notably the appointments of Justices Holmes, Brandeis, and Cardozo), and the crisis of institutional legitimacy that resulted from the Court's steadfast refusal, prior to 1937, to uphold consistently governmental attempts to regulate business activity.

Its civil liberties–civil rights decisions, however, tended to remain rather conservative across the entire period analyzed. The Court consistently approved governmental power during times of war, even upholding the internment of Japanese-Americans during World War II. However, during the Stone Court, the Court's decisions became somewhat more moderate than they had been in previous years, due in part to the changing membership and the justices' realization that civil liberties claimants did not represent as great a danger to national security as they had previously thought.

Chapter 3 analyzes the content and change of the Court's agenda over time in more detail. It documents the change from a docket largely characterized by economics decisions to one dominated by questions of civil liberties and civil rights. These changes illustrate the Court's changing role within the American system of governance.

3

Contours of Judicial Attention: Composition and Dynamics of the Workload and the Agenda of the United States Supreme Court, 1888–1997

THIS CHAPTER ANALYZES THE COMPOSITION OF THE UNITED STATES SUPREME Court's agenda during the period from 1888 to 1997. This period comprises more than a century of Supreme Court jurisprudence, during which the Court's agenda was drastically changing from one dominated by economics cases to one dominated by civil liberties and civil rights cases.[1] These agenda changes portend larger developments in not only the surrounding environment in which the Court operated but also the changes in the institutional role that the Court fulfilled in the American political system. This chapter first discusses the process by which the data were collected and shown to be reliable by the original researchers. It then turns to analyze the changes within the Court's agenda and their determinants.

DATA COLLECTION PROCESS

In the fall of 1994, Professor Sandra L. Wood of the political science faculty at the University of North Texas sought to implement her idea of extending the United States Supreme Court database that Professor Harold J. Spaeth had initiated. The Spaeth database has been checked for reliability, and it has provided data for numerous studies.[2] Professor Spaeth had collected and coded decisions of the Supreme Court and classified them into various issue areas.[3] However, Spaeth's dataset initially included only decisions of the Court handed down since the beginning of the 1953 term year, marked by Earl Warren's becoming the tribunal's chief justice. Professor Wood herself had collected and coded data for her own dissertation following the protocol set out in the United States Supreme Court database for the period from 1937 to 1954.[4] Her proposal sought to extend the Spaeth dataset into the latter part of the nineteenth century so as to provide one dataset that was continuous for at least a century.

With the assistance of three political science doctoral students at the University of North Texas (Linda Camp Keith, Ayo Ogundele, and this writer), Professor Wood began to extend her data for the Supreme Court back to 1888. The beginning date was chosen because it represented the beginning of the Fuller Court, and it witnessed an increase in federal statutory law, thus increasing the demands on the Court's agenda. All cases in which the Court issued a formal opinion were coded ($N = 10,506$) from the case decisions as reported in the *Supreme Court Reporter*, memoranda cases were excluded. This task took the four members of the research group approximately nine months to complete.

Each of the research group members coded approximately one-quarter of the cases for the term year period from 1888 to 1937. The coders met periodically to discuss decision rules about how to code—for example, the direction of the decision, the issue area of the case, and so on. If a particularly difficult case was encountered, additional members of the research group (at least one, if not all three other members) would also code the case, and a consensus would be reached as to how to code the case. These cases numbered less than five out of approximately two hundred per term. Furthermore, the coders conducted periodic reliability checks in which a random sample of cases for a particular term year would be exchanged among the members, and the members' codings for the cases would be compared. We selected a random sample of 325 cases to test our intercoder reliability. The reliability scores for these checks indicated that there was very high agreement among the codes that research members assigned to the sample of cases: 99 percent overall, and 94 percent when considering only the issue area and the decision direction, the most difficult coding. When there were differences in coding, the research group discussed the matter and reached a consensus as to how to code the particular case in question and similar cases.

The items coded are noted on the code sheet sample located in Appendix A. Appendix B summarizes the coding protocol for each of these items. These items include, among others, the direction of the decision the Court has announced (liberal or conservative), how each justice voted, whether the justices wrote special opinions, and, if so, with whom, and which of the fourteen separate issue areas best described the subject matter of the decision. The fourteen issue areas followed the subject matter classifications set out in the codebook that accompanies the Spaeth dataset. These are: criminal procedure, civil rights, First Amendment, due process, attorney, union, economic, judicial power, federalism, interstate relations, federal taxation, miscellaneous, and separation of powers. All of these but the separation of powers issue area are included in Spaeth's data base.

The content of these issue areas bears explanation. Based on Spaeth's methodology and operationalizations, the fourteen issues were coded and categorized. Criminal procedure cases deal with the gamut of issues involving criminal procedural rights, such as the right to counsel and the right to a fair trial. Civil rights cases involve allegations of discrimination based on an immutable characteristic, such as gender, race, and disability. The types of issues involved in this category include voting rights, affirmative action, gender discrimination, immigration, and citizenship questions. First Amendment cases deal with issues of free expression and free association, including free speech, free press, right to assembly, right to petition, freedom of religion, and obscenity issues. Due process, the fourth issue category, involves issues of fairness in administrative procedures. Fifth, privacy decisions deal with matters of personal integrity, including abortion, contraception, and so on. The attorneys issue area includes decisions involving attorney's fees, admission to the bar, disciplinary actions, and advertising. Union cases deal with matters of arbitration, antitrust, bargaining and negotiation with employers, and the like involving the relationship between labor and management generally. The eighth issue category deals with economics cases. This issue category is quite varied, including within its ambit bankruptcy, mergers, governmental regulation of business, civil liability, securities regulation, patents, and copyrights. Judicial power cases deal with issues of civil and criminal procedure, mootness, venue, standing, judicial review, judicial administration, and comity. Federalism cases involve issues of federal preemption of state regulation or of state court jurisdiction and the general relationship between the federal government and the state governments. Interstate Relations cases are self-explanatory. Federal taxation cases deal with disputes regarding federal taxation of individuals or corporations. Separation of powers involves questions of the relative share of power that the institutions of the federal government possess. The miscellaneous case category is self-explanatory.[5]

SIZE AND COMPOSITION OF THE COURT'S CASELOAD

Total Reported Decisions

These analyses combine the three datasets discussed above (Spaeth, Wood, and Wood et al.) so as to examine the entire period from 1888 to 1997. Because very little empirical data exist concerning the behavior of the Court for the period 1888-1937, the size and composition of its caseload over time is first examined here. Vast changes have occurred in the number of cases in which the Court issued a formal opinion during this period.

As Figure 3-1 and Table 3-1 show, the number of cases decided follows a generally downward trend across the first two-thirds of the period examined, from 1888 to 1953. It hits both an historic high and low in this period. In 1890, the Court decided 291 cases; in 1913, 292. After 1913, the series declines rather consistently until 1917 and temporarily stabilizes. After 1925, however, the Court's caseload declines permanently: in no year since has it decided as many cases. It did so frequently before 1925. From that point until 1953, the series gradually declines. The Court issued 196 decisions in 1926 and only 87 cases in 1953, its nadir. Beginning in 1954, the Court's caseload appears to change course again and exhibits a moderate upward trend that stabilizes in 1972. After 1987, however, it appears to begin to decline precipitously once again; in fact, from 1989 to 1997, the Court has issued an average of about 109 decisions per term.[6]

Casper and Posner posit that four important variables influence the change in the Court's caseload. They are: "(1) the number and scope of federal rights, (2) the procedural devices that facilitate or obstruct the enforcement of federal rights, (3) the costs to litigants of asserting such rights at various stages of the litigation process, and (4) the certainty or definiteness of the rights."[7] Prior to 1925, the large number of decisions the Court issued is, in part, a function of the uncertainty of the law. The Court was then grappling with untested questions of law arising from the increased level of regulation of business activity during a period of unprecedented industrialism and Progressive efforts to reform the law. As a result, there were many unsettled areas of Constitutional jurisprudence, most notably the protection the Due Process Clause of the Fourteenth Amendment guarantees to economic concerns. Thus, the Court's caseload was large so that the Court was able to resolve these pressing issues.

Moreover, the Judiciary Act of 1925 greatly expanded the Court's discretionary jurisdiction, allowing it to whittle down the number of cases claiming space on its agenda to only important, unsettled issues of law.[8] Hence, the gradual but permanent decline in the number of opinions is most likely in part caused by the Court's new-found power arising from the act that allowed it to accept fewer cases to hear initially and, in turn, the number of decisions declined. Yet, the number of cases hovers around 150 per year (rather than declining even further) from 1929 to the post–World War II era, perhaps due to challenges brought against the public policies enacted as result of the Great Depression and the Depression's reflex, the New Deal. The national government was forced to implement social welfare legislation to meet the demands of that national crisis. But because the situation

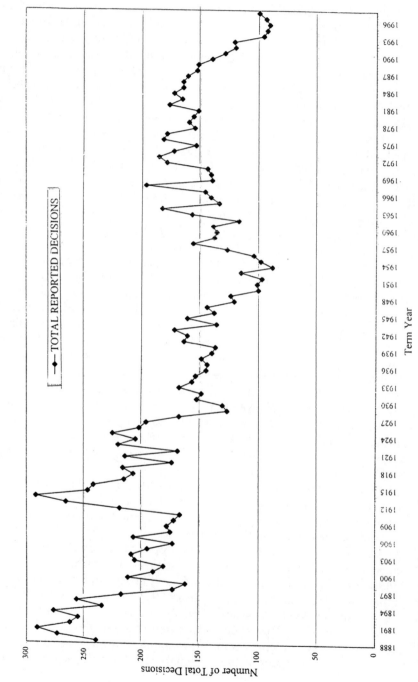

Figure 3-1. Caseload of the United States Supreme Court, 1888-1997

Table 3-1. United States Supreme Court's Agenda, 1888-1997

TERM YEAR	TOTAL REPORTED DECISIONS	ECONOMICS DECISIONS	JUDICIAL POWER DECISIONS	FEDERAL TAXATION DECISIONS	CRIMINAL PROCEDURE DECISIONS	CIVIL RIGHTS DECISIONS	FIRST AMENDMENT DECISIONS	PRIVACY DECISIONS	DUE PROCESS DECISIONS	FEDERALISM DECISIONS	INTERSTATE RELATIONS DECISIONS	SEPARATION OF POWERS DECISIONS	ATTORNEY DECISIONS	UNION DECISIONS	MISCELLANEOUS DECISIONS	ECONOMIC DIMENSION DECISIONS	CIVIL LIBERTIES-RIGHTS DIMENSION DECISIONS	JUDICIAL POWER DIMENSION DECISIONS	OTHER DIMENSION DECISIONS
1888	240	67.9	27.1	0.0	3.3	0.4	0.0	0.0	0.4	0.4	0.0	0.4	0.0	0.0	0.4	67.9	4.2	27.1	1.2
1889	274	66.4	22.3	0.0	4.7	1.5	0.0	0.0	1.8	2.6	0.7	0.0	0.0	0.0	0.0	66.4	8.0	22.3	3.3
1890	291	66.7	21.6	0.7	7.2	1.7	0.0	0.0	0.3	0.7	0.3	0.3	0.3	1.0	0.3	68.7	9.3	21.6	1.7
1891	263	76.0	15.2	0.4	4.9	1.5	0.4	0.0	0.4	0.4	0.4	0.0	0.4	1.0	0.0	77.8	7.2	15.2	0.8
1892	256	75.4	15.6	0.8	4.3	2.0	0.0	0.0	1.6	0.4	0.0	0.0	0.0	0.0	0.0	76.2	7.8	15.6	0.4
1893	277	64.3	20.6	1.8	10.5	0.4	0.0	0.0	0.4	0.4	0.4	0.4	1.1	3.0	0.4	70.1	11.2	20.6	1.5
1894	235	58.7	23.4	1.7	13.2	0.9	0.0	0.0	0.0	0.4	0.4	0.9	0.0	0.0	0.9	60.4	14.0	23.4	2.6
1895	257	52.1	21.4	2.7	17.1	1.2	0.8	0.0	0.8	1.6	0.8	0.8	0.4	1.0	0.8	56.3	19.8	21.4	3.9
1896	218	61.0	20.6	0.0	11.0	1.4	0.5	0.0	3.7	0.9	0.0	0.5	0.5	1.0	0.5	62.5	16.5	20.6	1.9
1897	173	68.8	17.3	0.0	11.0	1.7	0.0	0.0	1.2	0.0	0.0	0.0	0.0	0.0	0.0	68.8	13.9	17.3	0.0
1898	162	61.1	21.6	1.9	6.2	2.5	0.3	0.0	6.8	0.9	0.0	0.0	0.0	0.0	0.0	63.0	15.4	21.6	0.0
1899	212	59.9	23.6	2.4	3.8	0.5	0.5	0.0	7.1	1.9	0.5	0.5	0.0	0.0	0.5	62.3	11.8	23.6	2.4
1900	190	64.2	18.9	4.7	4.7	2.1	0.0	0.0	1.1	1.1	2.1	0.6	0.0	0.0	0.6	68.9	7.9	18.9	4.2
1901	181	66.9	23.2	1.7	4.4	1.1	0.0	0.0	1.1	0.6	0.6	1.0	0.0	0.0	0.0	68.5	6.6	23.2	2.3
1902	206	62.6	23.8	0.0	4.4	2.4	0.0	0.0	2.9	2.4	1.0	0.0	0.0	0.0	0.0	62.6	9.7	23.8	3.4
1903	209	63.6	18.7	1.9	6.7	5.3	0.0	0.0	2.9	1.0	0.0	0.0	0.0	0.0	0.0	65.6	14.8	18.7	1.0
1904	195	58.5	24.6	1.5	6.7	1.5	0.0	0.0	2.1	3.1	2.1	0.0	0.0	0.0	0.0	60.0	10.3	24.6	5.1
1905	173	64.7	19.1	0.6	7.5	0.6	0.0	0.0	2.9	1.7	2.9	0.0	0.5	1.0	0.0	65.3	11.0	19.1	4.6
1906	207	63.8	15.5	0.5	8.2	1.4	0.0	0.0	8.7	0.5	1.0	0.0	1.1	2.0	0.0	65.7	18.4	15.5	1.4
1907	175	57.1	24.0	0.6	8.6	0.6	0.6	0.0	4.6	2.3	0.6	0.0	1.1	2.0	0.0	60.9	13.7	24.0	2.9
1908	178	56.7	24.2	0.6	11.8	0.6	0.0	0.0	0.6	0.6	2.2	0.0	0.6	1.0	0.0	60.4	13.5	24.2	2.8
1909	172	58.7	19.2	1.2	12.2	2.3	0.0	0.0	5.2	0.6	0.0	0.0	0.0	0.0	0.0	61.5	19.8	19.2	0.6
1910	167	67.1	13.8	0.6	11.4	0.6	0.0	0.0	4.2	0.6	1.2	0.6	0.0	0.0	0.6	67.7	16.2	13.8	3.0

Table 3-1. United States Supreme Court's Agenda, 1888-1997

TERM YEAR	TOTAL REPORTED DECISIONS	ECONOMICS DECISIONS	JUDICIAL POWER DECISIONS	FEDERAL TAXATION DECISIONS	CRIMINAL PROCEDURE DECISIONS	CIVIL RIGHTS DECISIONS	FIRST AMENDMENT DECISIONS	PRIVACY DECISIONS	DUE PROCESS DECISIONS	FEDERALISM DECISIONS	INTERSTATE RELATIONS DECISIONS	SEPARATION OF POWERS DECISIONS	ATTORNEY DECISIONS	UNION DECISIONS	MISCELLANEOUS DECISIONS	ECONOMIC DIMENSION DECISIONS	CIVIL LIBERTIES-RIGHTS DIMENSION DECISIONS	JUDICIAL POWER DIMENSION DECISIONS	OTHER DIMENSION DECISIONS
1911	219	71.7	15.1	0.9	4.6	1.8	0.5	0.0	2.7	0.9	0.5	0.9	0.5	0.0	0.9	74.1	9.6	15.1	3.2
1912	266	63.5	12.8	0.8	11.7	1.9	0.4	0.0	8.3	0.0	0.0	0.0	0.8	2.0	0.0	67.0	22.2	12.8	0.0
1913	292	61.3	19.2	3.4	6.2	1.0	0.0	0.0	3.1	3.1	1.4	0.7	0.3	0.0	0.7	66.1	10.3	19.2	5.8
1914	247	68.8	14.2	1.6	5.3	1.6	2.0	0.0	1.6	2.0	1.2	0.4	0.4	1.0	0.4	71.9	10.5	14.2	4.0
1915	242	70.7	12.4	0.8	8.7	0.8	0.0	0.0	5.0	0.4	0.4	0.0	0.4	1.0	0.0	72.9	14.5	12.4	0.8
1916	215	66.5	20.0	0.9	4.7	0.9	0.0	0.0	2.3	1.9	0.0	0.0	0.0	0.0	1.9	67.4	7.9	20.0	5.6
1917	207	60.9	11.1	6.3	5.3	2.4	1.0	0.0	1.4	5.3	2.9	1.9	0.0	0.0	1.9	67.1	10.1	11.1	12.0
1918	216	66.2	11.1	2.8	7.4	0.9	0.5	0.0	7.4	2.3	0.9	1.9	0.5	1.0	0.0	70.4	16.2	11.1	3.2
1919	174	56.9	13.2	4.0	6.9	1.7	0.9	0.0	4.6	9.2	2.3	0.0	0.0	2.0	0.0	64.1	13.2	13.2	11.5
1920	214	57.9	15.9	5.6	7.9	0.9	0.0	0.0	2.3	6.1	0.9	0.0	0.5	0.0	0.5	63.6	12.1	15.9	8.0
1921	169	56.2	10.1	10.1	7.1	1.2	0.9	0.0	3.6	7.1	2.4	0.5	1.1	0.0	0.0	66.3	11.8	10.1	9.5
1922	220	71.2	11.4	3.2	5.0	2.3	0.0	0.0	4.1	1.4	0.0	0.0	0.0	1.0	1.5	75.9	12.3	11.4	1.4
1923	205	66.3	14.1	3.9	5.9	4.9	0.9	0.0	0.5	1.0	1.5	1.5	0.5	0.0	0.0	70.2	11.2	14.1	5.4
1924	225	49.8	20.0	8.0	6.2	2.7	0.0	0.0	6.2	5.3	0.4	0.0	0.0	0.0	1.0	57.8	15.6	20.0	5.8
1925	202	62.8	11.1	11.1	8.5	0.0	0.4	0.0	0.5	2.5	1.5	1.0	1.0	2.0	0.0	76.9	9.0	11.1	6.0
1926	196	60.2	8.2	6.1	16.3	2.0	0.0	0.0	5.6	1.0	0.0	0.0	0.0	0.0	1.0	66.3	24.0	8.2	1.0
1927	168	45.8	15.5	10.1	4.8	1.8	0.0	0.0	4.2	14.9	1.2	0.0	0.6	1.0	0.0	57.5	10.7	15.5	16.1
1928	127	56.7	11.8	11.0	3.9	3.9	1.6	0.0	2.4	6.3	0.8	0.0	0.8	0.0	0.0	69.5	11.8	11.8	7.1
1929	131	58.0	11.5	16.0	4.6	0.0	0.0	0.0	1.5	0.0	3.8	0.0	0.0	0.0	4.6	74.0	6.1	11.5	13.0
1930	153	49.0	3.9	27.5	7.8	2.6	0.7	0.0	3.9	2.6	1.3	4.6	0.7	1.0	0.0	78.1	15.0	3.9	3.9
1931	149	59.1	9.4	16.1	6.0	3.4	0.0	0.0	2.0	0.7	0.7	0.0	0.7	1.0	0.7	76.8	11.4	9.4	2.7
1932	168	51.8	10.7	23.8	6.0	3.6	0.0	0.0	3.0	0.0	1.2	0.7	0.0	0.0	0.0	75.6	12.5	10.7	1.2
1933	157	48.4	11.5	14.6	6.4	0.0	0.0	0.0	5.7	8.3	3.2	1.3	0.0	0.0	1.3	63.1	12.1	11.5	14.0

Table 3-1. United States Supreme Court's Agenda, 1888-1997

TERM YEAR	TOTAL REPORTED DECISIONS	ECONOMICS DECISIONS	JUDICIAL POWER DECISIONS	FEDERAL TAXATION DECISIONS	CRIMINAL PROCEDURE DECISIONS	CIVIL RIGHTS DECISIONS	FIRST AMENDMENT DECISIONS	PRIVACY DECISIONS	DUE PROCESS DECISIONS	FEDERALISM DECISIONS	INTERSTATE RELATIONS DECISIONS	SEPARATION OF POWERS DECISIONS	ATTORNEY DECISIONS	UNION DECISIONS	MISCELLANEOUS DECISIONS	ECONOMIC DIMENSION DECISIONS	CIVIL LIBERTIES-RIGHTS DIMENSION DECISIONS	JUDICIAL POWER DIMENSION DECISIONS	OTHER DIMENSION DECISIONS
1934	154	48.7	17.5	16.2	3.2	0.6	0.0	0.0	1.3	10.4	0.6	0.0	0.0	0.0	0.0	64.9	5.2	17.5	11.0
1935	145	52.4	8.3	24.1	2.1	1.4	0.7	0.0	0.0	6.2	2.1	2.8	0.0	0.0	2.8	76.6	4.1	8.3	13.8
1936	144	55.6	6.9	16.0	8.3	1.4	3.5	0.0	0.0	4.2	0.0	0.0	0.0	0.0	0.0	71.5	13.2	6.9	4.2
1937	149	49.7	6.7	23.5	7.4	0.0	0.7	0.0	1.3	4.0	2.0	2.0	0.0	0.0	2.0	73.2	9.4	6.7	10.1
1938	140	50.0	11.4	16.4	3.6	4.3	0.7	0.0	1.4	3.6	3.6	0.7	0.0	0.0	0.7	66.4	10.0	11.4	8.6
1939	137	49.6	13.1	17.5	5.1	0.0	3.6	0.0	1.5	2.9	2.2	0.0	0.0	0.0	0.0	67.2	10.2	13.1	5.1
1940	164	37.8	15.2	25.0	7.3	1.8	1.8	0.0	0.6	4.9	3.0	0.0	0.0	0.0	0.0	62.8	11.6	15.2	7.9
1941	161	51.6	11.2	13.7	9.3	2.5	4.3	0.0	0.6	4.3	1.2	0.0	0.0	0.0	0.0	65.2	16.8	11.2	5.6
1942	172	43.0	15.1	11.0	16.9	2.9	5.2	0.0	0.7	4.7	2.9	0.0	0.0	0.0	0.0	54.1	25.6	15.1	5.2
1943	136	44.1	14.7	11.0	13.2	3.7	2.2	0.0	3.7	5.1	2.5	0.0	0.6	0.0	0.0	55.1	19.9	14.7	8.1
1944	161	39.8	11.8	16.1	9.9	5.0	0.6	0.7	1.4	6.2	1.4	0.0	0.7	1.0	0.6	57.5	19.3	11.8	9.3
1945	138	39.1	7.2	13.8	15.2	2.9	3.6	0.0	0.7	4.3	1.4	0.0	0.0	1.0	0.0	54.6	23.9	7.2	5.8
1946	144	34.7	6.3	5.6	17.4	2.8	0.7	0.0	0.0	6.3	4.1	0.0	0.0	0.0	1.4	53.5	21.5	6.3	9.0
1947	121	37.9	11.6	4.1	29.8	8.3	2.5	0.0	2.4	2.5	1.6	0.0	0.0	0.0	0.8	38.8	40.5	11.6	7.4
1948	124	31.0	12.9	7.3	20.2	4.0	2.4	0.0	0.0	4.8	1.0	0.0	1.0	0.0	0.8	45.2	29.0	12.9	7.3
1949	100	40.6	16.0	8.0	14.0	7.0	7.0	0.0	4.0	8.0	4.0	0.0	0.0	1.0	0.0	41.0	35.0	16.0	9.0
1950	101	36.1	11.9	4.0	10.9	8.9	6.9	0.0	2.1	3.0	3.1	0.0	0.0	0.0	0.0	44.6	30.7	11.9	7.9
1951	97	31.3	12.4	4.1	23.7	8.2	7.2	0.0	2.6	1.0	3.5	0.0	1.7	1.7	0.0	40.2	41.2	12.4	4.1
1952	115	37.5	13.9	7.8	13.9	10.4	2.6	0.0	0.0	2.6	0.0	0.0	0.0	0.0	0.0	42.9	29.6	13.9	6.1
1953	88	23.5	10.2	3.4	18.2	9.1	5.7	0.0	3.1	6.8	0.0	0.0	0.0	6.8	1.1	47.7	34.1	10.2	7.9
1954	98	28.8	13.3	11.2	19.4	11.2	5.1	0.0	1.9	4.1	3.8	0.0	2.0	4.1	3.1	40.8	38.8	13.3	7.2
1955	104	25.2	14.4	6.7	13.5	12.5	4.8	0.0	1.9	2.9	3.8	0.0	0.0	9.6	1.0	45.1	32.7	14.4	7.7
1956	127	25.2	15.0	6.3	16.5	11.8	7.1	0.0	3.1	3.9	0.0	0.0	2.4	8.7	0.0	42.6	38.5	15.0	3.9

Table 3-1. United States Supreme Court's Agenda, 1888-1997

TERM YEAR	TOTAL REPORTED DECISIONS	ECONOMICS DECISIONS	JUDICIAL POWER DECISIONS	FEDERAL TAXATION DECISIONS	CRIMINAL PROCEDURE DECISIONS	CIVIL RIGHTS DECISIONS	FIRST AMENDMENT DECISIONS	PRIVACY DECISIONS	DUE PROCESS DECISIONS	FEDERALISM DECISIONS	INTERSTATE RELATIONS DECISIONS	SEPARATION OF POWERS DECISIONS	ATTORNEY DECISIONS	UNION DECISIONS	MISCELLANEOUS DECISIONS	ECONOMIC DIMENSION DECISIONS	CIVIL LIBERTIES-RIGHTS DIMENSION DECISIONS	JUDICIAL POWER DIMENSION DECISIONS	OTHER DIMENSION DECISIONS
1957	156	24.4	12.8	5.8	24.4	10.9	7.1	0.6	3.8	4.5	0.0	0.0	0.6	3.2	1.9	34.0	46.8	12.8	6.4
1958	138	37.0	13.8	4.3	20.3	5.8	8.0	0.0	0.0	4.3	1.4	0.0	0.0	3.6	1.4	44.9	34.1	13.8	7.1
1959	136	23.5	14.7	10.3	14.7	10.3	5.9	0.0	3.7	5.9	0.0	0.0	0.0	10.3	0.7	44.1	34.6	14.7	6.6
1960	139	20.1	8.6	7.9	23.0	11.5	16.5	0.0	0.7	2.9	0.0	0.0	0.0	7.9	0.7	35.9	51.7	8.6	3.6
1961	117	24.8	13.7	6.0	17.1	12.8	8.5	0.0	4.3	4.3	0.0	0.0	0.0	7.7	0.7	38.5	42.7	13.7	5.2
1962	157	23.6	12.1	5.7	16.6	18.5	6.4	0.0	1.9	7.0	1.6	0.0	0.6	7.0	0.9	36.9	43.4	12.1	7.6
1963	183	18.6	10.9	3.3	20.8	24.6	8.2	0.7	0.0	6.0	2.2	0.0	0.0	4.9	0.6	26.8	53.6	10.9	8.7
1964	134	17.2	15.7	7.5	13.4	20.1	9.7	0.0	1.5	2.2	1.4	0.0	0.0	9.0	1.1	33.7	45.4	15.7	5.1
1965	141	21.3	17.7	6.4	17.7	14.9	10.6	0.0	2.8	4.3	0.0	0.0	0.0	2.1	0.7	29.8	46.0	17.7	6.4
1966	146	17.1	16.4	1.4	27.4	14.4	15.8	0.0	0.0	2.1	0.0	0.0	0.7	4.8	0.0	24.0	57.6	16.4	2.1
1967	197	14.2	9.1	1.5	34.5	14.2	14.7	0.0	1.0	3.0	2.8	0.0	2.0	4.6	0.0	22.3	64.4	9.1	4.0
1968	140	13.6	17.1	2.9	28.6	19.3	8.6	0.0	2.1	4.3	0.0	0.0	1.4	2.9	1.0	19.4	58.6	17.1	5.0
1969	141	8.5	12.8	5.0	24.1	24.8	12.1	0.7	0.7	2.8	1.7	0.0	0.7	4.3	0.7	19.2	61.7	12.8	6.3
1970	144	12.5	14.6	3.5	19.4	20.8	16.7	0.6	2.8	0.7	2.2	0.0	0.0	3.9	0.7	23.0	60.4	14.6	2.1
1971	179	19.6	8.4	2.2	24.6	19.6	10.6	1.6	7.3	1.7	1.2	0.0	1.1	3.2	1.4	25.7	62.7	8.4	3.4
1972	186	16.1	12.9	2.7	21.5	21.0	10.2	1.2	4.8	2.2	0.6	0.0	1.2	4.6	0.0	23.1	59.1	12.9	4.9
1973	173	12.7	15.0	4.0	20.8	22.0	10.4	1.9	4.6	2.3	1.1	0.0	0.6	3.9	0.5	22.5	59.0	15.0	3.5
1974	154	18.2	14.9	3.2	18.8	20.1	5.2	1.6	4.5	7.1	1.1	0.0	0.0	2.7	0.0	25.9	50.5	14.9	8.3
1975	182	17.6	20.9	0.5	20.3	17.0	7.1	3.4	7.7	3.3	0.6	0.0	0.6	3.9	0.6	20.8	53.7	20.9	4.4
1976	179	10.6	13.4	2.2	23.5	24.0	8.4	0.6	4.5	4.5	0.6	0.0	2.6	3.9	0.0	17.3	63.8	13.4	5.6
1977	155	21.3	12.3	4.5	21.3	20.0	5.2	3.1	3.2	3.9	2.6	0.0	0.0	3.2	1.3	31.6	50.3	12.3	5.8
1978	160	18.1	11.3	2.5	21.3	25.0	5.6	3.1	6.3	2.5	0.6	0.0	0.0	3.8	0.0	24.4	61.3	11.3	3.1
1979	156	21.2	10.3	0.0	25.0	14.7	7.1	3.8	7.1	1.3	2.6	0.0	3.2	3.8	0.0	28.2	57.7	10.3	3.9

Table 3-1. United States Supreme Court's Agenda, 1888-1997

TERM YEAR	TOTAL REPORTED DECISIONS	ECONOMICS DECISIONS	JUDICIAL POWER DECISIONS	FEDERAL TAXATION DECISIONS	CRIMINAL PROCEDURE DECISIONS	CIVIL RIGHTS DECISIONS	FIRST AMENDMENT DECISIONS	PRIVACY DECISIONS	DUE PROCESS DECISIONS	FEDERALISM DECISIONS	INTERSTATE RELATIONS DECISIONS	SEPARATION OF POWERS DECISIONS	ATTORNEY DECISIONS	UNION DECISIONS	MISCELLANEOUS DECISIONS	ECONOMIC DIMENSION DECISIONS	CIVIL LIBERTIES-RIGHTS DIMENSION DECISIONS	JUDICIAL POWER DIMENSION DECISIONS	OTHER DIMENSION DECISIONS
1980	152	17.8	13.2	3.9	18.4	19.7	7.2	0.7	3.9	5.3	2.0	0.0	0.7	5.3	2.0	27.7	49.9	13.2	9.3
1981	177	15.8	16.4	1.7	15.3	20.9	7.3	2.3	5.6	3.4	2.3	0.0	1.7	5.6	1.7	24.8	51.4	16.4	7.4
1982	166	19.9	10.8	2.4	21.7	16.9	6.6	2.4	4.8	6.6	1.2	0.0	1.2	4.2	1.2	27.7	52.4	10.8	9.0
1983	173	16.2	9.8	2.3	30.1	16.8	6.9	1.2	6.4	4.0	1.7	0.0	1.2	3.5	0.0	23.2	61.4	9.8	5.7
1984	165	18.8	7.3	2.4	25.5	15.2	8.5	0.6	6.7	5.5	1.8	0.0	4.2	3.0	0.6	28.4	56.5	7.3	7.9
1985	165	10.3	12.7	3.0	28.5	19.4	8.5	0.6	4.2	6.1	0.6	0.0	2.4	2.4	1.2	18.1	61.2	12.7	7.9
1986	161	14.3	9.3	3.1	27.3	15.5	8.1	0.6	7.5	7.5	0.6	0.0	1.9	3.1	1.2	22.4	59.0	9.3	9.3
1987	153	17.0	16.3	2.0	20.3	14.4	7.8	1.3	5.9	5.9	0.7	0.0	2.0	5.2	1.3	26.2	49.7	16.3	7.9
1988	152	11.2	12.5	2.6	22.4	19.1	9.9	2.6	3.3	5.9	0.0	0.0	3.9	3.3	3.3	21.0	57.3	12.5	9.2
1989	140	17.9	13.6	5.0	27.9	6.4	10.0	2.9	2.9	6.4	1.4	0.0	2.9	2.9	0.0	28.7	50.1	13.6	7.8
1990	129	20.2	14.0	1.6	27.1	14.0	3.9	0.8	2.3	4.7	1.6	0.0	2.3	6.2	1.6	30.3	48.1	14.0	7.9
1991	120	23.3	14.2	3.3	21.7	16.7	6.7	2.5	5.0	4.2	0.0	0.0	1.7	0.8	0.0	29.1	52.6	14.2	4.2
1992	121	15.7	18.2	5.0	26.4	14.0	7.4	0.8	0.8	5.8	2.5	0.0	1.7	1.0	0.0	24.1	49.4	18.2	8.3
1993	96	22.9	11.5	2.1	26.0	16.7	4.2	3.1	3.1	5.2	1.0	0.0	2.1	1.0	1.0	28.1	53.1	11.5	7.2
1994	93	18.3	17.2	2.2	23.7	15.1	8.6	0.0	2.2	7.5	3.2	0.0	1.1	0.0	1.1	21.6	49.6	17.2	11.8
1995	91	18.7	15.4	4.4	24.2	12.1	5.5	1.1	5.5	6.6	2.2	0.0	0.0	4.4	0.0	27.5	48.4	15.4	8.8
1996	94	16.0	12.8	3.2	20.2	21.3	5.3	6.4	5.3	7.4	0.0	0.0	0.0	1.1	1.1	20.3	58.5	12.8	8.5
1997	100	16.0	21.0	3.0	28.0	20.0	2.0	0.0	4.0	1.0	2.0	0.0	0.0	2.0	1.0	21.0	54.0	21.0	4.0

was so unique, there were many unsettled questions that the Court ultimately had to review. Thus, the Court's caseload may have increased as a consequence.

Also, the moderate upward trend in the series that begins in 1954 may be due to the changing subject matter of the Court's decisions. The Court's civil liberties–civil rights jurisprudence, under Earl Warren, was allegedly liberal and, thus, announced that the Constitution gave petitioners greater rights than had been established previously. Therefore, the number of opinions that the Court issued would accordingly increase due to this expansion of constitutional guarantees. Yet, the series begins to decline in 1987, possibly because of the Rehnquist Court's more restrictive view of constitutional protections. This decrease in the number of opinions may also be due to the Court's having resolved many of the prevailing issues of civil rights and liberties, much as the Court during Fuller's and White's tenures did with respect to issues of economic regulation. Hence, the series may have stabilized as a result.

Issue Areas

While the overall number of reported decisions fluctuates within its overall downward trend across the period analyzed, the decisions themselves can be further analyzed according to the issue areas in which they fall. Figures 3-2 through 3-6 and Table 3-1 show the relative proportion of the Court's agenda for fourteen issue areas for the years 1888 to 1997, inclusive. The content of these issue areas is described above. Following the classification scheme that Spaeth originates,[9] the decisions were placed into one of the following issues areas: criminal, civil rights, First Amendment, due process, attorney, union, economic, judicial power, federalism, interstate relations, federal taxation, miscellaneous, and separation of powers.

Economics Decisions

The first finding that is most noticeable from the figures is that, as Figure 3-2 shows, economics cases constituted the largest proportion of all of these issue areas—usually an overwhelming majority of the decisions the Court announced for about 60 of the 110 years analyzed (1888–1950). Indeed, economics so overwhelmed the other series as to make them unreadable if they were plotted in one figure for this period. Thus, Figures 3-2 through 3-6 separately display the proportions for the other issue areas in a more readable form.

As one can see from Figure 3-2, the proportion of economics decisions displays a clear downward trend across the period and an especially strong

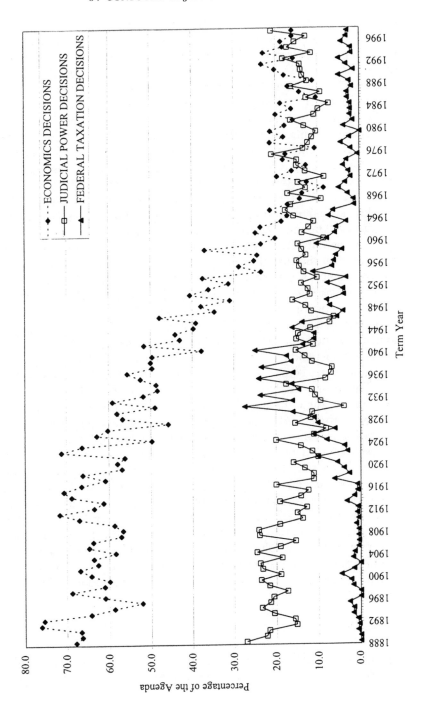

Figure 3-2. Composition of the Agenda of the United States Supreme Court, 1888-1997

downward trend from the mid-1930s through 1969. The series experiences
its historical high of 76 percent (199 decisions) in 1891 and its historic low
of 8.1 percent (3 decisions) in 1969. This decline continues even through
the period of the Great Depression, when one would expect the Court, as
the nation's highest judicial authority, to be deluged with requests from
parties seeking redress and the lower courts seeking guidance as to how to
resolve the unprecedented problems then facing the national economic order.

Pacelle examines the composition of the Court's agenda from 1933 to
1987. He categorizes the cases into slightly different issue areas than is done
in the present analysis.[10] For example, he disaggregates cases that the present
coding system would have coded as "economic" into five different categories. These are: U.S. regulation, state regulation, state as a litigant, United
States as a litigant, and ordinary economic.[11] The "State as a Litigant"
cases involve "boundary disputes between two states, navigable waters cases,
and state liability for certain actions."[12] These cases more closely correspond to what the current coding scheme would classify as "Interstate Relations." Hence, if the remaining case types (those other than the "State as
a Litigant" cases) are aggregated, then a valid comparison between Pacelle's
analysis and the present analysis can be made.[13]

Based on this redefinition of economics cases, Pacelle's results are quite
similar, although not identical, to those of the present analysis. Examining
the average percentage of cases across five term years, Pacelle reports that
economics cases comprised 55.4 percent of the Court's agenda for 1933–
37.[14] The present analysis indicates that the figure is 52.46 percent.[15] Both
Pacelle's and these findings do show the same steady decrease in the percentage of the agenda that the Court dedicated to economics cases. The
historic high for the series is found within the first period (1933–37) (Pacelle:
55.4 percent; present study: 52.46 percent). The most recent period (1983–
87) exhibits the series' historic low (Pacelle: 24.3; present: 15.32).[16] Throughout the entire period, the two analyses provide similar results and
implications: economics cases constituted about one-half of the cases that
the Court announced in the term years prior to the end of World War II,
but in more recent times constitute only about one-fifth of the Court's docket.
However, Pacelle's results do differ slightly from those of this analysis in
that his results tend to show larger absolute percentages. This discrepancy
may be an artifact of the differences in coding methodology between the
two studies.

Judicial Power

Figure 3-2 also displays the percentage of the Court's agenda constituted
by judicial power cases.[17] Such cases comprise a fairly significant propor-

tion of the Court's agenda during the years from 1888 to 1997. In the first half of the period analyzed, these cases experienced a moderate downward trend, ending in 1930. In 1888, the series begins with its period high proportion of 27 percent; in 1930 it experiences its historic low of 3.9 percent. Also, beginning in 1930, the series becomes rather volatile, but shows no significant net change. It exceeds 20 percent in 1975 and 1997, reaching a mark of 21 percent.

Federal Taxation

The third series shown in Figure 3-2 plots the proportion of federal taxation cases on the Court's agenda. The series shows a clear increasing pattern, especially after 1926. These cases reach their historic high—27.5 percent of the agenda—in 1930. This finding is consistent with theoretical expectations since the Sixteenth Amendment, providing for a Federal personal income tax, was adopted in 1913. The series falls off to 5.6 percent in 1946 and thereafter exceeds 10 percent only once—in 1954. In later years, it rarely exceeds 5 percent. There are several years in which no such cases were issued, all but one occurring before 1903.

Pacelle similarly finds that from 1933 to 1937, federal taxation cases consumed 17.8 percent of the Court's docket, the historic high.[18] Thereafter, the percentage dwindles to 8.4 percent between 1953 and 1957, and then to 3.2 percent during the term years 1983 to 1987. Pacelle's historic low occurs between 1978 and 1982, at 2.5 percent.[19] The present study, however, finds that the historic low is zero percent. This discrepancy may be explained by the different coding techniques of the two studies: Pacelle employs an average across five term years, while in the present study the results are reported for individual term years.

Similarly, the present investigation finds that the historic high occurred between 1933 and 1937, with federal taxation cases comprising 18.88 percent of the Court's docket on average across those five years, and that the series declines to consume only 6.68 percent of the Court's decisions on average by 1953–57, and only 2.56 percent by 1983–87. As Pacelle finds, the historic low occurred between 1978 and 1982, when these cases accounted for only 2.20 percent of the Court's agenda.

Criminal Procedure

Figure 3-3 plots the percentage of the agenda that criminal procedure, civil rights, and First Amendment cases comprise. Looking first at criminal procedure cases, one can see that this series demonstrates a strong upward trend, but a trend that does not become established until 1939. Before that

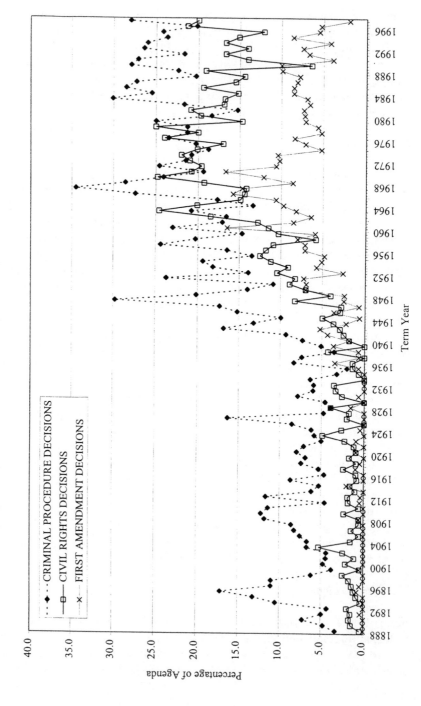

Figure 3-3. Composition of the Agenda of the United States Supreme Court, 1888-1997

term year, it exhibits occasional increases that raise it above its otherwise normal 5 to 10 percent. As the figure shows, the series demonstrates a rather strong upward trend, with large but temporary increases in the early 1890s, and in the 1960s, the latter perhaps due to the agenda priorities of the Warren Court. The series hits its high in 1967, capturing 34.5 percent of the Court's decisions that term year. As noted, criminal cases begin to garner significantly more space on the Court's agenda in the late 1930s, moving from 3.6 percent in 1938 to 20.2 percent only ten years later in 1948. The series exhibits a notable shift in its level in 1942; thereafter it never drops below 10 percent (rounded) of the Court's decisions. Although it continues to fluctuate rather strongly thereafter, the series never returned to the low levels observed in the 1930s and prior, and its mean steadily rises.

Pacelle categorizes "criminal" decisions slightly differently. He defines "Due Process" cases as those including "primarily, but not exclusively, criminal procedure cases. Among the areas are search and seizure, self-incrimination, death penalty, right to counsel, jury procedure, and double jeopardy. In addition, Due Process considerations in administrative proceedings are included." Pacelle also defines "criminal law" cases as those "that turned on a substantive interpretation of a criminal statute by the Court."[20] Those cases dealing with the fairness of administrative proceedings were coded herein as "due process" cases; all others were coded as "criminal procedure" cases.

Thus, the results in these four categories (Pacelle's "Due Process" and "Criminal Law," and "criminal procedure" and "due process" in the present analysis) are compared. Using once again the tack that Pacelle takes (employing the average percentage of the docket consumed across a five-year period), the results of the two studies are somewhat different overall. From 1933 to 1937 and from 1938 to 1942, the two studies' findings are quite similar: the five-year average for due process, criminal law, and criminal procedure is about 7 percent each.

From 1943 to 1947, however, they begin to diverge. Pacelle finds that these cases comprised 12.6 percent of the docket, whereas this study suggests that 17.10 percent of the Court's agenda was consumed by such cases. From 1948 to 1952, Pacelle's analysis finds that these cases consumed 18.30 percent of the Court's agenda, while the present study finds that they represent 16.54 percent of the docket. In the two succeeding five-year periods, Pacelle's results indicate that the series increases from 22 percent (for 1953 and 1957) to 24.10 percent (for 1958 to 1962) to 27.40 percent (for 1958 to 1962) to 34.1 percent (its historic high) for 1968 and 1972.[21]

However, the present analysis demonstrates that between 1948 and 1962 they remained relatively flat. The series comprises 16.54 percent from 1948 to 1952, 18.4 percent from 1953 to 1957, and 18.34 percent from 1958 to

1962. Between 1963 and 1967, however, these cases increase somewhat, comprising 22.76 percent of the docket; between 1968 and 1972, the figure climbs to 23.64 percent. Between 1973 and 1977, the series reverses course and declines to 20.94 percent.

From 1973 to 1977, these cases begin to consume less of the Court's docket. Pacelle finds that they are 29.8 percent of the Court's docket, whereas the present study finds that they are 20.94 percent of the agenda. Between 1978 and 1982, their decline continues. The present study finds that they represent 20.34 percent of the decisions announced, while Pacelle notes that the figure is 28.6 percent. But both studies indicate that the series then rebounds. Pacelle finds that they comprise 31.3 percent of the Court's agenda from 1982 to 1988; the present study 25.11 percent, its historic high.[22]

Hence, as I have found with other issue areas, the two studies' findings do diverge. Although they do agree generally as to whether there is a trend occurring and its direction, the studies disagree as to the magnitude of the proportion of the Court's docket that these cases comprise, differences reaching as high as 7 percent. They also disagree as to when the series' historic high occurs. Pacelle states that it occurs from 1968 to 1972, whereas the present study finds that it occurs during the five-year period from 1982 to 1988. Again, these discrepancies may be due to different coding methodology, disagreements as to what category a decision best fits in, differences in simple calculation of the percentages, or some combination of these factors.

Civil Rights

Figure 3-3 also shows the frequency of civil rights cases on the Supreme Court's agenda. As the figure shows, the series attains 5 percent or greater only twice (in 1903 and 1944) during the fifty-eight term years from 1888 and 1945. Its historic low of zero percent occurs several times during this period, observed first in 1925. After 1945, the series becomes a continuous part of the Court's agenda. Civil rights cases then begin to experience an upward trend in 1947, attaining 8.3 percent in that year, 8.9 percent in 1950, 10.4 percent in 1952, 12.5 percent in 1955, and 18.5 percent in 1962. The series hits an historic high in 1978 of 25.0 percent of the decisions that the Court announced in that term year. This latter mark is nearly matched in the term years 1963 (24.6 percent), 1969 (24.6 percent), and 1976 (24.0 percent).

This upward movement in the proportion of civil rights cases that the Court decided supports McCloskey's observations that the Court's priorities were changing from one focused on economics questions to issues of civil rights, due in part to the questions of most pressing concern and conflict within the American political structure as a whole.[23] The Court, as the nation's highest conflict resolution institution, would naturally begin to consider those questions that were being increasingly debated in the larger political context. Indeed, the Court did not begin to consider them until they were arising in other political venues. Prior to the 1950s, the extant political culture did not support the expansion of civil rights, being more concerned with how best to handle the challenges that growing industrialism presented to the nation, whether through vigorous economic regulation or through other policies. Hence, the increase in the proportion of civil rights cases that the Court considered, beginning in the 1950s, reflects a fundamental change in the substance of the Court's agenda from one concerned with issues related to the regulation of business activity to one dominated by questions of civil rights and civil liberties.

Pacelle examines the percentage of civil rights cases on the Court's agenda across time. He labels such cases "equality" cases, which are "characterized as civil rights and involve alleged discrimination on the basis of race, gender, age, disability, or similar factors."[24] Until 1968, he finds these cases did not consistently consume more than 10 percent of the Court's docket. From 1933 to 1962, civil rights cases, in an average per term year, comprise 3.38 percent of the total decisions of the Court. Even after 1962, such cases exceed 15 percent only once (1983–87).[25]

Pacelle's findings do differ rather substantially from those found in this study, however. From 1933 to 1962, the results of the present analysis are about double those of Pacelle (compare 2.7 percent with 4.51 percent for 1943 to 1947; compare 5.1 percent with 11.1 percent for 1953 to 1957). Moreover, whereas Pacelle finds that the historic high for the series (16.6 percent) occurred between 1983 and 1987, the historic high in the present study occurred between 1968 and 1972 (21.1 percent), followed closely by the averages observed during 1973 to 1977 (20.62 percent) and 1978 to 1982 (19.44 percent).[26] During the period in which Pacelle finds the apogee of civil rights cases (1983-1987), this study finds that such cases began to decline in frequency, consuming an average of 16.26 percent of the agenda.[27] Nevertheless, Pacelle's finding that civil rights cases do not begin to become more frequent until the 1960s is confirmed herein.

First Amendment

The third series that Figure 3-3 plots is First Amendment cases. Like civil rights decisions, First Amendment cases do not begin to significantly increase their share of the Court's agenda until the 1950s; indeed, they usually do not even initially appear on the agenda before 1935.[28] It is not until the 1950s that these cases regularly exceed 5 percent of the agenda. Not until 1965 do such cases consistently comprise 10 percent or more of the

Court's term decisions. The series high is observed in 1970 (16.7 percent), and there are many term years before 1935 in which no First Amendment cases were decided. As discussed above, the Court was previously more concerned with resolving economic issues. This series parallels the changes observed in the relative share of the agenda that civil rights decisions comprise. Again, these findings confirm Pacelle's results and McCloskey's observations about the growth of civil rights decisions during the last forty years.[29]

Privacy

The first issue area plotted in Figure 3-4 depicts the proportion of privacy cases from 1888 to 1997. The most apparent finding when one examines this series is that in the majority of term years, the Court's agenda does not include any such decisions because Supreme Court precedent did not formally recognize the right of privacy until 1965 when, in *Griswold v. Connecticut*, the Court held unconstitutional a state statute that made the use and prescription of contraceptives illegal.[30] Although there are three single termyear increases (1945, 1957, and 1964), the series does begin to increase, although only marginally, in 1970. However, it begins to decline soon thereafter, in 1979. Moreover, its historic high is only 3.8 percent, also observed in 1979. Thus, privacy cases have not comprised even a modest portion of the Court's agenda across the 110 term years analyzed.

Pacelle examines the relative frequency of First Amendment and privacy cases. He labels these "Substantive Rights" cases, and aggregates them into a single issue area along with decisions involving "[i]ndividual rights to an abortion, rights of privacy, and cases involving conscientious objectors and alleged Communists are also included."[31] Hence, to make a valid comparison, Pacelle's "Substantive Rights" cases will be compared with the five-year averages within the First Amendment and privacy issue areas in the present investigation.

The results of the two studies show differences and similarities, as with previous issue areas. The historic low for both Pacelle and the present study is observed in the earliest five-year period (1933–37).[32] Similarly, both studies' results indicate that the historic high occurred between 1968 and 1972 (Pacelle: 16.2 percent; here: 6.11 percent). Thereafter, both studies find that the percentage of these cases increases consistently through the period from 1973 to 1977, when it begins to decline. In the last five-year period Pacelle discusses (1983–87), he finds that such cases comprise only 10.7 percent of the docket; the present study finds they that represent 4.41 percent of the tribunal's agenda.[33]

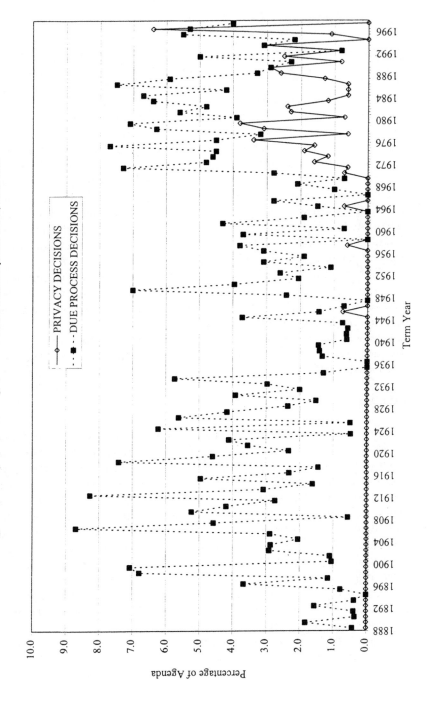

Figure 3-4. Composition of the Agenda of the United States Supreme Court, 1888-1997

Due Process

Figure 3-4 also plots the annual proportions of due process cases. The first finding one notices is that the proportion of the Court's agenda fluctuates rather wildly (between zero and 9 percent) across the entire period at hand. There is no apparent upward or downward trend that one can discern from the figure, as there clearly is with economics decisions. The series' maximum occurs in 1906, comprising 8.7 percent of the Court's decisions. There appears to be a downward trend from about 1900 to 1940. There are several term years (1894, 1935, 1936, 1947, 1958, 1963, and 1966) in which the Court announced no due process decisions. However, much like the other issue areas of civil liberties, civil rights, and First Amendment cases, the series does experience a jump in level beginning in 1967. From 1967 until 1997, this issue area consumes at least a modest portion of the Court's agenda, although it declines near the end of the series, comprising only 4.0 percent of the Court's decisions in 1997.

The findings for the two studies do differ in terms of the magnitude of the percentages across time. The present study's findings are generally smaller than are those of Pacelle, although the difference is often only two or three percentage points. The two studies agree, however, in that they both affirm the timing and the general trend in the growth and then the decline in First Amendment and privacy cases on the Court's docket across the period from 1933 to 1987.

Federalism

Figure 3-5 plots the proportions of federalism, interstate relations, and separation of powers cases. Among the three series, federalism cases clearly occur most frequently. Beginning around 1916, federalism cases trend erratically upward, although the slope of the series line is not terribly steep. There are several large increases in the 1920s and 1930s, although the series is rather dynamic during those years. This finding supports Pacelle's finding of an increase in such issues on the Court's docket.[34] It also bolsters Schwartz's observation that the Court was moving, albeit slowly, toward a philosophy supportive of social welfare, which could be best effectuated by bolstering the national government's power.[35] The series stabilizes in 1954, begins to decline in 1963, and then describes a upward trend again in 1971. Its historic high of 14.9 percent occurred in 1927, and in several term years, it consumes no space on the Court's agenda.

Pacelle finds that federalism cases decline over the period from 1933 to 1987.[36] His results indicate that the historic high is observed between the

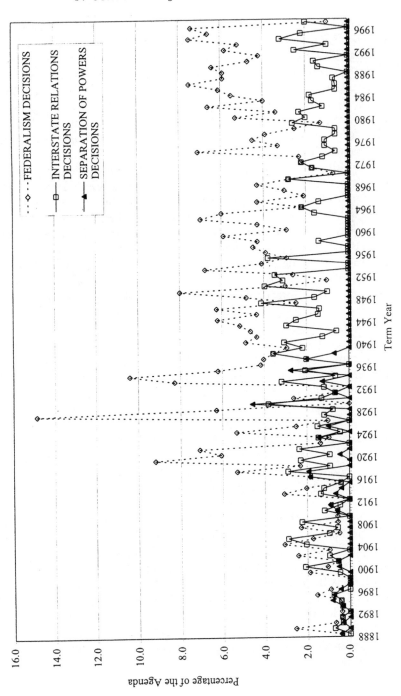

Figure 3-5. Composition of the Agenda of the United States Supreme Court, 1888-1997

years of 1933 and 1937. Thereafter, the series declines to 5.4 percent, between 1968 and 1972, after which it rebounds somewhat to 10.0 percent during 1983–87. This study similarly indicates that the series generally declines through 1968–72, consuming only 3.54 percent of the Court's docket. It then slowly returns to approximately the level first observed in 1933–37 (6.62). The present study's findings suggest that the historic high for federalism cases occurred in 1933–37, similar to those of Pacelle.[37] The studies also agree that the historic low occurs between 1968 and 1972, although once again there are differences in the absolute magnitude of the results.

In this context, however, the differences often reach eight or nine percentage points. Part of this discrepancy can be accounted for by the different methodologies of the studies. Pacelle coded only cases whose opinions were at least a page long, whereas in the present study all cases were coded regardless of the opinion's length.[38] Further, the different researchers involved may simply have disagreed as to what category the decision best represented. Some decisions that one researcher may place in the federalism category may also be placed in economics, for example. These differences in coding may explain the different results of the two studies.

Interstate Relations

As Figure 3-5 shows, interstate relations cases do not consume more than 4 percent of the Court's agenda during the period at hand. From 1888 to 1930, such cases do not demonstrate a clear trend. They comprise less than 2 percent of the Court's docket on average up until 1930. Then, there was a temporary increase in their proportion, lasting through the end of World War II and ending in 1950, when the series begins to trend downward to a point of less than an average of 1.5 percent of the Court's agenda through 1997. The series high is experienced in 1947 when these cases comprise 4.1 percent of the Court's decisions. Thereafter, the series declines substantially.

No direct comparison can be made between these findings and those of Pacelle because of his coding scheme. He operationalizes "State as a Litigant" cases as including "boundary disputes between two states, navigable waters cases, and state liability for certain actions."[39] In the present study, only the first two categories are included in the operationalization of "Interstate Relations" cases. The third category, involving state liability, is included within the "Economics" issue area herein. Based on the data displayed in Table 3-1, these latter decisions comprise the bulk of the three types of cases. Hence, any comparison between the findings of the two studies would be misleading.

Separation of Powers

Finally, separation of powers cases are even less frequently on the Court's agenda than are interstate relations cases, as Figure 3-5 shows. The series' historic high occurs in 1929, when it comprised 4.6 percent of the Court's docket. In several term years, the Court issued no separation of powers rulings. Thus, the series' showing no such cases after 1954 is somewhat misleading for these types of cases, since no direct comparison can be made between the pre- and postwar periods. Pacelle finds that the series increases, although only modestly, from 1933 to 1982. Between 1933 and 1937, the percentage of these cases on the Court's docket was 0.4 percent; between 1983 and 1987, it only reached 1.2 percent.[40]

One should note that Spaeth[41] did not include an issue area for such cases in his original dataset. The research team at the University of North Texas, headed by Dr. Sandra L. Wood, chose to create such a category because they encountered a nontrivial number of such decisions.

Union

Figure 3-6 displays the proportion of the Court's agenda dedicated to two relatively infrequent series: attorney cases and union cases. The proportion of union cases remains near zero until 1936, when the series becomes a visible proportion of the Court's caseload. It fluctuates from about 2 percent to about 10 percent until 1960, when it subsides to a relatively steady 2 to 5 percent per term year. The series' high occurs in 1959 at 10.3 percent. In this and other series, there are several term years in which the Court issued no decisions in this issue area.

This finding of an increase in the series in the late 1930s confirms Pacelle's results and Schwartz's observations as to the fundamental change in the Court's priorities in the Roosevelt era.[42] The Court had for the first time adopted a judicial philosophy that was supportive of New Deal and regulatory legislation and, indeed, a social welfare state, as opposed to the laissez-faire philosophy that had dominated the Court's decision-making beginning most prominently in the late 1800s.[43] This change apparently led it to devote some agenda space to union-related issues. The liberalism of these decisions will be discussed in the next chapter.

Attorney

Figure 3-6 also displays the proportion of attorney cases. Only after the end of World War II do such cases consume even a tiny portion of the Court's

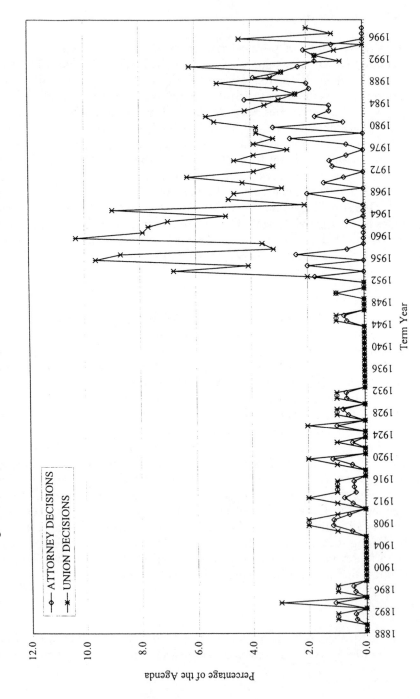

Figure 3-6. Composition of the Agenda of the United States Supreme Court, 1888-1997

agenda. There are relatively large increases in 1952 (1.7 percent), 1954 (2.0 percent), and 1956 (2.4 percent), but these decline quickly. Prior to that time, there are very small and fleeting changes in the proportion of the Court's agenda dedicated to attorney cases. Only in 1979 does the series begin to demonstrate anything resembling a trend; it reaches its historic high of 4.2 percent in 1984.

MAJOR ISSUE AREAS

To determine more clearly the trends in the various types of decisions that the Court issued across the 110 years analyzed in the present study, the fourteen issue types are aggregated into four major categories, following Pacelle's and Schubert's methodology. In Pacelle's analysis of the major issue dimensions, he aggregates "Due Process," "Substantive Rights," and "Equality" in a "Civil Liberties" dimension, and "Internal Revenue," "State Regulation," "United States as a Litigant," "State as Litigant," and "Ordinary Economic" into an "Economic" dimension.[44]

Schubert finds that two major scales, the "C" scale and the "E" scale, dominated Supreme Court decision-making from 1946 to 1969. Schubert's "C" scale is comprised of the justice's views on the broad range of civil liberties and civil rights issues. The scale, therefore, "consists of claims to personal (as distinguished from property) rights and freedoms."[45] These are the rights of free speech, press, religion, assembly, and petition located in the First Amendment. They also include rights of due process and racial equality listed in the Fourth through Eighth Amendments (as against the federal government), and the Fourteenth Amendment (as against the state governments).[46] Schubert's "E" scale, moreover, deals with the justices' views on matters of economic regulation. Schubert "group[s] together sets of cases which involved disputes between unions and employers; governmental regulation of business activities; fiscal claims of workers against employers; and disputes between small businessmen and their corporate competitors."[47]

Schubert theorizes the existence of four subscales beyond the major "C" and "E" scales. He finds some evidence of the "F" scale, dealing with matters of governmental taxing authority.[48] Schubert also posits three other subscales: the "N" (federalism), "A" (judicial activism), and, "J" (judicial centralization) subscales.[49] There is no substantial empirical support for the existence of these latter scales, however.

The Content of the Issue Areas

The fourteen disaggregated issue areas used in the present investigation are aggregated as follows: decisions in criminal procedure, civil rights, First

Amendment, privacy, and due process cases are combined into an overall civil liberties–civil rights dimension; decisions in attorney, union, economics, and federal taxation cases are combined into an overall economics dimension; decisions in judicial power cases are combined into a single dimension; and decisions in federalism, interstate relations, separation of powers and miscellaneous cases are combined into a dimension labeled "other" to indicate the rather diverse, residual nature of the cases that the dimension comprised. Interstate relations decisions (what Pacelle calls "State as a Litigant" cases) are not included in the aggregated economic dimensions herein because such cases are conceptually distinct from the other issue types within that dimension.

Economics Decisions

Figure 3-7 shows the proportions of the Court's agenda due to each of the four major areas during each of the term years from 1888 to 1997. Figures 3-8 through 3-11 plot the individual major issue dimensions over this time period. As Figures 3-7 and 3-8 clearly show, economic decisions overwhelmingly dominated the Court's agenda for more than sixty years (1888–1948). The series hovers around 65 percent during this period. During the Great Depression era (1929–39), the series temporarily increases to well over 70 percent of the Court's docket.

These findings are theoretically consistent. In addition to the political and legal demands that the Great Depression caused on the Court's docket, the Progressive movement, and subsequent reforms, may have caused the Court to be concerned primarily with questions of economics. Progressivism sought to "restrict the excesses of big business by attacking monopolies, settling industry-wide strikes, and conserving natural resources. These efforts produced a considerable expansion of federal power. . . ."[50] The Progressive reforms involved setting maximum work-week length, and minimum wages, prohibiting child labor, prescribing working conditions, and even regulating labor-management relations, each of which was brought to the Court for a ruling on its constitutionality.[51] Thus, the Court's agenda was dominated by challenges to such legislation.

However, in the late 1940s, economics decisions begin a sharp downturn (see Figure 3-8 and Table 3-1), gaining stability in the late 1970s and 1980s, and attaining an average of 24.74 percent of the Court's agenda through 1997. These findings demonstrate the validity of the much-discussed transition that occurred in the Court's post–World War II agenda,[52] with civil liberties–civil rights decisions moving to win the lion's share of the Court's agenda thereafter.[53] The historic high for economic dimension cases

Figure 3-7. Composition of the Agenda of the United States Supreme Court
Based on Major Issue Dimensions, 1888-1997

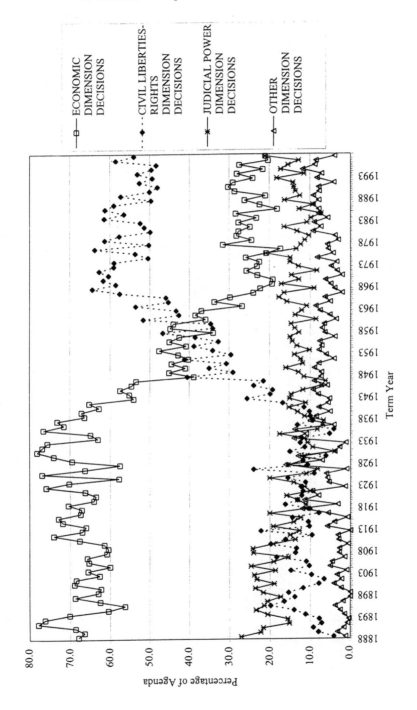

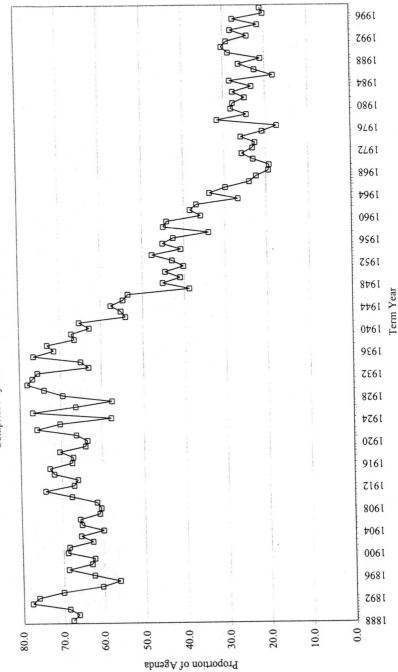

Figure 3-8. Proportion of United States Supreme Court's Agenda Comprised by Economics Decisions, 1888-1997

occurs in 1930, when they comprise 77.1 percent of the Court's rulings. The overall low occurs in 1976, at 17.3 percent of the tribunal's agenda.

Pacelle operationalizes his economic dimension somewhat differently than does the present investigation. He includes within his operationalization these issue areas: "Internal Revenue," "State Regulation," "State as Litigant," "United States as Litigant," and "Ordinary Economic."[54] Strangely, however, he fails to include decisions within the "U.S. Regulation" issue area, which theoretically should be aggregated with the other issue area decisions. To compare more directly the findings of this study with his, all these categories, with the exception of "State as Litigant," are combined. The "State as Litigant" issue area is excluded because of its inclusion of cases dealing with boundary disputes between states, which are not theoretically associated with the remainder of the decisions that involve state liability. Such cases are separately considered herein in the "Interstate Relations" category. Cases involving border disputes comprise a maximum of 2.4 percent in any five-year period. On average, they comprise about 1.2 percent of the Court's annual docket. Hence, their exclusion presents no significant problems of comparison or interpretation.

Pacelle's combined findings are comparable to those in the present investigation. Both his findings and the present findings indicate that economic cases have declined consistently since 1933 to a point where they comprise about one-quarter of the Court's docket between 1983 and 1997. The historic high for Pacelle (73.2 percent) and this study (71.34 percent) occurs between 1933 and 1937. The historic low for Pacelle (28.7 percent) and this study (22.08 percent) also occurs within the same five year period (1968–72).[55] Thereafter, both studies indicate that the series begins to increase modestly. It does not return to the levels observed during the 1930s, when it comprised nearly three-quarters of the Court's docket. Hence, both studies confirm McCloskey's observation that economics cases, while once occupying the preeminent place on the Court's docket, have substantially declined, giving way to civil rights and liberties decisions.

Civil Liberties–Civil Rights

As Figure 3-9 shows, the series depicting civil rights and civil liberties decisions is relatively flat through 1936. From 1888 to 1936, the series attains or exceeds approximately 20 percent only four times (1895, 1909, 1912, and 1926). The series average during this time is about 12 percent. The series' minimum occurs in 1935, at 4.1 percent, when economics cases dominate the Court's docket. Many of these cases during this time involve questions of free speech, often regarding the limit of Constitutional guarantees during times of war.[56]

A strong, upward trend for civil liberties–civil rights begins in 1937. For

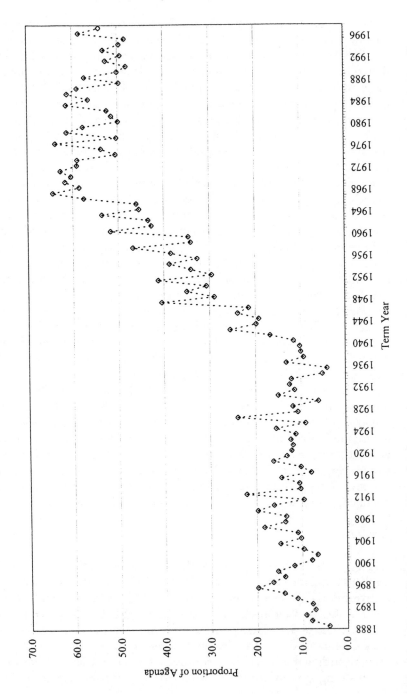

Figure 3-9. Proportion of United States Supreme Court's Agenda Comprised by Civil Liberties-Civil Rights Decisions, 1888-1997

example, the Court's changing priorities may be illustrated by its ruling in
Palko v. Connecticut, holding that the Bill of Rights protected "fundamental
rights" from the actions of state governments and establishing the doctrine
of selective incorporation of constitutional guarantees.[57] This decision is a
landmark ruling, for it created precedent on which later civil liberties jurisprudence will later be erected.[58] The series reaches its historic high of 64.4
percent in 1967, and stabilizes in the late 1970s and 1980s at slightly more
than one-half of the agenda. In recent years, civil liberties–civil rights decisions nearly achieve the percentage of the Court's agenda that economics
decisions reached between the 1890s and 1930s.

Pacelle finds that the series describes an upward trend, beginning in
1933. Between 1933 and 1937, civil liberties-civil rights cases comprise only
9.30 percent of the Court's docket.[59] Thirty years later (between 1963 and
1967), the figure climbs exactly forty points (to 49.30). The next five term
years show an increase even over this high point. Civil liberties–civil rights
decisions comprise 62.30 percent of the Court's decisions on average between 1973 and 1997. Thereafter, the series begins to decline, although
only modestly. By 1983–87, such cases consume on average 58.60 percent
of the Court's agenda.[60]

The present study largely confirms Pacelle's findings. Its results suggest
several conclusions about the Court's changing priorities with regard to
civil liberties–civil rights. First, as McCloskey observes, these decisions were
not a high priority for the Court prior to 1937.[61] The Court's attention was
structurally limited by its consideration of economics issues. This is an expected finding because the nation, and thus the Court, was grappling with
novel questions of the constitutional limits of economic regulation during a
period when the nation overall was becoming much more industrialized
and commercial, and when it was enduring the economic and political challenges of the Great Depression. Second, the present results suggest that
there has been a steady, upward trend in the average percentage of civil
liberties–civil rights decisions the Court has announced, beginning in 1937.
By that time, the Court had resolved many pressing economic questions
and began to dedicate at least a growing portion of its agenda to issues that
had begun to become more prominent in the national policy-making process. Similar to Pacelle's findings, the historic high is observed between 1968
and 1972 (60.16 percent); the historic low between 1933 and 1937 (8.80
percent). Thereafter, again as Pacelle's results imply, the series begins to
decline, although only marginally. Between 1983 and 1987, the series accounts for an average of 56.0 percent of the Court's agenda. Again, as I
have found in other issue areas, there are slight differences in magnitude
between the results of the present study and those of Pacelle perhaps due,
in part, to different coding procedures.

The economics and civil liberties–civil rights patterns confirm Pacelle's findings concerning the transition in the Court's agenda that occurred in the late 1930s and 1940s, and reaffirm Schubert's description of the post–World War II Court as one whose workload was dominated mostly by economics and civil liberties–civil rights decision-making. Further, the overall trends in the proportions of these decision types support the conclusions of McCloskey, who suggests that economics issues dominated the Court's agenda from the latter part of the nineteenth century until the time of the New Deal, when civil liberties and civil rights issues began to be prevalent and, eventually, to dominate the body of decisions that the Court announced.

Judicial Power

The third most important major issue in Supreme Court decisions (quantitatively) is judicial power. As Figure 3-10 shows, the series is relatively stable from 1888 to 1907, hovering around 20 percent of the Court's docket. From 1908 to 1939, the percentage of judicial power decisions slopes fairly gently downward. Thereafter, it slopes very gently upwards until the 1970s, after which it stabilizes. The gentle upward trend supports the growing, although modest, concern of the Court with issues of judicial power and, more generally, governmental power that surrounded the New Deal era. Only once does the series exceed 25 percent of the Court's agenda (in 1888). After 1925 and until the early 1960s, it stays below 20 percent, usually below 15 percent. However, from 1957 to 1997, it is typically between 15 and 20 percent, and exceeds 20 percent on several occasions. Its historic high is observed in 1888, at 27.1 percent; its historic low in 1930, at 3.9 percent.

Other

The remainder of the Court's agenda is accounted for by the proportion of the decisions in the residual "other" dimension. As Figure 3-11 depicts, the series is quite volatile, especially in the late 1920s and early 1930s, experiencing its historic high in 1927 of 16.1 percent. Typically, however, these decisions account for less than 6 percent of the Supreme Court's agenda throughout the entire period analyzed here.

CHAPTER SUMMARY

This chapter analyzes the long-term trends in the caseload and types of issues the United States Supreme Court has decided across the period from 1888 to 1997. Generally, the caseload of the Court has experienced a downward

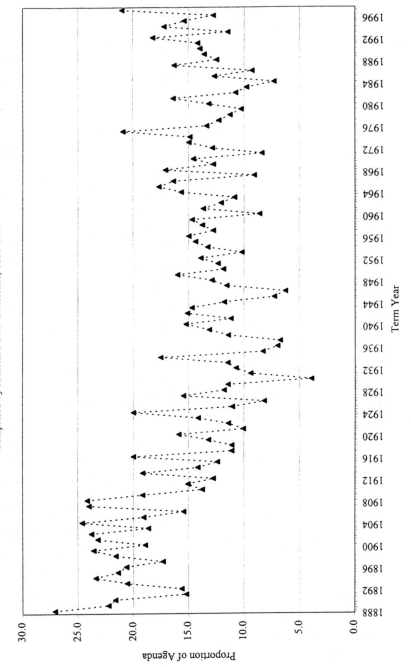

Figure 3-10. Proportion of the United States Supreme Court's Agenda Comprised by Judicial Power Decisions, 1888-1997

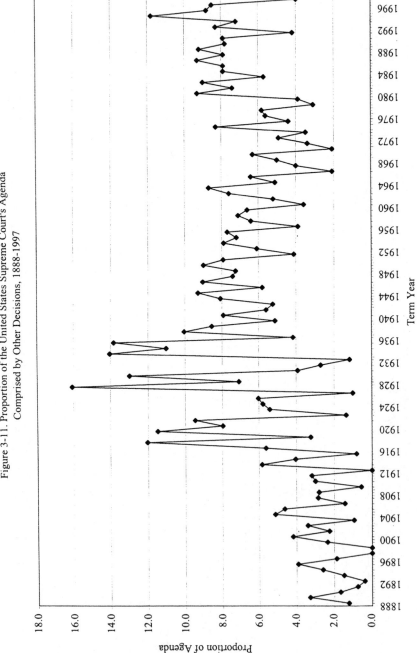

Figure 3-11. Proportion of the United States Supreme Court's Agenda Comprised by Other Decisions, 1888-1997

trend from its maximum in 1914 perhaps due in part to the institutional changes that accompanied the Judiciary Act of 1925. Specifically, we find that economics cases tend to overwhelm the remaining issue areas, as Pacelle finds and McCloskey predicts, through the end of World War II, possibly due to the challenges of the Great Depression and the pubic policies arising from the New Deal. Thereafter, civil liberties–civil rights cases become predominant in the Court's agenda and economics cases begin to wane, a finding that also confirms McCloskey's observations and Pacelle's results. Moreover, judicial power cases comprise an average of about 15 percent of the Court's agenda across the 110 term years analyzed in this study.

4

Going Their Own Way:
Unanimity of United States Supreme Court
Decision-Making, 1888–1997

THE RESEARCH EFFORT IN THIS CHAPTER INVESTIGATES PATTERNS OF CHANGE and stabilization in the unanimity that the Supreme Court's decisions represent from 1888 to 1997. To do so, it first discusses the proportions of the Court's decisions that were unanimous, and then those in which the justices dissented or concurred and filed dissenting or concurring opinions. Overall, the Court's decisions during the twentieth century began to move away from the historical tradition of predominantly unanimous decisions[1] and towards those in which concurrences and dissents occurred.[2]

UNANIMITY EXPLORED

There are fewer unanimous decisions in the post-1940 period than there are in previous years (Figure 4-1). Unanimity is of particular concern to scholars studying the Court because its absence indicates that the Court is departing from concerns of institutional solidarity to begin to express the individual policy views of the justices. Pritchett indicates that nonunanimous decisions are the only window on the justices' differing policy perspectives, because if one studies unanimous decisions only there is no variance in the voting behavior of the justices to examine.[3] Hence, nonunanimous cases represent the boundary of the Court's agreement on important questions of public policy.

From the perspective of the justices, unanimous decisions increase the authority of the Court's decisions. Judge Learned Hand declared that nonunanimous decisions were "disastrous" because they vitiate "the impact of monolithic solidarity on which the authority of a bench of judges so

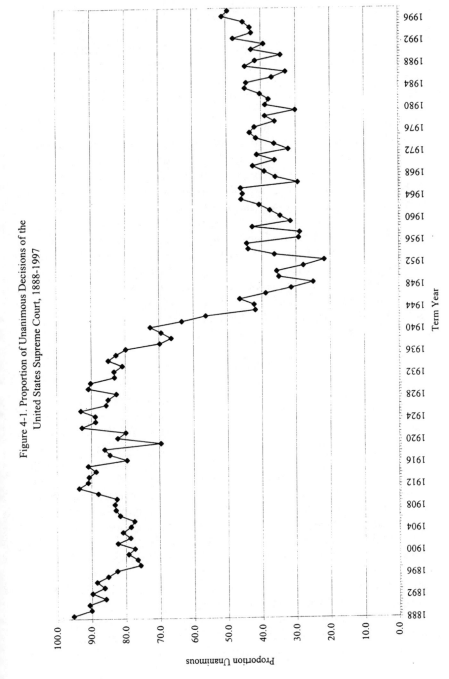

Figure 4-1. Proportion of Unanimous Decisions of the United States Supreme Court, 1888-1997

largely depends."[4] Taft "'expected [the chief justice] to promote teamwork [e.g., unanimity] by the Court so as to give weight and solidarity to its opinions.'"[5] If the justice did not strongly believe that the majority erred in some important concept, Taft believed that a justice "should be a good member of the team, silently acquiesce in the views of the majority, and not to try to make a record for himself by dissenting."[6] Hence, during his tenure Taft socialized his brethren into the "no-dissent-unless-absolutely necessary tradition and most of them learned it well."[7] This long-standing preference for unanimous decisions continued to be part of the Court's norms beyond Taft's stint as chief justice, although some chief justices viewed it more favorably than others.[8] Thus, scholars and some of the justices of the pre-1940's themselves underscore the importance of unanimous decisions.

However, there is a price to be paid for unanimous decisions. They often require the justices to sacrifice some of their individual expressiveness so that a consensus can be formed among the Court, serving to dilute the policy views of the justices.[9] Oliver Wendell Holmes, Jr., "gazing mournfully upon the wreck of one of his own original drafts, described this process as pulling out all the plums and leaving the dough."[10] Therefore, unanimous decisions sometimes misleadingly portray the Court as announcing a policy stand that all the justices wholeheartedly support when in fact the justices may be privately divided on the question.

UNANIMITY EXAMINED

The unit of analysis for this investigation of unanimity is the case decision reported in the *Supreme Court Reporter*. Decisions in which there were no dissenting votes cast are considered herein as unanimous. Table 4-1 shows the percentage of such decisions that garnered 9-0, 8-0, 7-0, 6-0, and 5-0 votes aggregated across the term years 1888 to 1997. Decisions with less than nine votes occur because justices, for various reasons, do not participate in the decisional process. Such reasons may include their recusal because of a prior involvement with the case, or they simply were too ill to participate. For example, Howell Jackson (who served on the Fuller Court between 1893 and 1895) spent much of the time in California after he joined the Court recuperating from tuberculosis.[11] Decisions that received fewer than five majority votes are not considered binding rulings of the Court, but are only considered judgments in which the lower court's ruling is affirmed.[12] Thus, they are excluded from this analysis.

In the present study, the majority of unanimous decisions received either a 9–0 or an 8–0 vote. In 1910, 38.3 percent of the Court decisions received a 7–0 vote, a historic high. Thereafter, they occur consistently

Table 4-1. Percentage of Unanimous Decisions and Concurring Votes and Decisions of the United States Supreme Court, 1888-1997

TERM YEAR	TOTAL REPORTED DECISIONS	UNANIMOUS	9-0 VOTES	8-0 VOTES	7-0 VOTES	6-0 VOTES	5-0 VOTES	AT LEAST ONE CONCURRING VOTE	ONE CONCURRING VOTE	TWO CONCURRING VOTES	THREE CONCURRING VOTES	FOUR CONCURRING VOTES	FIVE CONCURRING VOTES	SIX OR MORE CONCURRING VOTES	AT LEAST ONE CONCURRING OPINION	ONE CONCURRING OPINION	TWO CONCURRING OPINIONS	THREE CONCURRING OPINIONS	FOUR OR MORE CONCURRING OPINIONS
1888	240	95.4	90.4	3.8	1.3	0.0	0.0	1.8	1.8	0.0	0.0	0.0	0.0	0.0	0.0	0.0	0.0	0.0	0.0
1889	274	90.1	81.4	8.0	0.7	0.0	0.0	1.4	0.7	0.0	0.0	0.0	0.0	0.0	0.4	0.4	0.0	0.0	0.0
1890	291	90.7	77.3	10.0	3.1	0.3	0.0	2.7	2.3	0.3	0.3	0.0	0.0	0.0	0.7	0.7	0.0	0.0	0.0
1891	263	85.9	71.9	6.8	6.5	0.8	0.0	0.8	0.8	0.0	0.4	0.0	0.0	0.0	0.4	0.4	0.0	0.0	0.0
1892	256	89.8	80.9	7.4	1.2	0.4	0.0	2.2	1.1	0.7	0.0	0.4	0.0	0.0	0.0	0.0	0.4	0.0	0.8
1893	277	86.3	22.4	57.0	5.8	1.1	0.0	1.3	1.3	0.0	0.0	0.0	0.0	0.0	1.6	0.4	0.0	0.0	0.0
1894	235	88.5	12.8	71.5	4.3	0.0	0.0	2.3	1.6	0.4	0.4	0.0	0.0	0.0	0.9	0.9	0.0	0.0	0.0
1895	257	85.2	56.8	25.7	2.7	0.0	0.0	3.7	2.8	0.5	0.5	0.0	0.0	0.0	0.8	0.8	0.0	0.0	0.0
1896	218	82.6	76.1	5.5	0.9	0.0	0.0	5.2	4.0	0.0	1.2	0.0	0.0	0.0	1.8	1.2	0.5	0.6	0.0
1897	173	75.7	69.4	5.8	0.6	0.0	0.0	1.2	0.6	0.6	0.0	0.0	0.0	0.0	0.6	1.4	1.1	0.0	0.0
1898	162	76.5	71.0	4.9	0.6	0.0	0.0	5.7	3.8	1.4	0.5	0.0	0.0	0.6	1.9	0.5	0.0	0.0	0.0
1899	212	79.2	70.8	6.6	1.9	0.0	0.0	5.3	3.7	0.0	0.0	1.6	0.0	0.0	1.6	0.6	0.5	0.0	0.0
1900	190	77.4	70.5	5.8	1.1	0.0	0.0	4.4	2.8	1.1	0.0	0.0	0.0	0.0	0.6	1.9	0.0	0.5	0.0
1901	181	82.3	56.4	21.0	4.4	0.6	0.0	7.3	4.4	1.0	1.0	0.5	0.5	0.0	2.4	0.5	0.0	0.0	0.0
1902	206	78.6	39.3	35.4	3.4	0.5	0.0	8.6	5.7	1.9	1.0	0.0	0.0	0.0	1.0	0.5	0.0	0.0	0.0
1903	209	80.9	72.2	7.2	1.4	0.0	0.0	6.2	4.6	1.0	0.0	0.5	0.0	0.0	0.5	4.0	0.0	0.0	0.0
1904	195	78.5	75.9	2.6	0.0	0.0	0.0	8.1	5.8	1.7	0.6	0.0	0.0	0.0	4.0	0.5	0.0	0.0	0.0
1905	173	77.5	74.0	2.9	0.6	0.0	0.0	7.7	6.3	0.5	1.0	0.6	0.0	0.0	0.5	2.3	0.0	0.0	0.0
1906	207	81.6	70.0	11.1	0.5	0.0	0.0	4.6	3.4	0.6	0.0	0.0	0.0	0.0	2.3	0.6	0.0	0.0	0.0
1907	175	82.9	80.0	2.9	0.0	0.0	0.0	2.2	1.7	0.6	0.0	0.0	0.0	0.0	0.6	0.0	0.0	0.0	0.0
1908	178	83.1	74.2	9.0	0.0	0.0	0.0	7.0	5.2	1.7	0.0	0.0	0.0	0.0	0.0	2.4	0.0	0.0	0.0
1909	172	82.6	44.8	36.6	1.2	0.0	0.0	3.0	2.4	0.6	0.0	0.0	0.0	0.0	2.4	0.0	0.0	0.0	0.0
1910	167	88.0	41.9	7.8	38.3	0.0	0.0	0.5	0.0	0.5	0.0	0.0	0.0	0.0	0.5	2.4	0.0	0.0	0.0
1911	219	93.6	39.3	54.3	0.0	0.0	0.0	0.5	0.0	0.5	0.0	0.0	0.0	0.0	0.5	0.0	0.5	0.0	0.0

Table 4-1. Percentage of Unanimous Decisions and Concurring Votes and Decisions of the United States Supreme Court, 1888-1997

TERM YEAR	TOTAL REPORTED DECISIONS	UNANIMOUS	9-0 VOTES	8-0 VOTES	7-0 VOTES	6-0 VOTES	5-0 VOTES	AT LEAST ONE CONCURRING VOTE	ONE CONCURRING VOTE	TWO CONCURRING VOTES	THREE CONCURRING VOTES	FOUR CONCURRING VOTES	FIVE CONCURRING VOTES	SIX OR MORE CONCURRING VOTES	AT LEAST ONE CONCURRING OPINION	ONE CONCURRING OPINION	TWO CONCURRING OPINIONS	THREE CONCURRING OPINIONS	FOUR OR MORE CONCURRING OPINIONS
1912	266	91.0	86.1	4.1	0.4	0.4	0.0	4.5	4.1	0.4	0.0	0.0	0.0	0.0	0.0	0.0	0.0	0.0	0.0
1913	292	90.8	89.4	1.4	0.0	0.0	0.0	2.1	1.4	0.7	0.0	0.0	0.0	0.0	1.0	1.0	0.0	0.0	0.0
1914	247	88.7	70.0	18.2	0.4	0.0	0.0	2.0	1.6	0.0	0.0	0.4	0.0	0.0	0.0	0.0	0.0	0.0	0.0
1915	242	90.9	76.9	14.0	0.0	0.0	0.0	2.1	1.7	0.4	0.0	0.0	0.0	0.0	0.4	0.4	0.0	0.0	0.0
1916	215	79.5	73.5	5.6	0.5	0.0	0.0	2.8	2.8	0.0	0.0	0.0	0.0	0.0	0.5	0.5	0.0	0.0	0.0
1917	207	84.5	74.4	9.7	0.5	0.0	0.0	2.4	1.9	0.5	0.5	0.0	0.0	0.0	0.0	0.0	0.0	0.0	0.0
1918	216	86.1	83.8	2.3	0.0	0.0	0.0	3.2	1.9	0.9	0.0	0.0	0.6	0.0	0.5	0.5	0.0	0.0	0.0
1919	174	69.5	64.9	4.0	0.6	0.0	0.0	4.6	2.9	0.6	0.0	0.6	0.0	0.0	2.4	0.6	0.6	0.0	1.2
1920	214	82.2	72.4	8.4	1.4	0.0	0.0	10.3	3.3	7.0	0.6	0.0	0.0	0.0	4.2	2.3	1.9	0.0	0.0
1921	169	79.9	70.4	9.5	0.0	0.0	0.0	7.7	7.1	0.0	0.0	0.0	0.0	0.0	1.2	1.2	0.0	0.0	0.0
1922	220	92.7	90.9	1.8	0.0	0.0	0.0	1.4	0.9	0.5	0.0	0.0	0.0	0.0	0.0	0.0	0.5	0.0	0.0
1923	205	88.8	85.9	2.9	0.4	0.0	0.0	2.9	2.0	0.0	0.0	0.0	0.0	0.0	1.5	1.0	0.0	0.0	0.0
1924	225	88.9	61.3	27.1	0.0	0.0	0.0	0.9	0.9	0.5	0.5	0.0	0.0	0.0	0.0	0.0	0.0	0.0	0.0
1925	202	93.1	86.6	6.4	0.5	0.0	0.0	4.0	3.0	1.0	1.0	0.0	0.0	0.0	1.5	1.5	0.0	0.0	0.0
1926	196	85.7	82.1	2.6	1.2	0.5	0.0	6.6	4.1	0.6	0.0	0.5	0.0	0.0	0.5	0.5	0.0	0.0	0.0
1927	168	85.1	78.0	6.0	0.8	0.0	0.0	2.4	1.8	1.6	0.8	0.0	0.0	0.0	1.2	1.2	0.0	0.0	0.0
1928	127	82.7	79.5	2.4	9.2	0.0	0.0	4.7	2.4	2.3	1.5	0.0	0.0	0.0	1.6	1.6	0.0	0.0	0.0
1929	131	90.8	40.5	41.2	3.9	0.0	0.0	6.1	2.3	0.0	0.0	0.0	0.0	0.0	2.3	2.3	0.0	0.0	0.0
1930	153	90.2	82.4	3.9	0.7	0.0	0.0	0.7	0.7	0.7	0.6	0.0	0.0	0.0	0.7	0.7	0.0	0.0	0.0
1931	149	83.2	50.3	32.2	0.6	0.0	0.0	1.3	3.0	1.2	0.0	0.0	0.0	0.0	1.3	1.3	0.0	0.0	0.0
1932	168	83.3	79.2	3.2	1.3	0.0	0.0	5.4	2.5	1.9	0.6	0.6	0.0	0.0	1.2	0.6	0.6	0.0	0.0
1933	157	80.9	76.4	3.2	0.0	0.0	0.0	5.7	2.6	2.6	0.0	1.3	0.0	0.0	3.2	1.3	0.0	0.0	1.9
1934	154	85.1	81.2	3.9	0.7	0.0	0.0	5.8	2.6	0.0	0.6	0.0	0.0	0.0	1.9	1.9	0.0	0.0	0.0
1935	145	82.8	73.1	9.0	0.7	0.0	0.0	6.2	1.4	0.0	2.1	2.8	0.0	0.0	2.1	1.4	0.0	0.7	0.0

Table 4-1. Percentage of Unanimous Decisions and Concurring Votes and Decisions of the United States Supreme Court, 1888-1997

TERM YEAR	TOTAL REPORTED DECISIONS	UNANIMOUS	9-0 VOTES	8-0 VOTES	7-0 VOTES	6-0 VOTES	5-0 VOTES	AT LEAST ONE CONCURRING VOTE	ONE CONCURRING VOTE	TWO CONCURRING VOTES	THREE CONCURRING VOTES	FOUR CONCURRING VOTES	FIVE CONCURRING VOTES	SIX OR MORE CONCURRING VOTES	AT LEAST ONE CONCURRING OPINION	ONE CONCURRING OPINION	TWO CONCURRING OPINIONS	THREE CONCURRING OPINIONS	CONCURRING OPINIONS FOUR OR MORE
1936	144	79.9	42.4	33.3	4.2	0.0	0.0	5.6	2.8	1.4	0.7	0.7	0.0	0.0	0.7	0.7	0.0	0.0	0.0
1937	149	69.8	18.1	23.5	27.5	0.7	0.0	14.8	10.7	2.7	1.3	0.0	0.0	0.0	5.4	3.4	2.0	0.0	0.0
1938	140	66.4	5.7	47.9	11.4	1.4	0.0	14.3	6.4	5.7	1.4	0.7	0.0	0.0	9.2	7.1	2.1	0.0	0.0
1939	137	69.3	19.7	44.5	4.4	0.7	0.0	13.9	9.5	2.9	0.7	0.7	0.0	0.0	3.6	3.6	0.0	0.0	0.0
1940	164	72.6	59.1	11.6	1.8	0.0	0.0	7.9	4.3	3.0	0.6	0.0	0.0	0.0	3.0	3.0	0.6	0.0	0.0
1941	161	63.4	34.8	23.6	3.7	1.2	0.0	13.7	6.2	3.1	3.1	1.2	0.0	0.0	8.0	6.2	2.3	0.6	1.2
1942	172	56.4	12.8	38.4	4.1	1.2	0.0	16.9	9.9	5.8	0.6	0.6	0.0	0.0	11.0	8.1	3.7	0.0	0.0
1943	136	41.9	36.0	3.7	2.2	0.0	0.0	24.3	13.2	7.4	2.9	0.7	0.0	0.0	15.4	11.0	2.5	0.7	0.0
1944	161	42.2	37.3	3.7	0.6	0.6	0.0	35.4	23.6	9.3	2.5	0.0	0.7	0.0	18.6	15.5	5.8	0.6	0.0
1945	138	46.4	0.0	39.9	5.8	0.7	0.0	29.0	17.4	7.2	3.6	0.0	0.0	0.0	21.7	15.2	0.7	0.7	0.0
1946	144	38.9	35.4	3.5	0.0	0.0	0.0	28.5	23.6	2.8	1.4	0.7	0.8	0.0	20.2	18.1	5.0	1.4	0.0
1947	121	31.4	24.8	4.1	1.7	0.8	0.0	31.4	16.5	7.4	0.8	5.8	0.0	0.0	24.0	18.2	8.9	0.8	0.0
1948	124	25.0	22.6	0.8	1.6	0.0	0.0	33.9	16.1	10.5	4.8	2.4	0.0	0.0	25.0	14.5	6.0	0.8	0.8
1949	100	35.0	4.0	24.0	7.0	0.0	0.0	20.0	10.0	7.0	2.0	1.0	0.0	0.0	12.0	5.0	2.0	1.0	0.0
1950	101	35.6	26.7	6.9	2.0	0.0	0.0	27.7	14.9	9.9	2.0	1.0	0.0	0.0	18.8	15.8	2.1	0.0	0.0
1951	97	27.8	11.3	13.4	3.1	0.0	0.0	22.7	8.2	8.2	4.1	2.1	0.9	0.0	13.4	11.3	2.6	0.0	1.0
1952	115	21.7	16.5	3.5	1.7	0.0	0.0	21.7	11.3	5.2	4.3	0.0	0.0	0.0	13.9	9.6	0.0	1.7	0.0
1953	88	36.3	26.1	6.8	3.4	0.0	0.0	20.4	12.5	6.8	1.1	0.0	1.0	0.0	12.5	12.5	0.0	0.0	0.0
1954	98	43.9	5.1	37.8	0.0	0.0	0.0	20.4	12.2	5.1	3.1	0.0	0.0	0.0	13.3	9.2	4.1	0.0	0.0
1955	104	44.3	33.7	8.7	1.9	0.0	0.0	20.2	14.4	4.8	0.0	1.6	0.0	0.0	13.4	11.5	1.9	0.0	0.0
1956	127	29.2	15.0	12.6	1.6	0.0	0.0	21.3	10.2	7.1	2.4	1.3	0.0	0.0	15.8	13.4	2.4	0.0	0.0
1957	156	28.9	24.4	4.5	0.0	0.0	0.0	22.4	12.8	3.2	5.1	1.3	0.0	0.0	12.2	7.7	4.5	0.0	0.0
1958	138	42.7	35.5	5.8	1.4	0.0	0.0	23.9	13.8	4.3	2.2	2.2	0.7	0.7	17.4	15.2	2.2	0.0	0.0
1959	136	31.6	26.5	5.1	0.0	0.0	0.0	29.3	11.0	8.1	4.4	5.1	0.7	0.0	19.1	11.8	5.9	0.7	0.7

Table 4-1. Percentage of Unanimous Decisions and Concurring Votes and Decisions of the United States Supreme Court, 1888-1997

Term Year	Total Reported Decisions	Unanimous	9-0 Votes	8-0 Votes	7-0 Votes	6-0 Votes	5-0 Votes	At Least One Concurring Vote	One Concurring Vote	Two Concurring Votes	Three Concurring Votes	Four Concurring Votes	Five Concurring Votes	Six or More Concurring Votes	At Least One Concurring Opinion	One Concurring Opinion	Two Concurring Opinions	Three Concurring Opinions	Four or More Concurring Opinions
1960	139	34.6	28.8	2.9	2.2	0.7	0.0	28.1	10.8	11.5	3.6	2.2	0.0	0.0	24.4	17.3	5.0	1.4	0.7
1961	117	37.6	14.5	7.7	14.5	0.9	0.0	37.7	19.7	7.7	6.0	4.3	0.0	0.0	22.2	16.2	3.4	2.6	0.0
1962	157	40.7	29.9	8.9	1.9	0.0	0.0	28.6	15.3	8.9	2.5	0.6	1.3	0.0	21.1	15.3	4.5	1.3	0.0
1963	183	45.9	35.0	8.2	0.0	1.6	1.1	27.8	15.8	6.0	2.7	1.1	2.2	0.0	20.3	12.6	6.6	1.1	0.0
1964	134	45.5	35.1	3.0	6.7	0.0	0.7	36.4	9.7	11.9	11.2	2.2	0.7	0.7	27.7	15.7	7.5	4.5	0.0
1965	141	46.0	31.2	9.9	3.5	0.7	0.7	29.0	16.3	5.7	2.8	2.1	1.4	0.7	20.6	12.8	5.7	2.1	0.0
1966	146	29.5	24.7	2.7	2.1	0.0	0.0	28.1	15.1	7.5	4.1	1.4	0.0	0.0	20.5	16.4	2.7	0.7	0.7
1967	197	36.0	16.8	16.2	2.5	0.5	0.0	38.5	18.8	9.6	7.1	2.5	0.5	0.0	25.7	16.2	5.1	3.0	1.4
1968	140	39.2	16.4	16.4	5.0	0.7	0.7	44.9	25.0	12.1	5.0	2.1	0.7	0.0	34.8	24.3	7.9	2.1	0.5
1969	141	42.5	3.5	31.9	5.7	0.7	0.7	41.9	22.0	9.2	5.0	4.3	0.7	0.7	26.9	16.3	7.8	2.8	0.0
1970	144	36.2	27.8	5.6	2.8	0.0	0.0	50.0	22.9	13.2	8.3	2.8	1.4	1.4	34.7	20.1	10.4	3.5	0.7
1971	179	41.3	17.3	3.9	20.1	0.0	0.0	38.0	19.6	9.5	5.6	2.2	1.1	0.0	26.4	18.4	5.6	1.7	0.7
1972	186	32.2	26.3	2.7	2.7	0.5	0.0	30.2	15.6	5.4	4.8	2.2	1.1	1.1	19.9	13.4	6.5	0.0	0.0
1973	173	36.3	27.7	5.2	1.7	1.7	0.0	31.7	15.0	7.5	4.6	4.6	0.0	0.0	27.7	21.4	4.0	1.2	1.1
1974	154	41.5	26.1	12.3	2.6	0.0	0.5	31.0	14.9	6.5	7.1	1.9	0.6	0.5	23.3	18.8	2.6	1.9	0.0
1975	182	43.3	20.3	20.3	1.1	1.6	0.0	43.8	19.2	15.9	3.8	4.4	0.0	0.0	32.4	20.3	11.0	0.5	0.6
1976	179	41.9	30.7	8.4	1.7	1.1	0.0	41.4	19.0	11.2	6.1	3.4	1.7	0.6	27.4	16.2	7.3	3.4	0.5
1977	155	36.1	20.6	14.2	1.3	0.0	0.0	39.4	14.2	12.3	5.2	5.8	1.3	0.0	31.3	13.5	14.2	1.9	1.7
1978	160	38.9	22.5	13.8	1.3	0.0	1.3	43.2	20.6	11.9	5.0	4.4	1.3	0.6	38.7	27.5	8.1	2.5	0.6
1979	156	30.1	20.5	6.4	0.6	1.3	1.3	39.7	16.0	12.2	8.3	1.3	1.3	0.0	32.7	20.5	9.6	2.6	0.0
1980	152	38.8	26.3	11.2	0.0	1.3	0.0	46.7	20.4	15.8	5.9	2.6	2.0	0.0	41.3	25.0	12.5	2.6	1.2
1981	177	37.8	31.6	4.0	1.1	1.1	0.0	44.7	23.7	10.2	5.1	2.3	3.4	0.0	36.3	24.9	7.9	2.8	0.7
1982	166	40.3	34.9	3.6	1.2	0.6	0.0	37.3	18.1	7.2	6.6	4.2	0.6	0.6	30.7	23.5	4.2	3.0	0.0
1983	173	44.6	37.0	5.2	1.2	1.2	0.0	38.2	21.4	5.8	4.0	3.5	2.3	1.2	27.7	20.8	5.2	1.7	0.0

Table 4-1. Percentage of Unanimous Decisions and Concurring Votes and Decisions of the United States Supreme Court, 1888-1997

TERM YEAR	TOTAL REPORTED DECISIONS	UNANIMOUS	9-0 VOTES	8-0 VOTES	7-0 VOTES	6-0 VOTES	5-0 VOTES	AT LEAST ONE CONCURRING VOTE	ONE CONCURRING VOTE	TWO CONCURRING VOTES	THREE CONCURRING VOTES	FOUR CONCURRING VOTES	FIVE CONCURRING VOTES	SIX OR MORE CONCURRING VOTES	AT LEAST ONE CONCURRING OPINION	ONE CONCURRING OPINION	TWO CONCURRING OPINIONS	THREE CONCURRING OPINIONS	FOUR OR MORE CONCURRING OPINIONS
1984	165	44.2	24.2	15.8	3.6	0.6	0.0	33.9	13.3	11.5	6.1	2.4	0.6	0.0	30.9	23.6	6.7	0.0	0.6
1985	165	36.9	28.5	3.6	2.4	1.2	1.2	41.8	15.8	12.7	6.1	4.2	2.4	0.6	36.4	26.1	7.3	3.0	0.0
1986	161	32.9	26.1	3.7	2.5	0.6	0.0	39.6	21.1	9.9	4.3	2.5	0.6	1.2	36.0	24.2	9.3	1.9	0.6
1987	153	44.5	17.6	24.2	1.3	0.7	0.7	36.7	14.4	11.8	6.5	3.3	0.7	0.0	31.3	22.2	7.2	1.3	0.6
1988	152	41.6	33.6	5.3	0.7	2.0	0.0	46.0	23.0	8.6	7.2	5.9	1.3	0.0	37.5	27.6	6.6	3.3	0.0
1989	140	34.3	33.6	0.7	0.0	0.0	0.0	42.1	20.0	10.0	6.4	5.0	0.0	0.7	38.5	24.3	11.4	2.1	0.7
1990	129	42.7	34.1	7	1.6	0	0	31.8	17.8	7	3.9	2.3	0.8	0.0	25.7	22.5	1.6	1.6	0.0
1991	120	39.2	30	9.2	0	0	0	44.1	14.2	17.5	5.8	3.3	2.5	0.8	34.2	19.2	12.5	2.5	0.0
1992	121	47.9	46.3	0.8	0.8	0	0	41.4	17.4	11.6	6.6	3.3	1.7	0.8	38.0	24.8	9.9	2.5	0.8
1993	96	42.7	41.7	1	0	0	0	52.1	14.6	16.7	9.4	5.2	4.2	2.0	40.6	19.8	17.7	3.1	0.0
1994	93	43.1	39.8	2.2	1.1	0	0	43.0	22.6	8.6	8.6	3.2	0	0.0	40.9	28	9.7	1.1	2.1
1995	91	45.1	41.8	1.1	0	0	2.2	35.2	9.9	8.8	9.9	3.3	0	3.3	29.7	14.3	12.1	3.3	0.0
1996	94	51.1	48.9	0	1.1	1.1	0	30.8	8.5	12.8	7.4	0	2.1	0.0	26.7	21.3	4.3	0	1.1
1997	100	49.5	49.5	0	0	0	0	39.0	16	13	1	5	1	3.0	36.1	25	9	0	2.1

through 1997. Decisions with a 6–0 vote are first observed in 1890 and then occasionally through 1936. They begin to occur more frequently in 1937, although they remain comparatively quite rare. From 1968 to 1997, most terms saw at least one 6–0 vote. Their historic high is observed in 1988 (2.0 percent). It is not until 1963, however, that a 5–0 is first registered. Such votes are, through 1997, an infrequent occurrence, not exceeding 2.2 percent in any one term year.

Overall, from 1888 to 1997, unanimity on the United States Supreme Court decreases substantially. As Figure 4-1 shows, over 75 percent of the Court's annual decisions were unanimous until 1937. In many of the term years from 1888 to 1937, the unanimity rate hovers near 80 percent (see Table 4-1). The series' historic high is observed in 1888 when 95.4 percent of the Court's decisions were unanimous, followed closely by 93.6 percent of the decisions in 1911, after which the series is relatively stable through 1935. After 1936, however, it drops quite consistently until 1952, when it reaches its historic low of 21.7 percent. Then, the series begins to recover and stabilize at a much lower level (typically 30 to 40 percent) than that observed during the more consensual years observed prior to the mid-1930s. From 1952 to 1966, there are some moderate swings in the series, but nothing like the downward change that occurred from 1937 to 1952. This moderating influence may be due to the more effective leadership that Chief Justice Earl Warren provided after Chief Justice Fred Vinson retired, since Vinson is considered by many scholars not to have been an effective leader of the Court.[13] After 1952, only one change in the unanimity rate from one term year to the next exceeds 9 percent (from 1965 to 1966, 16.5 percent). From 1967 to 1997, the average rate of unanimous decisions is 40.41 percent. Hence, in the latter nineteenth and the early twentieth centuries, the Court's decisions are predominantly unanimous. Beginning in the 1940s and continuing through the 1990s, however, the Court's decisions become typically nonunanimous.

Schubert first notes the trend in the level of, and timing in changes to, the unanimity of the Court's decisions for the period 1946–69.[14] Epstein, Segal, Spaeth, and Thomas G. Walker report data that document that trend through the early 1990s.[15] These latter authors' data are very nearly, but not quite, identical to those of the present study because their data do not include non-orally argued per curiam opinions as this study does.

The Influence of the Chief Justice on Unanimity

At least two significant studies have tried to explain this dramatic change in the unanimity of Supreme Court decision-making. Walker, Epstein, and William J. Dixon analyze the decline in unanimity since the early 1940s.

They find that Chief Justice Stone's particular social and task leadership style significantly contributed to a decline of consensus on the Court when compared with prior years.[16] Effective chief justices must be able social leaders, who are able to ameliorate the "'negative aspects of conference' through activity [that] 'relieves tension, shows solidarity, and makes for agreement.'"[17] For example, during the Fuller Court, there may have been relatively few concurring opinions written because of the able social and task leadership that Fuller provided.[18]

Chief justices must also be effective task leaders. In that role, they attend to the business of the Court, ensuring that cases are processed and decisions announced.[19] To do so, task leaders "initiate and receive more interaction than others" in conference.[20] "Usually, [he] makes more suggestions, gives more opinions, and successfully defends his ideas more often than others. Usually, he is regarded as having the best ideas for the decision of the cases and is highly esteemed by his associates."[21] Therefore, effective chief justices must be skilled social and task leaders to be able to minimize the disruptive effects of conflict among the justices and, thus, foster unanimity in the Court's decision-making.

Chief Justice Stone was not a particularly good social leader because he was unable, or perhaps simply unwilling, to "smooth ruffled tempers, relieve tensions and maintain solidarity" among the justices.[22] "He was also a vain, sensitive man whose ego was easily bruised, who sometimes responded to criticism sarcastically, and who did not hide his low opinion of the abilities of some of his colleagues."[23] He also was not an able task leader because he failed not only to formulate clearly enough his position on the cases to be discussed in conference, but also he did not structure the discussion among the other justices well.[24] Stone's "leadership problems were not in writing persuasive opinions but in conference discussion. His presentation of cases as chief justice tended to be rambling, and in conference he did not remain above the fray so that he might later be in a position to reconcile differences among his colleagues."[25] Thus, Chief Justice Stone's peculiar leadership style is associated with the decline in unanimity on the Court since the early 1940s.

Haynie extends Walker, Epstein, and Dixon's analysis by examining the decline of unanimity during the Hughes Court (1930–40). She, too, asserts that the leadership style of the chief justice can significantly affect the occurrence of conflict on the Court and, thus, the level of unanimity.[26] Chief Justice Charles Evans Hughes retained tight control over conference discussion, which may have actually heightened tensions among the justices.[27] Although Hughes is considered by other scholars to have been an able social and task leader for the Court,[28] Haynie suggests that Hughes's own words, speaking to the concept of dissensus generally, belie a somewhat more expressive tendency.[29] Hughes writes: "[a] dissent in a court of last resort is an appeal to the brooding spirit of the law, to the intelligence of a future day when a later decision may possibly correct the error into which the dissenting judge believes the court to have been betrayed."[30] Hence, the institutional preference for unanimous decisions has been drastically reduced, especially since the 1930s, reflecting in part the change in leadership on the Court.[31]

Unanimity on the Supreme Court, 1888–1946

The average rates of unanimity for each of the four pre-1945 chief justice courts were calculated to depict this pattern over the period of time that is primarily analyzed here. The average rate of unanimity for the Fuller Court (1888–1909) is 83.24 percent. The White Court (1910–20) average increases very slightly from that for the Fuller Court to 85.09 percent. A similar slight increase occurs in the Taft Court (1921–29), which observed an average unanimity rate of 87.5 percent. Thus, for thirty-two term years (1888–1929), more than 80 percent of the Court's decisions are unanimous, and there was no significant sign of any decrease in this high level of consensus. However, Hughes's service as chief justice (1930–40) is associated with a decline in unanimity; the Court average is 78.5 percent, a decrease of 10.2 percent from the Taft Court level. In similar fashion, Stone's tenure witnessed a continuation of that decline to an average of 50.06 percent, reflecting a change of 36 percent from the average observed during the Hughes Court. Both decreases play a key role in the analyses of Walker, Epstein, and Dixon, and Haynie.[32]

CONCURRING VOTES

If a justice does not agree with the reasoning of the Court's opinion, he or she can concur. Justices may choose to cast concurring votes because they disagree with the Court's opinion but may defer writing separate opinions, perhaps because a concurring opinion may be seen as weakening the Court's opinion.

The coding scheme for the present analysis specified two types of concurring votes. Following the protocol of Spaeth,[33] the justices' votes are scored as a "regular concurrence" if the justice agreed with Court's opinion and with its disposition and, thus, joined the majority but wrote a separate opinion as well.[34] A "special concurrence" is noted if the justice agreed with the Court's disposition of the case but not its opinion.[35] A concurring justice is considered to be a member of the majority coalition in terms of the case vote.

Figure 4-2 shows the percentage of cases with at least one concurring vote (either a regular or a special concurring vote) from 1888 to 1997. As one can see, there is a dramatic increase in the series across the period of analysis. Up until 1936, concurring votes are an infrequent occurrence, due to the strong norms of unanimity that prevailed on the Court up until the 1930s and the skilled leadership of Fuller, White, and Taft.[36] Indeed, the chief justice court averages support those interpretations. For example, the Fuller Court average percentage of decisions with at least one concurring vote is 4.07, while the rate for the White Court declines somewhat to 3.41 percent; however, the last five years of the White Court witnesses an increase in these votes. For the Taft Court, the average returns to the exact level observed during the Fuller Court (4.07 percent). However, the Hughes Court witnesses an 82 percent relative change in the series' average, increasing to 7.41 percent. The Stone Court additionally shows a dramatic increase as well: 23.86 percent of the decisions have at least one concurring vote during its five term years, a relative change of 222 percent.

Overall, the series exceeds 10 percent only once (in 1920) through 1936. Thereafter, however, the series begins to trend sharply upward.[37] In 1936, the rate was 5.6 percent; in 1937, the rate climbs to 14.8 percent. Between 1951 and 1958, the series stabilizes around 25 percent. Then, it begins to increase once again. The historic high is observed in 1993 (52.1 percent). It declines slightly from that level through 1997, hitting the mark of 39.0 percent. Overall, then, the rate of concurring votes has increased dramatically, most clearly from 1937 to 1944.

CONCURRING OPINIONS

There may be times when a justice not only wishes to express his disagreement with the Court's opinion (although not with the case's result) but also to state the reasons why he believes the majority's reasoning is in error. He may do so by writing a concurring opinion. Pritchett posits that concurring opinions are a sign of judges who fervently support the influence of reason in decision-making, and who feel a profound responsibility for their role in the law's development.[38]

Figure 4-3 and Table 4-1 report the percentage of decisions with at least one concurring opinion. As the figure clearly shows, concurring opinions are consistently infrequent until 1937. The series nears 5 percent only twice prior to that term year. There is a modest increase in the series during the last two years of the White Court (1919–20). The series continues to climb through 1936, although only modestly. Thereafter, the series begins to trend consistently upward. It never declines below 10 percent after 1941, the year in which Franklin D. Roosevelt nominated Harlan Fiske Stone as

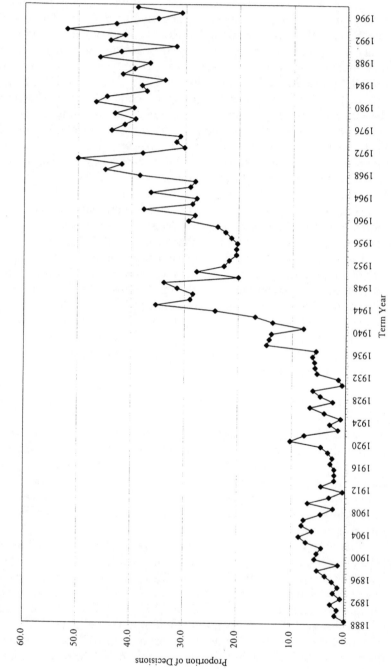

Figure 4-2. Proportion of United States Supreme Court Decisions
With At Least One Concurring Vote, 1888-1997

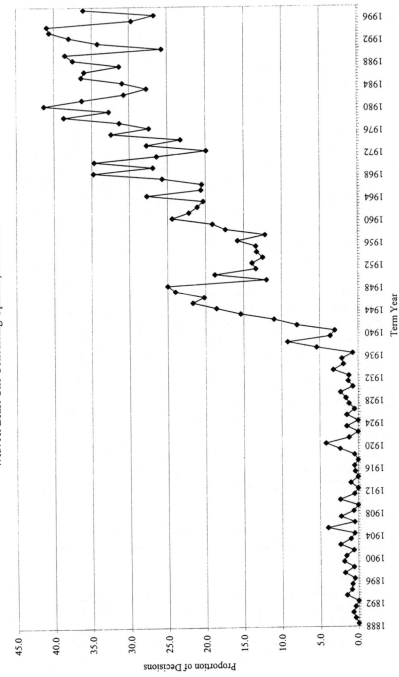

Figure 4-3. Proportion of United States Supreme Court Decisions
With At Least One Concurring Opinion, 1888-1997

chief justice. Pritchett finds a similar increase in the rate of concurring opinions during the Roosevelt years.[39] The series average from 1941 to 1997 is 25.66 percent. The series' historic high occurs in 1980, at 41.3 percent. This series generally reflects the overall decline in unanimity in the Court's decisions since the 1930s.

As before, the chief justice court averages provide an overall indication of the institutional changes in the Court's decision-making during the pre-1946 period. The Fuller Court average is 1.04 percent.[40] The White and Taft Court years see the rate of concurring opinions remain stable at 1.08 percent. Under Hughes, however, the Court's rate increases to 2.94 percent. The series continues to increase during Stone's tenure to 14.94 percent, an extraordinary relative increase of over 400 percent. Indeed, Stone apparently affected the series level because it is 3.0 percent in 1940, but by 1941 (the first year that Stone served as chief justice) it jumps to 8.0 percent.

Epstein, Segal, Spaeth, and Walker also report the increase in the proportion of cases with at least one concurring opinion beginning in the 1930s in their analysis of Albert P. Blaustein and Roy M. Mersky's data.[41] Their proportions, however, are smaller in magnitude than those of the present study. This difference is perhaps due to the fact that the data they analyze, for the pre-1953 period, include only signed opinions of the Court, whereas the present analysis includes *all* opinions of the Court.[42]

Haynie models this increase in the percentage of concurring opinions filed since the 1930s. She asserts that the decline in the norms of consensus on the Court began during the Hughes Court, and finds the peculiar social and task leadership of Chief Justice Hughes increased the occurrence of concurring opinions by 20 percent during his tenure from 1930 to 1940.[43] Although the chief justice is not the sole factor influencing the change in patterns of unanimity on the Court, Haynie states that Hughes's leadership style is a crucial variable affecting the rise of dissensus, first expressed in more frequent concurring opinions observed since the 1930s.[44] Hence, Haynie concludes that the decline of unanimity on the Court began during Hughes's tenure. However, Walker, Epstein, and Dixon argue that Hughes was an effective task leader due in part to his concise and persuasive case summaries that he presented in conference and the taut running of conference.[45]

Furthermore, during Hughes's period as chief justice, the Court was under attack from the Congress and particularly Franklin Roosevelt for consistently striking down New Deal legislation. The Hughes Court may then have first realized that it was no longer insulated from the politics that engulfed the other two branches.[46] Indeed, from 1936 to 1938, the rate of concurring opinions increased from 2.8 percent to 12.1 percent. This awakening among the justices may have contributed to the rancor that first appeared in the Hughes Court in the form of an increased rate of concurring opinions. Similarly, Haynie finds that Stone's tenure is associated with an increased percentage of decisions with at least one concurring opinion by 18 percent, while Warren's tenure is associated in time with a 5.8 percent increase.[47] Thus, dissensus on the Supreme Court was first expressed under White, continued during the leadership of Charles Evans Hughes, consolidated under Harlan Fiske Stone, and then stabilized under Earl Warren.[48]

Although the data used in this study were somewhat differently generated, the findings, not surprisingly, are generally consistent with previous studies. However, there are some differences. Perhaps the most significant difference is the finding that the White Court saw a modest increase in the frequency of concurring opinions, which neither Walker, Epstein, and Dixon nor Haynie analyze.[49] This study, also, finds that there is no apparent large increase in the percentage of cases with at least one concurring opinion immediately associated with the beginning of the Hughes Court in 1930, but the series does indeed increase during the period of his control, especially in the latter years of his tenure. The average percentage of decisions with at least one concurring opinion increases from 1.08 percent during Taft's tenure to 2.94 percent during Hughes's stint as chief justice, a relative increase of 172 percent (see Table 4-1).

The present analysis also confirms that the tenure of Chief Justice Stone (beginning in 1941) is associated with even larger increases in the series. From 1942 to 1943, for example, the series increases by 4.4 percent. Overall, the average percentage of decisions with at least one concurring opinion increases dramatically under Stone. Whereas the figure is 2.94 for Hughes, the average concurrence rate during the years of the Stone Court is 14.94 percent. Therefore, Haynie's findings are echoed by the present study's results.[50]

DISSENTING VOTES: BEHIND THE PURPLE CURTAIN

Pritchett argues that to truly understand the interactions that occur among the justices, one must look to nonunanimous decisions.[51] "For the fact of disagreement demonstrates that the members of the Court are operating on different assumptions, that their inarticulate major premises are dissimilar, that their value systems are differently constructed and weighted, that their political, economic, and social views contrast in important respects."[52] A nonunanimous decision "admits the public to the Supreme Court's inner sanctum" that lies behind the purple curtain.[53] This is particularly true of decisions with dissenting votes. In contrast to the traditions of other legal systems,[54] the norms of the American judicial process do not insist that

Table 4-2. Percentage of United States Supreme Court Decisions With Dissenting Votes and Opinions, 1888-1997

TERM YEAR	AT LEAST ONE DISSENTING VOTE	ONE DISSENTING VOTE	TWO OR MORE DISSENTING VOTES	TWO DISSENTING VOTES	THREE DISSENTING VOTES	FOUR DISSENTING VOTES	AT LEAST ONE DISSENTING OPINION	ONE DISSENTING OPINION	TWO DISSENTING OPINIONS	THREE DISSENTING OPINIONS	FOUR DISSENTING OPINIONS
1888	4.6	2.9	1.7	1.7	0.0	0.0	2.5	2.5	0.0	0.0	0.0
1889	9.9	3.3	6.6	2.9	3.6	0.0	5.5	5.5	0.0	0.0	0.0
1890	8.9	4.1	4.8	2.4	2.1	0.3	5.5	5.2	0.3	0.0	0.0
1891	14.1	8.7	5.3	2.7	2.3	0.4	8.0	7.2	0.8	0.0	0.0
1892	9.8	4.3	5.5	4.7	0.8	0.0	7.4	6.6	0.4	0.4	0.0
1893	13.7	4.3	9.4	6.5	2.2	0.7	8.3	7.9	0.4	0.0	0.0
1894	11.5	6.0	5.5	3.0	1.7	0.9	8.1	6.4	0.9	0.0	0.4
1895	14.8	7.4	7.4	3.1	3.1	1.2	10.1	8.2	1.9	0.0	0.0
1896	17.4	8.7	8.7	3.7	2.8	2.3	6.0	5.0	0.0	0.9	0.0
1897	24.3	9.8	14.5	9.2	4.0	1.2	11.0	11.0	0.0	0.0	0.0
1898	23.5	5.6	17.9	9.9	4.3	3.7	11.1	8.6	2.5	0.0	0.0
1899	20.8	9.0	11.8	5.7	3.8	2.4	6.1	5.2	0.9	0.0	0.0
1900	22.6	4.2	18.4	5.8	6.3	6.3	13.2	11.6	1.6	0.0	0.0
1901	17.1	3.9	13.3	8.3	2.2	2.8	8.3	7.2	0.0	0.0	0.6
1902	21.4	4.4	17.0	12.1	3.9	1.0	4.9	3.4	1.5	0.0	0.0
1903	19.1	4.8	14.4	6.2	4.8	3.3	8.6	7.7	1.0	0.0	0.0
1904	21.5	9.2	12.3	3.1	5.6	3.6	10.3	9.7	0.5	0.0	0.0
1905	22.0	4.6	17.3	6.9	6.4	4.0	11.0	10.4	0.6	0.0	0.0
1906	18.4	7.7	10.6	8.2	1.4	1.0	4.3	3.9	0.5	0.0	0.0
1907	17.1	8.6	8.6	5.1	1.7	1.7	8.6	6.3	1.7	0.6	0.0
1908	16.9	6.7	10.1	7.3	2.2	0.6	8.4	6.7	1.1	0.6	0.0

Table 4-2. Percentage of United States Supreme Court Decisions With Dissenting Votes and Opinions, 1888-1997

TERM YEAR	AT LEAST ONE DISSENTING VOTE	ONE DISSENTING VOTE	TWO OR MORE DISSENTING VOTES	TWO DISSENTING VOTES	THREE DISSENTING VOTES	FOUR DISSENTING VOTES	AT LEAST ONE DISSENTING OPINION	ONE DISSENTING OPINION	TWO DISSENTING OPINIONS	THREE DISSENTING OPINIONS	FOUR DISSENTING OPINIONS
1909	17.4	7.6	9.9	5.2	4.1	0.6	5.8	5.8	0.0	0.0	0.0
1910	10.2	6.6	3.6	2.4	1.2	0.0	6.0	6.0	0.0	0.0	0.0
1911	6.4	2.3	4.1	2.3	0.9	0.9	4.6	4.6	0.0	0.0	0.0
1912	9.0	3.8	5.3	2.3	1.9	1.1	4.1	4.1	0.0	0.3	0.0
1913	9.2	5.8	3.4	2.1	1.4	0.0	3.1	2.7	0.0	0.4	0.0
1914	11.3	3.2	8.1	3.6	2.8	1.6	7.3	6.9	1.2	0.0	0.0
1915	9.1	3.7	5.4	5.0	0.4	0.0	3.7	2.5	2.8	0.9	0.0
1916	20.5	6.0	14.4	6.0	5.1	3.3	9.8	6.0	1.9	0.0	0.0
1917	14.5	4.8	9.7	4.8	3.9	1.0	6.8	4.8	1.4	0.0	0.0
1918	13.9	5.6	8.3	3.2	2.8	2.3	6.5	5.1	2.3	0.0	0.0
1919	29.9	9.2	20.7	13.2	3.4	4.0	12.1	9.8	1.4	0.0	0.0
1920	17.8	5.6	12.1	5.6	4.2	2.3	6.1	4.7	1.2	0.6	0.0
1921	20.1	5.3	14.8	5.3	8.3	1.2	10.1	8.3	0.5	0.9	0.0
1922	7.3	1.4	5.9	4.5	1.4	0.0	5.0	3.6	2.4	0.0	0.0
1923	11.2	3.9	7.3	5.4	2.0	0.0	8.3	5.9	0.0	0.9	0.4
1924	11.1	6.2	4.9	2.2	1.8	0.9	5.3	3.6	1.0	0.0	0.0
1925	6.9	3.5	3.5	1.5	1.5	0.5	4.0	3.0	0.0	1.0	0.0
1926	14.3	4.1	10.2	4.1	4.1	2.0	9.2	8.2	0.0	0.6	0.0
1927	14.9	2.4	12.5	3.6	5.4	3.6	12.5	6.0	3.6	0.0	1.2
1928	16.5	6.3	10.2	3.1	6.3	0.8	11.8	8.7	3.1	0.0	0.0
1929	9.2	0.8	8.4	2.3	6.1	0.0	8.4	6.1	2.3	0.0	0.0

Table 4-2. Percentage of United States Supreme Court Decisions With Dissenting Votes and Opinions, 1888-1997

TERM YEAR	AT LEAST ONE DISSENTING VOTE	ONE DISSENTING VOTE	TWO OR MORE DISSENTING VOTES	TWO DISSENTING VOTES	THREE DISSENTING VOTES	FOUR DISSENTING VOTES	AT LEAST ONE DISSENTING OPINION	ONE DISSENTING OPINION	TWO DISSENTING OPINIONS	THREE DISSENTING OPINIONS	FOUR DISSENTING OPINIONS
1930	9.8	2.6	7.2	2.0	2.0	3.3	7.8	5.9	0.7	0.0	0.7
1931	16.1	6.0	10.1	3.4	5.4	1.3	10.7	10.1	0.7	0.0	0.0
1932	16.1	2.4	13.7	7.1	4.2	2.4	11.9	6.5	4.2	1.2	0.0
1933	19.1	5.7	13.4	2.5	5.7	5.1	12.1	10.8	0.0	1.3	0.0
1934	14.9	3.2	11.7	1.9	4.5	5.2	7.8	7.8	0.0	0.0	0.0
1935	17.2	1.4	15.9	2.8	8.3	4.8	13.8	11.0	2.1	0.7	0.0
1936	19.4	4.9	14.6	4.9	0.7	9.0	13.9	10.4	2.1	1.4	0.0
1937	30.2	9.4	20.8	14.8	4.0	2.0	22.8	20.1	2.7	0.0	0.0
1938	32.1	7.1	25.0	16.4	5.0	3.6	25.0	24.3	0.7	0.0	0.0
1939	29.2	12.4	16.8	5.8	9.5	1.5	16.8	16.8	0.0	0.0	0.0
1940	27.4	4.9	22.6	9.1	11.0	2.4	19.5	17.7	1.8	0.0	0.0
1941	35.4	5.0	30.4	9.3	11.2	9.9	32.3	26.7	2.5	3.1	0.0
1942	41.9	11.0	30.8	9.9	15.1	5.8	39.0	32.6	4.7	1.7	0.0
1943	55.9	14.7	41.2	16.2	13.2	11.8	50.0	40.4	7.4	2.2	0.0
1944	55.9	14.3	41.6	11.2	11.2	19.3	45.3	34.2	8.7	1.2	0.6
1945	52.2	19.6	32.6	15.9	16.7	0.0	49.3	44.2	3.6	1.4	0.0
1946	59.0	9.7	49.3	16.0	16.7	16.7	50.0	32.6	15.3	2.1	0.0
1947	68.6	11.6	57.0	19.8	17.4	19.8	52.9	43.0	8.3	1.7	0.0
1948	74.2	8.9	65.3	14.5	23.4	27.4	62.9	46.8	12.1	4.0	0.0
1949	60.0	25.0	35.0	23.0	10.0	2.0	56.0	38.0	15.0	3.0	0.0
1950	63.4	11.9	51.5	13.9	21.8	15.8	54.5	37.6	14.9	0.0	1.0

Table 4-2. Percentage of United States Supreme Court Decisions With Dissenting Votes and Opinions, 1888-1997

TERM YEAR	AT LEAST ONE DISSENTING VOTE	ONE DISSENTING VOTE	TWO OR MORE DISSENTING VOTES	TWO DISSENTING VOTES	THREE DISSENTING VOTES	FOUR DISSENTING VOTES	AT LEAST ONE DISSENTING OPINION	ONE DISSENTING OPINION	TWO DISSENTING OPINIONS	THREE DISSENTING OPINIONS	FOUR DISSENTING OPINIONS
1951	70.1	14.4	55.7	21.6	23.7	10.3	51.5	35.1	7.2	3.1	3.1
1952	73.9	19.1	54.8	27.8	20.9	6.1	58.3	43.5	13.9	0.9	0.0
1953	60.9	10.3	50.6	21.8	18.4	10.3	55.2	44.8	8.0	2.3	0.0
1954	53.7	11.6	42.1	20.0	21.1	1.1	44.2	31.6	12.6	0.0	0.0
1955	55.3	5.8	49.5	14.6	22.3	12.6	48.5	38.8	6.8	1.0	1.0
1956	69.0	15.9	53.2	19.8	23.0	10.3	61.1	47.6	11.9	1.6	0.0
1957	70.4	13.2	57.2	18.4	19.1	19.7	59.9	45.4	10.5	3.9	0.0
1958	55.9	7.4	48.5	11.8	18.4	18.4	47.8	37.5	8.8	1.5	0.0
1959	67.9	13.4	54.5	14.9	20.9	18.7	62.7	43.3	16.4	3.0	2.2
1960	65.0	11.7	53.3	16.1	18.2	19.0	64.2	43.1	14.6	2.2	0.0
1961	58.1	19.7	38.5	23.1	11.1	4.3	53.0	44.4	7.7	0.9	0.0
1962	59.0	17.9	41.0	19.2	13.5	8.3	48.1	43.6	4.5	0.0	0.0
1963	53.9	12.8	41.1	16.7	16.1	8.3	52.2	41.1	8.9	2.2	0.0
1964	54.5	19.7	34.8	16.7	10.6	7.6	49.2	37.9	8.3	1.5	0.8
1965	54.4	18.4	36.0	15.4	10.3	10.3	50.7	40.4	5.1	2.2	1.5
1966	69.9	19.2	50.7	11.6	21.2	17.8	66.4	53.4	9.6	3.4	0.0
1967	63.0	25.0	38.0	19.3	17.2	1.6	54.2	44.3	6.8	3.1	0.0
1968	59.4	16.7	42.8	21.0	18.1	3.6	58.0	37.0	15.9	3.6	0.7
1969	54.4	11.0	43.4	24.3	19.1	0.0	54.4	39.7	11.8	2.9	0.0
1970	61.4	14.3	47.1	12.1	14.3	20.7	64.3	39.3	17.1	5.0	1.4
1971	51.7	14.4	37.4	14.9	10.9	11.5	59.8	37.9	15.5	2.9	1.7

OF TIME AND JUDICIAL BEHAVIOR

Table 4-2. Percentage of United States Supreme Court Decisions With Dissenting Votes and Opinions, 1888-1997

TERM YEAR	AT LEAST ONE DISSENTING VOTE	ONE DISSENTING VOTE	TWO OR MORE DISSENTING VOTES	TWO DISSENTING VOTES	THREE DISSENTING VOTES	FOUR DISSENTING VOTES	AT LEAST ONE DISSENTING OPINION	ONE DISSENTING OPINION	TWO DISSENTING OPINIONS	THREE DISSENTING OPINIONS	FOUR DISSENTING OPINIONS
1972	67.8	11.7	56.1	13.3	25.0	17.8	67.2	38.9	20.6	5.6	1.1
1973	64.0	15.1	48.8	8.1	22.7	18.0	64.5	45.3	14.0	4.1	0.6
1974	59.7	18.1	41.6	10.7	19.5	11.4	54.4	37.6	15.4	1.3	0.0
1975	57.5	8.9	48.6	24.6	15.6	8.4	53.6	39.1	11.7	2.8	0.0
1976	57.7	12.6	45.1	16.6	15.4	13.1	58.9	41.1	10.9	6.9	0.0
1977	61.8	9.9	52.0	17.8	23.0	11.2	64.5	47.4	14.5	2.6	0.0
1978	61.5	13.5	48.1	11.5	19.6	16.7	60.3	45.5	11.5	3.2	0.0
1979	69.2	12.2	57.1	15.4	24.4	17.3	73.1	51.9	14.7	3.8	1.3
1980	62.9	12.6	50.3	15.4	23.1	11.9	65.7	51.0	12.6	2.1	0.0
1981	62.4	11.8	50.6	10.6	20.6	19.4	64.7	48.2	13.5	1.8	0.6
1982	60.0	12.7	47.3	10.3	18.2	18.8	61.8	46.7	13.3	1.8	0.0
1983	54.1	9.4	44.7	12.4	16.5	15.9	56.5	42.9	11.8	0.6	0.6
1984	53.6	9.8	43.8	13.1	19.0	11.8	58.2	41.8	11.1	2.6	1.3
1985	63.2	10.4	52.8	10.4	20.9	21.5	67.5	42.9	20.9	3.7	0.0
1986	66.9	4.4	62.5	13.8	22.5	26.3	70.6	51.3	17.5	1.9	0.0
1987	50.7	8.1	42.6	14.2	19.6	8.8	54.7	46.6	8.1	0.0	0.0
1988	57.7	6.0	51.7	10.1	18.8	22.8	61.1	44.3	16.1	0.7	0.0
1989	65.9	7.2	58.7	13.8	15.2	29.7	64.5	51.4	12.3	0.7	0.0
1990	61.7	14.0	47.7	15.0	17.7	15.0	56.6	41.1	13.2	2.3	0.0
1991	51.6	6.9	44.7	13.5	23.1	8.1	60.8	49.2	10.8	0.8	0.0
1992	47.3	9.6	37.7	13.0	11.8	12.9	53.9	43.0	5.8	1.7	1.7
1993	52.8	13.2	39.6	18.2	12.0	9.4	55.2	43.8	8.3	3.1	0.0
1994	55.2	11.2	44.0	12.8	11.2	20.0	57.1	44.1	10.8	2.2	0.0
1995	56.3	12.4	43.9	16.5	7.5	19.9	55.0	41.8	9.9	3.3	0.0
1996	56.9	10.6	46.3	11.4	11.4	23.5	50.0	33.0	14.9	2.1	0.0
1997	56.3	9.6	46.7	9.6	17.8	19.3	50.0	35.0	14.0	1.0	0.0

judges hide the existence of disagreement among their colleagues behind the pretense of unanimity.[55] If Supreme Court justices disagree not only with the majority's reasoning but also its disposition of the case, they may vote in dissent. They may choose not to express the reasons for their votes and, thus, not write a separate opinion outlining their positions on the case. A justice voting in dissent gives an even stronger statement of his or her disagreement with the majority than when writing a concurring opinion. In dissent, he records his opposition to the means *and* the ends of the Court's opinion. Having expressed their disagreement with the majority's position, justices oftentimes do not file another dissent again when a succeeding case involves the same question of law.[56]

Figure 4-4 displays the percentage of decisions with at least one dissenting vote filed from 1888 to 1997 (see also Table 4-2). As the figure clearly shows, the justices dissent at a modest rate until 1930. The average percentage of cases with at least one dissenting vote is 16.67 percent for the Fuller Court and about 13 percent for the White[57] and Taft Courts each. For the last five years of the White Court, the series average is 19.3 percent. Handberg reports that the average for that period is 21.4 percent.[58] In the present study, the dissent rate is initially 20.5 percent, and declines to 14.5 percent in 1917 and to 13.9 percent the following year. But then, the series rebounds to 29.9 percent in 1919, attaining 17.8 percent in the final year of the White Court, 1920. Handberg finds that the dissent rate varied from about 26 percent in 1916 to a high of about 39 percent in 1919. The rate then declines to around 18 percent in 1920.[59]

The results of the present study confirm the timing of this rise and fall of the dissent rate during the last half of the White Court, although there are differences in magnitude between the two studies' results. These differences may be due to several factors. First, Handberg only examines nonunanimous decisions. The dissent rate that he discusses may be simply the frequency of dissenting votes in such cases. Second, it may include both the frequency of dissenting votes and dissenting opinions. Third, it may be that Handberg is simply characterizing the dissent rate in only economic cases. His description of the data may, thus, be somewhat ambiguous. This increase in the division within the last natural court of the White Court is an unexpected finding. During these years, the Court began to move away from the strict adherence to the economic doctrine of laissez-faire and began to support Progressive reforms, upholding antitrust laws and governmental regulation of business activity.[60] In *Wilson v. New*, for example, the Court upheld the constitutionality of the Adamson Act, a provision of which set the maximum number of hours railroad employees could be required to work in a day.[61]

Moreover, there were changes in the Court's membership during this

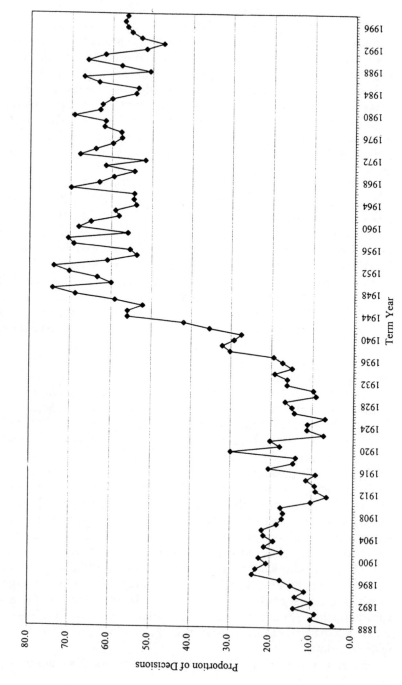

Figure 4-4. Proportion of Decisions of the United States Supreme Court With At Least One Dissenting Vote, 1888-1997

time. Justice Hughes joined the Court in 1910; Justice Brandeis in 1916. Although Hughes was more moderate than Brandeis, Hughes voted with the liberal wing of the Court, which Oliver Wendell Holmes led. However, Willis Van Devanter (in 1911) and James McReynolds (in 1914) joined the White Court's conservative wing.[62] The confluence of these two developments (the beginnings of a more liberal policy perspective and the change in the Court's membership) may have been associated with a moderate increase in conflict within the high tribunal, thus leading to this increased rate of dissenting votes. However, the Court was still largely operating under the norms of consensus. Thus, the justices may have not felt completely free to dissent whenever they wanted to do so. The increase in the dissent rate during the White Court may, therefore, represent the Court's attempt to reconcile these competing interests within the structural and historical constraints that then prevailed. Hence, the decline in unanimity that prior studies find to have begun during the Hughes Court or the Stone Court may have had its precursors in the White Court.[63]

The finding of a decline in the dissent rate during the Taft Court from that observed during the last half of the White Court is expected, too. The average rate during the Taft Court is about 13 percent, a relative change of about 33 percent. During Taft's tenure as chief justice, the Court returns to its consistent conservative policy perspective.[64] Also, two of the ardently conservative "Four Horsemen" were nominated to the Court (George Sutherland and Pierce Butler in 1922) during this period, joining strong conservatives James McReynolds, Willis Van Devanter, and Chief Justice William Howard Taft.[65] Thus, the Taft Court was more cohesive in its membership and its policy perspective, leading to more cohesive voting behavior and, thus, fewer dissenting votes being filed.

When one examines the years of the Hughes Court, however, there is a dramatic increase over the rate observed during the Taft Court: 21.05 percent of the decisions had at least one dissenting vote filed with them. This rate represents a relative increase of 70 percent over the series' average level during Taft's tenure. Thus, the dissent rate during the Hughes Court is more similar to that found during the last five years of the White Court. Stephen G. Halpern and Kenneth N. Vines, and Blaustein and Mersky report similar levels for the rate of dissenting votes during the Hughes Court, with a large increase in the rate of dissenting votes occurring after 1930.[66]

Across the entire period, the justices dissent more frequently than they cast concurring votes, strangely enough. Given the norms of consensus prevailing prior to the 1930s, one would expect justices to concur more often than they dissent because concurrences ostensibly announce to the public and other political actors less conflict with the majority than do dissents. After 1930, the series increases dramatically, until 1948 when it reaches a new equilibrium.

As one can see from the figure, the increase is particularly steep following the 1941 term year, when Chief Justice Stone assumed the helm of the
Court. The dissent rate under Stone increases even beyond the unprecedented levels observed during Hughes's tenure. The average dissent rate
for Stone is 48.26 percent, a phenomenal relative change of 129 percent
from that during Hughes's leadership. Moreover, the legacy that Stone left
on the Court is still apparent on the contemporary Court. From 1948 to
1997, for example, the series average is 60.28 percent (see Table 4-2). Hence,
about two-thirds of the Court's decisions on average then have at least one
dissenting vote expressed and, thus, some amount of dissensus noted, as
compared to the pre-1930 period when only about 15 percent of the Court's
decisions did.

Pritchett examines the newfound tendency of the justices appointed by
Franklin Roosevelt, from 1937 to 1947, to dissent more frequently than
justices had in the past.[67] He, too, reports an increase in the dissent rate
beginning in 1930.[68] Although the findings of this study and that of Pritchett
differ slightly in terms of magnitude,[69] they do agree as to the existence of
an increase in that rate in 1930, a slight decrease after the 1938 term, and
then a large increase beginning in 1941, culminating in about 60 percent of
the decisions handed down during the 1946 term having at least one dissenting vote.[70] More illustrative of the level of conflict that pervaded the
Stone Court perhaps is the justices' tendency to depart from the institutional custom of dissenting only in matters of importance.[71] They began to
dissent more frequently over matters that were not always vital.[72] Hence,
the change in the rate of dissent was not only a quantitative one but also
one involving a qualitative transformation.

THE JUDGES' BILL AND DISSENSUS

Scholars have examined the influence of the Court's changing jurisdiction,
and thus its agenda, on the dissent rate. Halpern and Vines investigate the
effect of the Judges' Bill. Prior to that statute being enacted, the Court's
jurisdiction mostly consisted of obligatory cases, which often represented
well-settled issues of the law. The decisions on such cases presumably did
not cause a great deal of conflict among the justices.[73] Those authors find
that the promulgation of the act did affect the rate of dissent subsequently.
As expected, the largest effect comes in cases that the Court was obliged to
hear, rather than in those on its discretionary docket.[74]

Halpern and Vines suggest that the act may have signaled the justices
that they should adopt a new, more active role. "The Act's supporters ad-
vanced a conception of the Court as an institution which should reserve its
judgments only for the most important national policy questions," thereby

changing the place of the Court as an institution within the American system of governance.[75] Hence, the act's rationale made it more acceptable, if not expected, that the justices would more frequently dissent. Justice Cardozo once remarked that cases of national importance are "not necessarily and ineluctably subject to one 'correct' solution."[76] Thus, the act may have contributed to a change in the Court's role conception, which was exacerbated by the political turmoil in which the Court was soon to find itself in the mid-1930s.

However, Walker, Epstein, and Dixon discount the impact of the act on the dissent rate. They assert that a significant escalation in the dissent rate did not occur until the early 1940s even though the Court's discretionary jurisdiction expanded following the act.[77] They dismiss the hypothesized effect that Halpern and Vines attribute to the act because the dissent rate shortly thereafter returned to the levels observed prior to the statute's passage. Moreover, Haynie does not find that the act significantly increased the rate of dissensus on the Court.[78] Indeed, Figure 4-4 supports these latter studies' conclusions about the alleged effect that the act had on the dissent rate on the Court. It had some effect, but the change immediately after its passage was not substantial. A larger increase in dissents developed some fifteen years later.

Yet one should not entirely discount the act's effect in implying a new role for the Court to play in the resolution of conflict within the political system. This change in role conception may have taken several term years to percolate and develop, and its effect may only have been expressed much later. Indeed, it may be more clearly expressed in the Court's policy preferences. This delayed effect may partially explain the increased dissent rate that Walker, Epstein, and Dixon, Halpern and Vines, and this study find in the early 1940s.

MULTIPLE DISSENTS

One aspect of the qualitative change that occurred in the Court's decision-making during the pre-1945 period involves multiple dissents. Multiple dissents indicate a more divided Court than decisions in which there is only one dissenting vote or none at all. As Figure 4-5 and Table 4-2 show, the historic high for decisions with two or more dissenting votes occurs in 1948, when 65.3 percent of the Court decisions contain two or more dissenting votes. The series historic low is observed in 1888, when only 1.7 percent of the decisions have such voting patterns.

Decisions with a 5-4 vote are particularly illustrative of the division among the justices because such votes represent the boundary of the Court's dissensus; this is the maximum possible dissensus that can occur and the

Figure 4-5. Proportion of United States Supreme Court Decisions With Two or More Dissenting Votes, 1888-1997

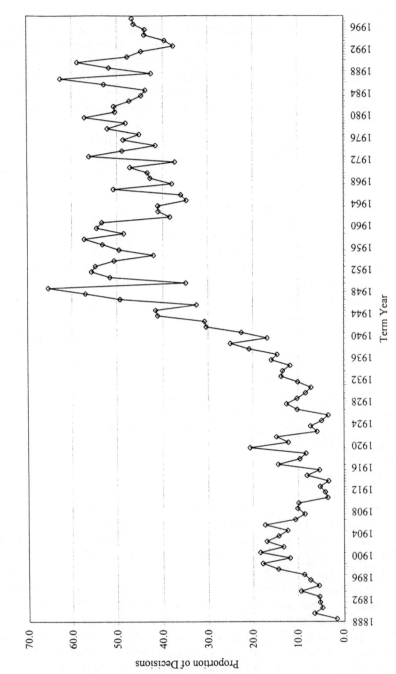

Court's opinion can still have any precedential value. Table 4-2 shows that the series high for 5-4 decisions is observed in 1989, when 29.7 percent of the Court's decisions have such votes.

There are several years in which no 5-4 decisions are announced. Three term years during Fuller's (1888, 1889, and 1892) and Taft's (1922, 1923, and 1929) tenures have no 5–4 decisions; the White Court has two years (1913 and 1915) with none of those decisions. On the other hand, the Hughes and the Stone Courts have at least one such decision during each of their respective term years. The average percentage of 5-4 decisions in the Fuller Court is 1.73. It declines somewhat to 1.50 percent for the White Court and even further, to 0.87 percent, for the Taft Court. This latter finding is not unexpected given Taft's view of dissenting votes. One would predict that he would particularly disfavor 5-4 decisions because of the level of division within the Court such decisions announce to the public and other policy actors. The Hughes Court sees an increase in the proportion of 5-4 decisions. Its rate is 3.69 percent, a relative increase of 135 percent from the average observed across the three prior chief justice courts. The rate during the Stone Court climbs to 9.36 percent, a relative change of 154 percent. Hence, from 1930 to 1946, the rate of 5–4 decisions increases relatively an incredible 583 percent. Clearly, 5–4 decisions are a rather infrequent occurrence prior to 1930 due to the norms of consensus that pervaded the Court.[79] Even so, the Fuller Court has a higher percentage of such opinions than the rates found for the White or Taft Courts. This result is somewhat surprising given the norms of consensus that allegedly were stronger during the earlier Courts. Perhaps the large amount of regulatory legislation brought to the Court for review first during the Fuller Court may affect this increased dissent rate.[80] Thus, the Court becomes much more sharply divided in its voting behavior during the post-1946 period.

Similarly, Pritchett finds an increased rate of 5–4 decisions during the Roosevelt years.[81] He finds that the average rate of 5–4 decisions during the Hughes Court was 3.55 percent, as opposed to 3.69 percent in the present study. He reports an increased rate during the Stone Court (12.80 percent), as opposed to 9.36 percent here.[82] This discrepancy may be due to Pritchett's analysis only including nonunanimous cases, whereas the present study includes all opinions. Therefore, this study agrees with Pritchett's findings of increased division among the justices and the timing of that increase from 1930 to 1946.

The promulgation of the Judges' Bill in 1925, too, may be associated with an increase in the frequency of multiple dissents.[83] To more clearly assess the effect of the act, the averages for each chief justice court prior to 1946 are calculated. The Fuller Court average is 10.50 percent, while that for the White Court declines to 8.32 percent. To parse out the effect of the

Judges' Bill, Taft's tenure as chief justice is split into halves: 1920–26 and 1927–29.[84] The division point of 1927 is chosen because some of the cases that the Court decided in 1926 predated the act.[85] From 1921 to 1926, 7.77 percent of the Taft Court decisions have multiple dissent votes included in them. From 1927 to 1929, however, the figure rises 2.6 percentage points to 10.37, a relative change of 33 percent. Thus, the act did not appear to substantially increase the multiple dissent rate, as Halpern and Vines assert. However, as Figure 4-5 shows, the 1926 term year shows an increase in the rate of multiple dissents over the rate for the past four term years and a reversal in the direction of the series. After 1925, it begins to turn upward.

For the Hughes Court, the average observed is 15.62 percent, a relative increase of 51 percent over that for the Taft Court. While this change is rather large, it does not compare to the magnitude of changes seen during the Stone Court, when 35.32 percent of the cases involve multiple dissents, which represents a relative change of 126 percent from the prior Court's average.

Overall, the series from 1926 to 1960 trends upward, although the change from one term year to the next is not all that large. The steepest increases in the series occur after 1941, lending credence to Walker, Epstein, and Dixon's assertion that Stone's leadership style permanently altered the norms governing the voting behavior of the justices.[86] However, the effects of the Judges' Bill and of Hughes should not be overlooked since the series begins to increase, albeit modestly, after 1925. Hence, the growing percentage of cases with two or more dissenting votes since 1926 documents the expanding level of dissensus that characterizes the voting of, and the interpersonal relations among, the Court's justices.[87]

THE DECLINE OF CONSENSUAL NORMS

In addition, these results shed light directly on those studies that attempt to discover the cause of the "mysterious demise of consensual norms" during the 1930s and 1940s.[88] The last five years of the White Court (1916–20) appear to have initiated a decline in the norms of consensus that had prevailed until that time, perhaps due to the particular members then serving on the Court and a subsequent, temporary change in its policy preferences.[89] Also, this study's findings generally support Haynie's conclusion that suggest Hughes's tenure, beginning in 1930, is associated with a continuing decline of consensus that was later institutionalized under Chief Justice Stone. Although Haynie examines only dissenting opinions (as opposed to analyzing dissenting votes too), her analysis suggests that Hughes's distinctive leadership style contributed to the decline in the norm of consensus. Hughes's interpersonal style and judicial inclinations, thus, allowed for a more individualistic environment in which dissenting votes flourished.[90]

On the other hand, Walker, Epstein, and Dixon suggest that Hughes did not contribute to the rise of dissensus on the Court.[91] However, their methodology largely involves analysis of graphs depicting the number of dissenting opinions per one hundred majority opinions, whereas Haynie employs a more formal time series methodology to demonstrate the effect of Hughes and Stone on the dissent rate of the Court. Hence, Haynie's findings are strongly confirmed by the present analysis, while those of Epstein, Walker, and Dixon are less clearly supported in the present study.

DISSENTING OPINIONS

Perhaps the clearest expression of a justice's disagreement with the majority is represented by a dissenting opinion. Rather than quietly recording his conflict with the majority by issuing a dissenting vote, he publicly announces his disagreement and the reasons for it, thus clearly demonstrating the lack of cohesion on the Court and the reasons for it. The norms of consensus on the Court that discourage the writing of dissenting opinions largely prevailed until the 1940s because they were perceived to weaken the authority of the Court's opinion and, indeed, the Court as an institution if it were seen to be divided concerning an issue. On the other hand, some authors of dissenting opinions (such as Charles Evans Hughes) argue that their opinions look to the future and the development of the law.

Figure 4-6 displays the percentage of decisions with at least one dissenting opinion. As one can clearly see, the series does not exceed 15 percent prior to 1934. Through the Fuller, White, and Taft Courts and the first four years of the Hughes Court, dissenting opinions are an infrequent event in Supreme Court decision-making. Thus, consensus prevails on the high tribunal until that point in time. The averages for those three chief justice courts illustrate that notion. The percentage of cases with at least one dissenting opinion during the Fuller Court is 7.86 percent. It declines during the White Court to 6.37 percent. The rate during the last five years of the White Court is 8.26 percent. The series increases slightly, to 8.29 percent, during the Taft Court.

Thereafter, however, the series dramatically increases through 1997. The largest increases occur from 1935 through 1948. The figure rises rather abruptly to 14.74 percent during the Hughes Court. This represents a relative increase of 78 percent. The Stone Court's dissent rate is extraordinary: 43.18 percent of the decisions on average have at least one dissenting opinion during his tenure. This rate represents a relative change of 193 percent from that observed during the Hughes Court. Epstein, Segal, Spaeth, and Walker report similar data, documenting the magnitude of dissenting opinions and the timing of their increase during the Hughes and the Stone Courts.[92]

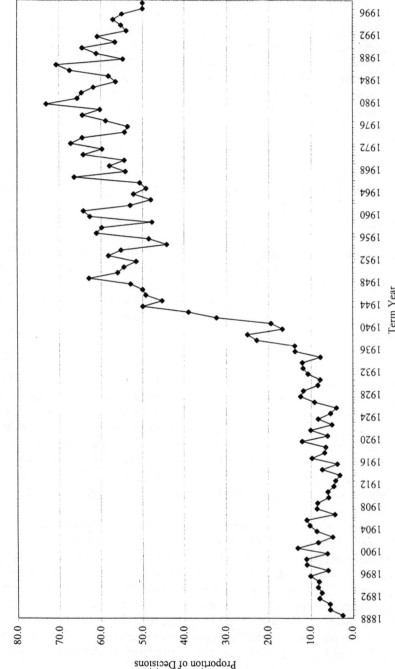

Figure 4-6. Proportion of United States Supreme Court Decisions
With At Least One Dissenting Opinion, 1888-1997

Once again, this analysis confirms the findings of Haynie. While Stone's tenure is associated with an increase in the rate of the decline of consensus on the Court, Haynie argues this decline was initiated during Hughes's tenure. When Stone assumed the Court's helm in 1941, that trend toward allowing, if not expressly encouraging, individual expression through dissent that Hughes had begun continued.[93] Stone's views on dissent are quite clear. He states: "[s]ound legal principles ...never sprang full-fledged from the brains of any man or group of men. They are the ultimate result of the abrasive force of the clash of competing and sometimes conflicting ideas. . . ."[94] For Stone, "conflict represented intellectual, not personal, differences."[95] Therefore, the unique leadership styles of both Hughes and Stone and their perspectives on dissents are associated, at least in part, with this dramatic increase in the dissent rate.

Moreover, one should bear in mind the unique political, social, and legal circumstances in which the Court then operated. "Basically the dissents and concurrences which characterize the Roosevelt Court reflect the conflicts of a society faced with unprecedented new problems of public policy and the deadly earnest in which the Court is considering proposed solutions."[96] The present findings bear out these differences by empirically demonstrating the transformation that they wrought on the decisional trends of the Supreme Court. This change manifests itself in large increases in the rate of concurring votes and opinions, and dissenting votes and opinions, as compared with their relative infrequency in the prior forty-three term years that extend back to Melville Fuller's time as chief justice of the United States.

CHAPTER SUMMARY

This chapter examines the trends in the institutional-level decision-making of the United States Supreme Court from 1888 to 1997. The results presented in the chapter demonstrate that the Court's decisions have become much more nonunanimous over time, most particularly since the 1930s. While the norms of consensus hold the Court together during the Fuller and Taft Courts, those institutional customs begin to unravel during the last half of the White Court, beginning in 1916. Chief Justices Fuller and Taft socialized the justices on their Courts into a tradition of not dissenting unless it were absolutely necessary to promote the legitimacy of the Court's decisions. They also sought to limit split votes so as to protect the Court's prestige by distinguishing it from the Congress or the presidency whose business is sullied by politics. While approximately 80 percent of the decisions during the Fuller and Taft Courts are unanimous, the rate begins to drop in the White Court, recovers during the Taft Court, descends again during the Hughes Court and continues to do so during the Stone Court, reaching by 1947 rates of only about 35 percent unanimous. The Court's decisions remain stable at that approximate level of unanimity from 1947 to 1989, and then increase somewhat to about 50 percent by 1997.

This nonunanimity that describes the Court's decisions since the 1940s is expressed in a rising tide of concurring and dissenting votes and opinions. The decline of consensus on the Court is illustrated by the growing rate of concurring votes and opinions and dissenting votes, beginning at the midway point of the White Court (1916). While Taft serves as a mediating influence to dampen the conflict on the Court, Hughes's tenure is associated with the unanimity rate returning to the depressed levels first observed during the latter years of the White Court. Haynie suggests that this decline occurs because Hughes's distinctive leadership style—that resolved conflict among the justices but also fostered an atmosphere in which individual expression by the justices was encouraged—is associated with this increase in the rate of concurring votes and opinions and, thus, the continued erosion of the long-standing norms of consensus in Supreme Court decision-making.[97]

This trend of declining consensus is in full bloom during the tenure of Harlan Fisk Stone (1941–45). The chapter shows that the rate of dissenting votes and opinions flourishes during his tenure. Walker, Epstein, and Dixon attribute that rise to Stone's belief that dissent was beneficial for the intellectual growth of the Court and the doctrine the Court announced in its decisions.[98] Thus freed from the time-honored restraints of consensus, the justices began to dissent at a significantly higher rate during the five term years that Stone occupied the center chair. Whereas the average dissent rate during the pre-1930 chief justice courts is about 20 percent, the post-1945 rate hovers near 65 percent. It continues to do so through 1989 but then reaches 50 percent in 1997.

Split opinions provide a unique opportunity to gaze into the justices' minds and examine their policy orientations. Chapter 5 examines the liberalism of the Court's decisions in each of the issue areas discussed in chapter 3 from 1888 to 1997. It also provides an analysis of the trends in the Court's decision-making in the four aggregated issue dimensions introduced in that chapter. This is done to provide a glimpse into the Court's changing perspective on vitally important issues of public policy with which the nation wrestled over time. These include such large-scale social events as the Panic of 1893, the Spanish-American War, the election of Progressive Theodore Roosevelt to the presidency in 1904, two world wars, the Great Depression, Franklin Roosevelt's New Deal social welfare program, and Roosevelt's attempt to pack the Court in 1937 (perhaps the largest threat to the Court's independence and legitimacy during its history), which have occurred during the 110 term years analyzed in this study.

5

Who Wins and Who Loses across Time: Liberalism of United States Supreme Court Decision-Making, 1888–1997

THIS CHAPTER EXAMINES THE POLICY CONTENT OF THE SUPREME COURT'S decision-making over time. It analyzes the liberalism of the rulings the Court has issued from 1888 to 1997 in each of the issue areas discussed in chapter 3. It then examines the liberalism of the Court's decisions in each of the four aggregated issue areas introduced in chapter 3. It speculates as to the reasons for the changes observed in the Court's liberalism during a period in which the nation endured the Panic of 1893, the Spanish-American War (1898), two world wars, a Great Depression, and a president's attack on the legitimacy of its Supreme Court (1937).

POLITICS, LIBERALISM, AND THE SUPREME COURT

Beyond examining the rates of dissents or concurrences, one can also examine the decisional trends of the United States Supreme Court by analyzing its policy outputs over time. A key concept here is the common one of "liberalism." It is now routine, although once it was quite controversial, to classify Supreme Court decisions as "liberal" or "conservative" because they favor or oppose certain policy interests.[1] This controversy arises out of a myth that the Court is an apolitical institution, whose prestige and image are not to be sullied by the worldly interaction of the Congress or the president. "Every Court prior to the Roosevelt Court had enjoyed the protection of perhaps the most potent myth in American political life—the myth that the Court is a non-political body, a sacred institution on which politics must not lay its profane hands."[2] The justices are thereunder presumed simply to find and apply the law without reference to their own individual

129

attitudes on the matter but with exclusive reference to the dictates of the Constitution and precedent.[3]

But the Court cannot be an apolitical institution, Pritchett argues, because it must eventually resolve the most important political questions of the day.[4] "[J]udicial decisions are not babies brought by constitutional storks, but are born out of the travail of economic circumstance. . . . [J]udges are human, and . . . the judicial power need be no more sacred in our scheme than any other power."[5] Hence, the Supreme Court and its decisions are inherently political and, thus, the liberalism of the latter can, and should, be systematically analyzed.

Nevertheless, the Court is somewhat constrained by the judicial functions it must complete. It must base its decisions on the rule of law; and because of the limiting language of the Constitution, it can issue decisions only in cases or controversies.[6] Therefore, while the Court's decisions are driven largely by the justices' public policy preferences, they presumably operate within a more restrained environment than does the president or Congress because of the institutional checks circumscribing the Court's power.

In time serial analyses such as those presented in this study, there is the question of the comparability of the liberalism rates reported for the Courts in different periods. Because of the changing issue content of the cases brought to the Court across this rather substantial analytical period, the difficulty of the Court's issuing a liberal decision in a particular issue area may not be the same throughout the period studied. Baum suggests that to truly understand the change in the Court's policy preferences over time, one must measure the degree to which policy change exists, or simply the difficulty of the justices casting a liberal vote.[7] Baum devises a method to measure policy change of the Court from 1945 to 1985, by subtracting the change in each of the member's voting behavior from the change in the Court's decision-making due to personnel changes.[8] He finds that his method of correction does not produce any fundamental differences in the Court's policy trends, although there are slight modifications suggested by his analysis.

While the Court did in fact hear different issues across the period analyzed, the cases are most likely equally difficult due to the changing norms of society. While a decision to uphold legislation outlawing child labor or an antilynching law was no doubt difficult to issue in 1905, such cases would be relatively trivial for the Court to decide today. However, other novel issues have replaced those prior issues that may have caused the Court difficulty in past years. There is now, for example, an ongoing debate about the constitutionality of abortion or other privacy claims that appears to be of similar difficulty to the civil liberties–civil rights claims that earlier Courts heard. Hence, although there may be a need for very slight modification of the liberalism rates, they appear to be comparable across the present period of analysis.

Liberalism Defined

To begin, it is necessary to define how the policy content of the decisions of the Supreme Court is measured. Political liberalism is a syndrome of attitudes that is associated with support for the interests of the downtrodden or less powerful in society, in contrast to the elites or those holding powerful positions in the social order.[9] Ulmer classifies the former as "underdogs" and the later as "upperdogs" to illustrate their perceived relative position within society.[10] Pamela Johnson Conover and Stanley Feldman state that "liberals seem to favor change and progress even at the expense of governmental involvement; conservatives, on the other hand, wish to preserve traditional arrangements particularly those threatened by governmental involvement."[11] In this analysis, "liberal" decisions are operationalized following these general concepts and the issue-specific definitions set out in the Spaeth Supreme Court database that advance the interests of the "underdogs" in the American political system.[12]

In economics cases, for example, a decision that approves an expansive degree of governmental regulation of economic activity is considered to be a liberal decision. Second, cases involving attorneys are liberal if they favor the interests of the attorneys because attorneys are thought to be "underdogs" with respect to the government, much as labor is an underdog to management.[13] Third, union cases are liberal if they uphold the rights of the union to organize and operate, and if they generally benefit the union's interests. Federal taxation decisions, the fourth issue area, are liberal if they uphold the interests of the federal government as opposed to the interests of the taxpayer, because it favors expanded governmental power, in the same vein as with economics decisions.

Fifth, in criminal procedure cases, those decisions that favor or benefit the accused are liberal, which usually involves a diminution of governmental power. In civil rights cases (the sixth issue area), those decisions that lead to expansion of civil rights are considered to be liberal. For First Amendment cases, those decisions that protect claims of freedom of speech and strike down governmental attempts to regulate speech are considered to be liberal. The eighth issue category is for privacy cases, which are liberal if they uphold claims of privacy as against intrusion by governmental officials.

Ninth, decisions dealing with questions of judicial power are liberal if they serve to expand the level of a court's authority, because the courts are part of the larger governmental structure. Federalism decisions, the tenth issue category, are liberal if they uphold the federal government's claims of power as against those of a state government. Interstate relations and separation of powers cases are not considered in this analysis of the liberalism of the Court's decisions, since no liberal content can be theoretically ascribed to such decisions presently.

There is also a residual category ("other," listed in Table 5-1) that contains all the decisions that do not fall within any of the above categories. Since their content is a combination of a myriad of issues, this category resists systematic examination and, thus, no policy orientation is attributed to such cases in this analysis.

Liberalism in Individual Issue Areas

Table 5-1 reports the percentage of decisions in each of these single issue areas that are decided in the liberal direction from 1888 to 1997. Figures 5-1 through 5-11 display the percentage of liberal decisions for these individual issue areas during that period. Since the Court's decisions predominantly involved economic issues up to the 1940s, they are examined first.

ECONOMICS

Figure 5-1 shows the liberalism of the Court's economic decisions across time. The series' historic high is observed in 1956, when 87.5 percent of the Court's economic decisions were liberal; the historic low occurs in 1995 (29.4 percent). The average percentage of liberal economic decisions for the Fuller Court is 54.76. The rate for the White Court is 59.94, only a slight increase over that for the Fuller Court. These results are somewhat unexpected because of the purported laissez-faire perspective of these Courts when considering economic issues.[14] These Courts appear to be more liberal than historical analyses have previously suggested.[15] The Taft Court's average percentage of liberal economic decisions is slightly lower than that for the White Court, at 52.58. This result may be due to the continuing conservatism of the Court, in particular due to the conservative policy preferences of Chief Justice Taft. The Hughes Court's average, on the other hand, is 66.96, representing an increase of 27 percent in the average proportion of liberal economic decisions. The Stone Court's average does not increase appreciably from that of the Hughes Court; that of the former is 67.36 percent. Thus, the Hughes Court's decision-making initiated a rather substantial change in the liberalism of economics decisions from the historic conservatism of the Court in prior years, a trend that the Stone Court, and the following Courts for that matter, continue.

Table 5-1. Percentage of Liberal Decisions of the United States Supreme Court in Indicated Issues, 1888-1997

TERM YEAR	TOTAL REPORTED DECISIONS	ECONOMIC	FEDERAL TAXATION	JUDICIAL POWER	CRIMINAL PROCEDURE	CIVIL RIGHTS	FIRST AMENDMENT	DUE PROCESS	PRIVACY	FEDERALISM	ATTORNEY	UNION	INTERSTATE RELATIONS	SEPARATION OF POWERS	OTHER
1888	240	45.4	0.0	26.2	50.0	0.0	0.0	0.0	0.0	0.0	0.0	0.0	0.0	0.0	0.0
1889	274	53.8	0.0	24.6	46.2	75.0	0.0	40.0	0.0	14.3	0.0	0.0	0.0	0.0	0.0
1890	291	45.9	50.0	17.5	28.6	40.0	100.0	0.0	0.0	100.0	0.0	0.0	0.0	0.0	0.0
1891	263	52.0	100.0	20.0	23.1	75.0	0.0	0.0	0.0	0.0	33.3	0.0	0.0	0.0	0.0
1892	256	42.0	100.0	7.5	36.4	0.0	100.0	0.0	0.0	100.0	0.0	0.0	0.0	0.0	0.0
1893	277	45.8	80.0	12.3	44.8	0.0	0.0	0.0	0.0	0.0	0.0	0.0	0.0	0.0	0.0
1894	235	52.6	50.0	23.6	29.0	50.0	0.0	0.0	0.0	100.0	100.0	0.0	0.0	0.0	0.0
1895	257	65.2	0.0	7.3	37.2	33.3	50.0	50.0	0.0	25.0	0.0	0.0	0.0	0.0	0.0
1896	218	57.9	0.0	13.3	50.0	66.7	0.0	50.0	0.0	100.0	0.0	0.0	0.0	0.0	0.0
1897	173	49.6	0.0	30.0	15.8	33.3	0.0	0.0	0.0	0.0	0.0	0.0	0.0	0.0	0.0
1898	162	56.6	66.7	17.1	60.0	50.0	0.0	36.4	0.0	0.0	0.0	0.0	0.0	0.0	0.0
1899	212	46.5	40.0	26.0	25.0	100.0	0.0	13.3	0.0	100.0	0.0	0.0	0.0	0.0	0.0
1900	190	62.0	55.6	16.7	11.1	0.0	0.0	0.0	0.0	50.0	0.0	0.0	0.0	0.0	0.0
1901	181	63.6	33.3	38.1	0.0	50.0	0.0	50.0	0.0	100.0	0.0	0.0	0.0	0.0	0.0
1902	206	64.3	75.0	22.4	33.3	18.2	0.0	16.7	0.0	40.0	0.0	0.0	0.0	0.0	0.0
1903	209	54.1	33.3	23.1	35.7	0.0	0.0	0.0	0.0	100.0	0.0	0.0	0.0	0.0	0.0
1904	195	54.0	100.0	25.0	23.1	0.0	0.0	25.0	0.0	66.7	0.0	0.0	0.0	0.0	0.0
1905	173	60.7	100.0	21.2	0.0	66.7	0.0	0.0	0.0	100.0	0.0	0.0	0.0	0.0	0.0
1906	207	56.8	100.0	15.6	29.4	100.0	0.0	33.3	0.0	100.0	50.0	100.0	0.0	0.0	0.0
1907	175	62.0	100.0	47.6	33.3	0.0	0.0	37.5	0.0	0.0	100.0	0.0	0.0	0.0	0.0
1908	178	62.4	100.0	9.3	38.1	0.0	0.0	0.0	0.0	0.0	0.0	0.0	0.0	0.0	0.0
1909	172	51.5	100.0	18.2	9.5	0.0	0.0	11.1	0.0	100.0	100.0	0.0	0.0	0.0	0.0
1910	167	70.5	100.0	21.7	10.5	0.0	0.0	0.0	0.0	0.0	0.0	0.0	0.0	0.0	0.0
1911	219	59.0	100.0	21.2	10.0	0.0	100.0	0.0	0.0	100.0	50.0	0.0	0.0	0.0	0.0
1912	266	46.2	50.0	14.7	19.4	0.0	100.0	22.7	0.0	0.0	100.0	0.0	0.0	0.0	0.0
1913	292	67.6	0.0	30.4	44.4	0.0	0.0	55.6	0.0	77.8	100.0	0.0	0.0	0.0	0.0
1914	247	59.3	0.0	25.7	15.4	75.0	0.0	50.0	0.0	60.0	0.0	0.0	0.0	0.0	0.0
1915	242	58.5	50.0	20.0	23.8	50.0	0.0	8.3	0.0	100.0	0.0	0.0	0.0	0.0	0.0
1916	215	65.7	100.0	23.3	20.0	0.0	0.0	20.0	0.0	100.0	0.0	0.0	0.0	0.0	0.0

Table 5-1. Percentage of Liberal Decisions of the United States Supreme Court in Indicated Issues, 1888-1997

TERM YEAR	TOTAL REPORTED DECISIONS	ECONOMIC	FEDERAL TAXATION	JUDICIAL POWER	CRIMINAL PROCEDURE	CIVIL RIGHTS	FIRST AMENDMENT	DUE PROCESS	PRIVACY	FEDERALISM	ATTORNEY	UNION	INTERSTATE RELATIONS	SEPARATION OF POWERS	OTHER
1917	207	59.5	61.5	17.4	27.3	60.0	0.0	33.3	0.0	63.6	0.0	0.0	0.0	0.0	0.0
1918	216	55.2	50.0	20.8	18.8	0.0	0.0	0.0	0.0	100.0	0.0	0.0	0.0	0.0	0.0
1919	174	64.6	57.1	21.7	16.7	66.7	0.0	12.5	0.0	68.8	0.0	0.0	0.0	0.0	0.0
1920	214	53.2	75.0	17.6	23.5	50.0	0.0	40.0	0.0	69.2	0.0	100.0	0.0	0.0	0.0
1921	169	58.9	52.9	23.5	8.3	100.0	0.0	16.7	0.0	58.3	0.0	0.0	0.0	0.0	0.0
1922	220	53.8	71.4	20.0	36.4	0.0	0.0	33.3	0.0	33.3	0.0	100.0	0.0	0.0	0.0
1923	205	61.0	25.0	27.6	8.3	10.0	0.0	0.0	0.0	100.0	0.0	50.0	0.0	0.0	0.0
1924	225	53.6	72.2	51.1	14.3	33.3	0.0	35.7	0.0	50.0	0.0	0.0	0.0	0.0	0.0
1925	202	46.8	66.7	31.8	35.3	0.0	0.0	0.0	0.0	50.0	100.0	0.0	0.0	0.0	0.0
1926	196	52.5	33.3	31.3	31.3	25.0	0.0	36.4	0.0	40.0	100.0	0.0	0.0	0.0	0.0
1927	168	50.6	64.7	53.8	25.0	0.0	0.0	28.6	0.0	100.0	0.0	0.0	0.0	0.0	0.0
1928	127	52.8	64.3	80.0	0.0	0.0	0.0	66.7	0.0	64.0	100.0	0.0	0.0	0.0	0.0
1929	131	43.2	81.0	20.0	33.3	0.0	0.0	50.0	0.0	87.5	0.0	0.0	0.0	0.0	0.0
1930	153	54.7	64.3	50.0	58.3	25.0	100.0	50.0	0.0	0.0	0.0	0.0	0.0	0.0	0.0
1931	149	58.0	62.5	21.4	22.2	40.0	0.0	33.3	0.0	75.0	0.0	0.0	0.0	0.0	0.0
1932	168	74.7	82.5	61.1	60.0	0.0	0.0	0.0	0.0	100.0	0.0	0.0	0.0	0.0	0.0
1933	157	63.2	60.9	61.1	50.0	0.0	0.0	44.4	0.0	0.0	0.0	100.0	0.0	0.0	0.0
1934	154	45.3	64.0	59.3	60.0	0.0	0.0	100.0	0.0	69.2	0.0	0.0	0.0	0.0	0.0
1935	145	68.9	37.1	36.4	100.0	50.0	100.0	0.0	0.0	75.0	0.0	0.0	0.0	0.0	0.0
1936	144	60.0	69.6	40.0	33.3	50.0	60.0	0.0	0.0	55.6	0.0	100.0	0.0	0.0	0.0
1937	149	73.0	77.1	50.0	54.5	0.0	100.0	100.0	0.0	66.7	0.0	0.0	0.0	0.0	0.0
1938	140	78.6	52.2	50.0	40.0	83.3	100.0	0.0	0.0	66.7	0.0	66.7	0.0	0.0	0.0
1939	137	77.9	79.2	33.3	71.4	0.0	80.0	0.0	0.0	80.0	0.0	100.0	0.0	0.0	0.0
1940	164	82.3	78.0	40.0	50.0	100.0	33.3	100.0	0.0	50.0	0.0	50.0	0.0	0.0	0.0
1941	161	75.9	68.2	33.3	53.3	75.0	42.9	0.0	0.0	62.5	0.0	50.0	0.0	0.0	0.0
1942	172	62.2	73.7	38.5	62.1	40.0	88.9	0.0	0.0	71.4	0.0	0.0	0.0	0.0	0.0
1943	136	68.3	80.0	40.0	27.8	60.0	66.7	0.0	0.0	50.0	0.0	100.0	0.0	0.0	0.0
1944	161	65.6	76.9	26.3	75.0	62.5	100.0	33.3	0.0	57.1	0.0	60.0	0.0	0.0	0.0
1945	138	64.8	78.9	60.0	57.1	50.0	100.0	0.0	100.0	60.0	100.0	69.2	0.0	0.0	0.0

Table 5-1. Percentage of Liberal Decisions of the United States Supreme Court in Indicated Issues, 1888-1997

TERM YEAR	TOTAL REPORTED DECISIONS	ECONOMIC	FEDERAL TAXATION	JUDICIAL POWER	CRIMINAL PROCEDURE	CIVIL RIGHTS	FIRST AMENDMENT	DUE PROCESS	PRIVACY	FEDERALISM	ATTORNEY	UNION	INTERSTATE RELATIONS	SEPARATION OF POWERS	OTHER
1946	144	71.0	62.5	33.3	28.0	0.0	0.0	100.0	0.0	77.8	0.0	64.3	0.0	0.0	0.0
1947	121	76.2	100.0	50.0	52.8	80.0	100.0	0.0	0.0	100.0	0.0	0.0	0.0	0.0	0.0
1948	124	70.2	100.0	68.8	52.0	60.0	33.3	33.3	0.0	66.7	0.0	14.3	0.0	0.0	0.0
1949	100	71.0	62.5	37.5	14.3	57.1	0.0	57.1	0.0	62.5	0.0	0.0	0.0	0.0	0.0
1950	101	53.7	100.0	50.0	54.5	44.4	42.9	25.0	0.0	66.7	0.0	20.0	0.0	0.0	0.0
1951	97	50.0	75.0	58.3	47.8	50.0	42.9	50.0	0.0	100.0	0.0	45.5	0.0	0.0	0.0
1952	115	44.4	66.7	56.3	25.0	83.3	66.7	33.3	0.0	33.3	0.0	66.7	0.0	0.0	0.0
1953	92	45.5	100.0	33.3	43.8	62.5	40.0	100.0	0.0	66.7	100.0	100.0	0.0	0.0	0.0
1954	100	73.9	90.9	30.8	52.6	63.6	80.0	100.0	0.0	100.0	0.0	80.0	0.0	0.0	0.0
1955	105	83.3	57.1	53.3	42.9	69.2	80.0	100.0	0.0	66.7	100.0	72.7	0.0	0.0	0.0
1956	145	87.5	75.0	47.4	66.7	46.7	55.6	100.0	0.0	80.0	0.0	40.0	0.0	0.0	0.0
1957	159	73.7	55.6	35.0	47.4	76.5	81.8	100.0	0.0	57.1	100.0	80.0	0.0	0.0	0.0
1958	141	70.6	83.3	36.8	50.0	62.5	81.8	0.0	0.0	100.0	0.0	64.3	0.0	0.0	0.0
1959	141	78.1	57.1	45.0	45.0	78.6	50.0	60.0	0.0	50.0	0.0	90.9	0.0	0.0	0.0
1960	143	53.6	90.9	25.0	62.5	62.5	34.8	100.0	0.0	75.0	0.0	88.9	0.0	0.0	0.0
1961	126	65.5	85.7	37.5	70.0	80.0	80.0	60.0	100.0	80.0	0.0	63.6	0.0	0.0	0.0
1962	163	81.1	100.0	47.4	76.9	96.6	90.0	66.7	0.0	63.6	0.0	66.7	0.0	0.0	0.0
1963	192	82.4	50.0	35.0	84.2	93.3	93.3	0.0	0.0	81.8	0.0	50.0	0.0	0.0	0.0
1964	139	78.3	80.0	38.1	55.6	74.1	76.9	100.0	0.0	100.0	0.0	33.3	0.0	0.0	0.0
1965	151	80.0	55.6	44.0	64.0	81.0	66.7	100.0	0.0	33.3	0.0	71.4	0.0	0.0	0.0
1966	165	80.0	50.0	37.5	65.0	71.4	78.3	0.0	0.0	66.7	0.0	44.4	0.0	0.0	0.0
1967	224	73.7	100.0	33.3	80.9	82.1	75.9	100.0	0.0	100.0	100.0	75.0	0.0	0.0	0.0
1968	168	66.7	85.7	29.2	67.5	81.5	91.7	0.0	0.0	50.0	0.0	33.3	0.0	0.0	0.0
1969	162	61.1	80.0	27.8	38.2	77.1	70.6	100.0	0.0	50.0	100.0	66.7	0.0	0.0	0.0
1970	193	54.3	50.0	19.0	32.1	56.7	52.6	100.0	0.0	0.0	100.0	28.6	0.0	0.0	0.0
1971	233	66.7	80.0	26.7	52.3	65.7	26.3	61.5	0.0	33.3	0.0	50.0	0.0	0.0	0.0
1972	247	66.7	80.0	20.8	32.5	51.3	52.6	66.7	100.0	75.0	0.0	37.5	0.0	0.0	0.0
1973	243	50.0	71.4	30.8	38.9	47.4	66.7	37.5	66.7	50.0	50.0	37.5	0.0	0.0	0.0
1974	201	50.0	100.0	26.1	48.3	58.1	62.5	71.4	0.0	72.7	0.0	66.7	0.0	0.0	0.0

OF TIME AND JUDICIAL BEHAVIOR

Table 5-1. Percentage of Liberal Decisions of the United States Supreme Court in Indicated Issues, 1888-1997

TERM YEAR	TOTAL REPORTED DECISIONS	ECONOMIC	FEDERAL TAXATION	JUDICIAL POWER	CRIMINAL PROCEDURE	CIVIL RIGHTS	FIRST AMENDMENT	DUE PROCESS	PRIVACY	FEDERALISM	ATTORNEY	UNION	INTERSTATE RELATIONS	SEPARATION OF POWERS	OTHER
1975	224	43.8	100.0	26.3	18.9	54.8	53.8	21.4	66.7	83.3	0.0	40.0	0.0	0.0	0.0
1976	222	36.8	75.0	25.0	35.7	41.9	46.7	37.5	16.7	50.0	100.0	57.1	0.0	0.0	0.0
1977	211	66.7	57.1	36.8	57.6	35.5	62.5	60.0	0.0	50.0	50.0	60.0	0.0	0.0	0.0
1978	212	41.4	50.0	16.7	44.1	42.5	22.2	40.0	60.0	50.0	0.0	50.0	0.0	0.0	0.0
1979	199	57.6	0.0	43.8	41.0	56.5	63.6	54.5	0.0	50.0	80.0	33.3	0.0	0.0	0.0
1980	230	51.9	50.0	25.0	39.3	30.0	45.5	16.7	0.0	100.0	100.0	75.0	0.0	0.0	0.0
1981	241	53.6	66.7	31.0	22.2	54.1	69.2	30.0	0.0	83.3	66.7	90.0	0.0	0.0	0.0
1982	238	54.5	75.0	44.4	22.2	53.6	45.5	37.5	25.0	83.3	0.0	57.1	0.0	0.0	0.0
1983	266	35.7	75.0	23.5	21.2	58.6	33.3	45.5	0.0	63.6	50.0	66.7	0.0	0.0	0.0
1984	273	41.9	100.0	41.7	31.0	60.0	57.1	36.4	0.0	57.1	28.6	50.0	0.0	0.0	0.0
1985	288	41.2	80.0	33.3	27.7	40.6	42.9	71.4	0.0	55.6	25.0	60.0	0.0	0.0	0.0
1986	251	39.1	80.0	20.0	36.4	56.0	46.2	50.0	100.0	60.0	66.7	80.0	0.0	0.0	0.0
1987	250	61.5	66.7	40.0	45.2	45.5	50.0	66.7	100.0	66.7	66.7	25.0	0.0	0.0	0.0
1988	232	52.9	75.0	36.8	26.5	48.3	46.7	20.0	50.0	44.4	75.0	0.0	0.0	0.0	0.0
1989	209	44.0	85.7	52.6	30.8	55.6	35.7	50.0	25.0	55.6	33.3	75.0	0.0	0.0	0.0
1990	178	50.0	0.0	66.7	40.0	61.1	40.0	33.3	25.0	50.0	0.0	50.0	0.0	0.0	0.0
1991	169	46.4	75.0	52.9	38.5	50.0	75.0	0.0	0.0	60.0	50.0	0.0	0.0	0.0	0.0
1992	148	47.4	83.3	45.5	37.5	29.4	55.6	33.3	33.3	71.4	100.0	50.0	0.0	0.0	0.0
1993	118	50.0	100.0	9.1	44.0	31.3	50.0	0.0	100.0	20.0	0.0	0.0	0.0	0.0	0.0
1994	102	47.1	50.0	31.3	40.9	28.6	75.0	33.3	100.0	42.9	0.0	0.0	0.0	0.0	0.0
1995	97	29.4	75.0	64.3	36.4	36.4	80.0	50.0	0.0	33.3	0.0	75.0	0.0	0.0	0.0
1996	103	60.0	66.7	25.0	26.3	40.0	20.0	40.0	16.7	42.9	0.0	0.0	0.0	0.0	0.0
1997	105	50.0	33.3	38.1	28.6	55.0	0.0	0.0	0.0	100.0	0.0	0.0	0.0	0.0	0.0

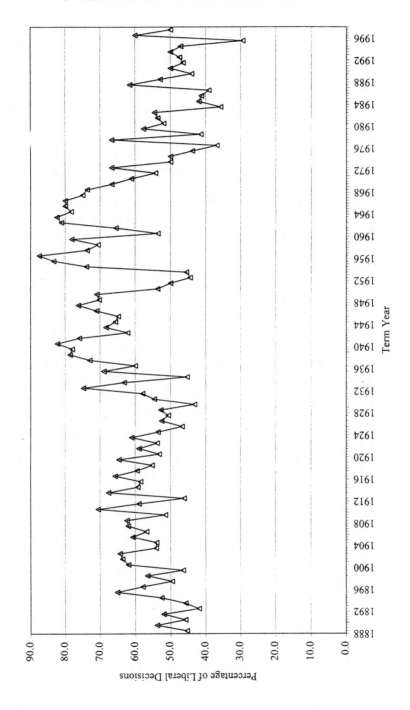

Figure 5-1. Percentage of Liberal Decisions of the
United States Supreme Court in Economics Cases, 1888-1997

As one can see, the series is somewhat dynamic through the 1930s. Prior to the 1931 term year, the series average is 55.62 percent. The pre-1930 historic low occurs in 1892 (42 percent). The pre-1930 historic high occurs in 1910, the first year of the White Court, with 70.5 percent of the Court's economic decisions being liberal. This latter result is a surprising finding given the generally conservative nature of the Court during White's tenure. Beginning in 1932, however, the series becomes more dynamic, trending sharply upward and reaching unprecedented levels by 1940. Many scholars suggest that the Court changed its posture toward economics issues abruptly when it began to engender high levels of public and political opposition, notably President Roosevelt's attempted Court-packing plan announced in April of 1937.[16] Although the series trends upward beginning in 1933, the series does increase surrounding Roosevelt's attack on the Court, and it continues to do so until 1940, when it reaches its highest point (82.3 percent) since 1888. This result supports the conclusion that the Supreme Court is attuned to changes in the political environment in which it operates.

After 1940, the series begins to decline to a low point in 1952 when only 44.4 percent of the decisions are liberal but then, only four terms later, the series attains its maximum. It then begins to decline sharply, reaching its historic low in 1995 of only 29.4 percent. This is an expected finding, since the Court was led, beginning in 1969, by conservatives Chief Justice Warren Burger and later, beginning in 1986, by Chief Justice William Rehnquist. The figure also illustrates the declining liberalism of the Warren Court's economic decisions, starting in 1965. Perhaps the Court then perceived that it should conserve its political capital for other matters, particularly civil liberties and civil rights issues that were then consuming large shares of its agenda.

Pritchett examines the Court's nonunanimous decisions only, and finds that the Court ruled in the liberal direction 68 percent of the time from 1936 to 1946. This result refers to an aggregate of cases involving issues of state taxation and regulation, as well as federalism.[17] Pritchett argues that the Court thereby adopted Holmes's conception of legislative supremacy and judicial restraint. Although it is difficult to parse out the differential effects of the issue types included in this analysis as opposed to those Pritchett examines, the results here appear to confirm Pritchett's findings since the average liberalism for economic and federalism decisions for the Stone Court is 66.15 (see Table 5-1).

FEDERAL TAXATION

Figure 5-2 displays the percentage of liberal decisions in federal taxation cases from 1888 to 1997. The series is quite volatile, which is due, in part, to the relative infrequency of tax decisions on the Court's docket, as is the case with many of the other, minor issue categories analyzed in the present study. The historic low of zero percent occurs first in 1895. The historic high (100 percent) occurs in several term years, first observed in 1891. However, this result is based upon a very small number of cases; in 1891, for example, the Fuller Court heard only one case. After 1916, the series becomes much more stable, most likely due to the higher number of decisions brought to the Court in the wake of the Sixteenth Amendment, providing for a federal income tax. The series then trends upward rather consistently until 1946 when it becomes somewhat more stable. In 1975, the series begins to decline and, by 1979, the percentage of liberal decisions is zero for the first time since 1914. Thereafter, the series once again begins to climb, but ultimately declines through 1997 reaching a rate of 33.3 percent.

The chief justice court averages provide a glimpse into these changes over time. The Fuller Court's average rate of liberalism is 53.81 percent, based on 53 decisions. There are only five term years (1888, 1889, 1896, 1897, and 1902) in which the Court considered no federal taxation decisions. The White Court's average increases to 63.06 percent for 51 decisions across the eleven term years. In only one year (1914) does the Court issue no liberal decisions for this issue area.

The Taft Court's liberalism rate descends slightly to 59.06, based upon a total of 136 decisions. The Taft Court is the first Court included in this study to issue at least one liberal tax decision during every term year. Perhaps this finding indicates that the Court was then becoming more liberal in its policy stances with regard to federal taxation.

The Hughes Court's liberalism rate, the first Court contained entirely in the Great Depression period, is 71.81, representing an increase of about 12 percent from that for the Taft Court. Moreover, the Hughes Court decided a larger number of federal taxation cases ($N = 274$), more than doubling the number on the Taft Court's docket. Similar to the Taft Court, each of the term years of the Hughes Court contain at least one liberal decision. Also, the rate for the Stone Court, composed of all Roosevelt appointees, increases modestly to 75.54. Yet, the Court heard only 101 federal taxation cases, a substantial decrease in the number of overall decisions.

These results are in some respects surprising and in others, they are expected. First, they are expected in that the series shows a generally increasing rate of liberal decisions. This result is theoretically consistent, given the changing membership on the Court. Second, from 1934 to 1946, the series is much more stable than it is in the prior or later years. This finding is also expected because of the increasing demands placed on the federal government arising from the burdens of the Great Depression. This result

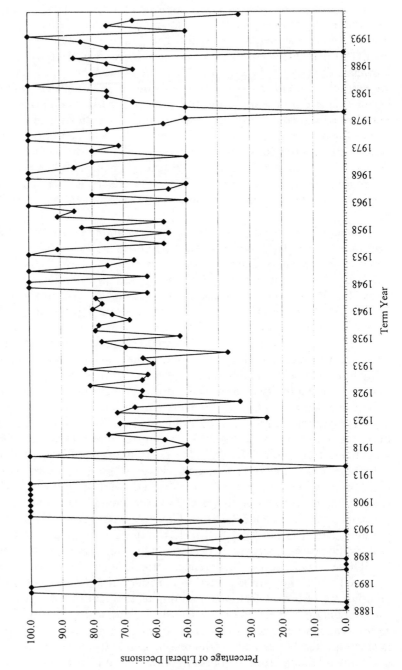

Figure 5-2. Percentage of Liberal Decisions of the
United States Supreme Court in Federal Taxation Cases, 1888-1997

is strengthened by Pritchett's similar finding that the Court ruled in the government's favor in 70 percent of nonunanimous federal taxation cases.[18] One would expect that the decisions would be liberal in policy orientation because such decisions strengthen the government's taxing power, thus providing much-needed revenue to the government to enable it to finance New Deal programs. The series does not begin to increase immediately after 1929 because it certainly took some time to develop and implement the policies needed to remedy the macroeconomic problems that the nation faced then, and even longer for the disputes to arrive at the Court for resolution. All the term years for that period achieve liberalism rates that are 50 percent or greater; nine of the sixteen years have rates that are 60 percent or greater. However, the series during the Warren Court appears to decline moderately. Additionally, the results are as one would expect based upon other analyses of the Court's policy preferences for this issue category.[19]

The results of this analysis of the liberalism of federal taxation decisions are somewhat surprising in several respects. During the Fuller, White, and Taft Courts, the series is no lower than 53 percent liberal. Indeed, during the White and Taft Courts, the average remains around 60 percent. These findings are surprising given the alleged conservatism of the Court's policy stances during the White and Taft Courts.[20] One would expect that the Court's decisions would be more consistently conservative than the results actually portray. This trend of increasing liberalism mirrors the rise of such policy outputs that occurs with respect to other issue areas, such as economic decisions.

Second, the Fuller Court's liberalism in these decisions is somewhat unexpected in that only four of the twenty-one term years in which the Court actually heard a federal taxation case (1895, 1899, 1901, and 1904) attain scores of less than 50 percent. It reaches a perfect liberal score (100 percent) in seven term years, although these scores represent no more than two decisions in any term year. These results, too, are surprising because of the putative conservatism that the Court expressed toward concerns of substantive due process, most clearly expressed in *Pollock v. Farmers' Trust Co.* (striking down a federal income tax law),[21] even when one discounts the findings in the years with only a handful of these decisions.

Third, as with other issue areas, the Burger (1969–85) and Rehnquist (1986–present) Courts are more liberal than one would anticipate given the alleged conservatism of both these chief justice courts. From 1969 to 1997, there are only three term years (1979, 1990, and 1997) whose rates are less than 50 percent. The remainder are 50 percent liberal or greater. During the first eleven years of the Rehnquist Court analyzed here, the series remains above approximately 65 percent liberal. Thus, this figure and its analysis belie a somewhat different description of the liberalism of the decisions of the Fuller, White, Taft (through the 1932 term), Burger, and Rehnquist Courts, while it may meet one's expectations based upon other studies of the post-1932 Taft Court and the Stone and the Warren Courts.

JUDICIAL POWER

Figure 5-3 plots the percentage of liberal decisions involving issues of judicial power. As the figure clearly shows, the series increases modestly until 1963, when it begins to decline. It does so until 1970, when it turns upward once again. Given the Fuller Court's alleged distaste for governmental intervention in the economy and the social order in general, it is expected that the Court's decisions in this area would be, in general, relatively conservative. The Court members may have felt a compulsion to deny their judicial colleagues powers that they denied to other governmental actors at various levels throughout the political system. The rates for only two of the twenty-two years comprising the Fuller Court exceed 30 percent. The historic low for the series (7.3 percent) is observed in 1895, during the heyday of the Fuller Court's battle with the Progressive forces. The average liberal percentage of the Fuller Court is 21.03, indicating that one out of five decisions of the Court was liberal.

The White Court is similarly conservative in its outlook on issues of judicial power. The series during White's tenure is somewhat more dynamic and it turns out to be very slightly more liberal too (21.32 percent on average). However, the series does increase during Chief Justice Taft's tenure (1921–29). It trends upward consistently and, in 1928, the series hits 80 percent, its historic high, in fifteen decisions. The series average during Taft's Court rises to 37.68, indicating that the Court became much more liberal over time as compared to its predecessors. The intervention of the passage of the Judges' Bill of 1925 may explain the increases in liberalism during this period because the Court may have had to resolve more controversial issues as a result.[22] The Court also may have perceived the act to imply that courts generally should be involved in more matters and, thus, be given more power of administration.

This trend toward expanded liberalism continues with the Hughes Court. The Court's average is 45.69, a change of 8 percent from that observed during the Taft Court. Although the series is on average larger in magnitude during the Hughes Court than it is during Taft's tenure, the series initially increases but then begins to decline in 1935 and does so through 1944. This diminished level of liberalism continues in the Stone Court; its average is 39.62, a slight decrease from the average observed during the Hughes Court. However, the figure indicates that the series is

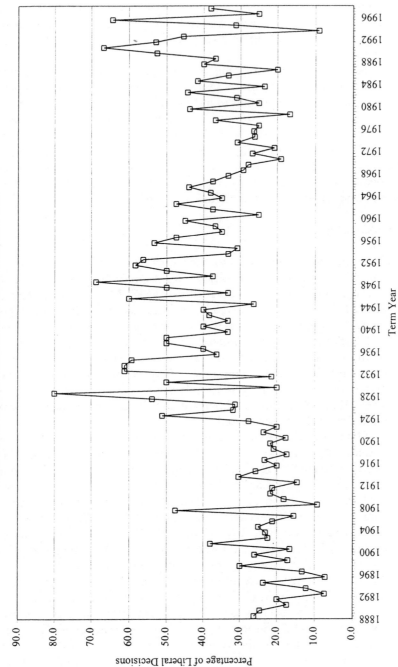

Figure 5-3. Percentage of Liberal Decisions of the
United States Supreme Court in Judicial Power Cases, 1888-1997

somewhat more consistent during the Stone Court than in the prior Court. Thus, the Stone Court perhaps consolidates the movement toward a greater degree of liberalism in these decisions that began with the Taft Court some twenty years earlier.

After the Stone Court, the series declines to 17.4 percent in 1970. In 1978, the lowest point in the series since 1908 is observed (15.8 percent). Thereafter, the series begins to increase rather consistently, indicating that the Burger and the Rehnquist Courts were moving toward a relatively in-creased level of liberalism. Indeed, the last term year of the Rehnquist Court (1997) analyzed here attains a moderate rate of 38.1 percent (in 22 deci-sions), although this does not exceed the much consistently higher rates of liberal decisions that are observed during the Taft and Stone Courts and, to a lesser extent, during the Hughes Court.

CRIMINAL PROCEDURE

In addition to these issue areas, the Court issues decisions involving ques-tions of criminal procedure. Figure 5-4 displays the percentage of liberal decisions in criminal cases from 1888 to 1997. There are three term years (1901, 1904, and 1928) in which the Court issued no liberal decisions in this area, although the Court did have the opportunity to hear such cases. Among the term years in which the Court issued at least one liberal deci-sion in this area, the historic low (8.3 percent) occurs in 1921 and in 1923. The series also hits its maximum of 100 percent in 1935. Excluding that term year (because it represents only three decisions), the historic high is observed in 1963, when 84.2 percent of the Court's criminal decisions fa-vored the rights of the accused.

Over time, the series is rather dynamic. From 1888 to 1928, the series declines. Beginning in 1928, however, the series increases dramatically, reach-ing 100 percent in 1935, when it begins to trend downward once again. From 1953, the year that Earl Warren took the center chair, the percentage of liberal decisions increases consistently and rather strongly until 1963, when it dips to 67.5 percent in 1968. From 1969 to 1997, the series exceeds the 50 percent point only twice. During the Burger Court years in particu-lar (1969–85), the figure indicates that the Court became more conserva-tive and the series declines rather precipitously from 1977 (57.6 percent liberal) to 1983 (21.2 percent liberal). The chief justice court averages for the Fuller, White, Taft, Hughes, and Stone Courts provide an overview of the changes in the Court's decision-making over time in matters of criminal law and procedure. The average liberalism rate for the Fuller Court is 31.41 percent, while that for the White Court is 20.89 percent, representing a relative move toward less liberalism (or more conservatism) of 33 percent.

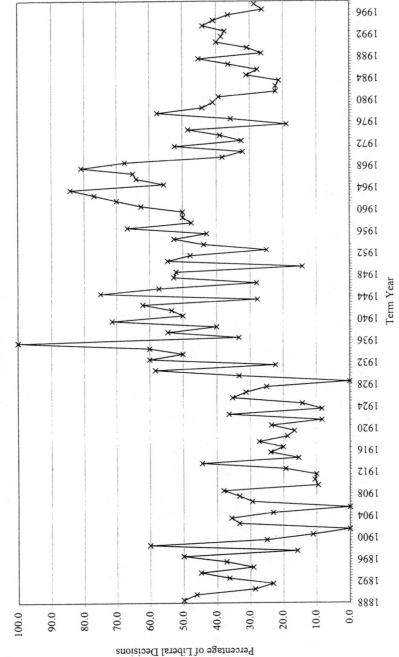

Figure 5-4. Percentage of Liberal Decisions of the
United States Supreme Court in Criminal Cases, 1888-1997

The Taft Court is nearly identical to the White Court, with its average liberalism rate being 21.36 percent. The Hughes Court, however, is substantially more liberal on average (54.52 percent). This represents an increase of 23 percent from the rate observed during the Taft Court. The Stone Court continues the Hughes Court's practice, with 55.06 percent of its decisions being liberal. However, Pritchett finds that the Court from 1941 to 1946 held for the accused in 41 percent of the nonunanimous cases involving questions of the right to counsel, jury trials, coerced confessions, search and seizure, and martial law.[23]

Additionally, this study and Epstein, Walker, and Dixon find that the liberalism of the Vinson Court's (1946–52) criminal procedure decisions declines through 1949, but then begins to increase in 1953 when Earl Warren is appointed chief justice.[24] In 1953, the series consistently increases until 1969, when it begins to decline rather quickly during the first term year of the Burger Court.[25] The series trends strongly downward, not surprisingly, during the Burger and the Rehnquist Courts, given the putative policy perspective of both those Courts.[26]

CIVIL RIGHTS

As chapter 2 discusses and chapter 3 demonstrates, there were very few civil rights cases on the Court's agenda prior to the 1940s. The Court's docket was filled with more pressing economic concerns as the nation strove to adapt to the challenges of growing industrialism and the Great Depression. Structural constraints, thus, prevented the Court, at least in part, from considering such questions. Moreover, the political context in which the Court engaged in decision-making simply was not conducive to hearing these issues debated. The Court under the helmsmanship of Fuller, White, and Taft held conservative policy preferences with respect to questions of civil rights and civil liberties generally. Perhaps the most noteworthy civil rights case that the Court decided during the pre-1940 period was *Plessy v. Ferguson*,[27] which certainly announced a conservative policy perspective on race relations as the nation was on the verge of new century. However, this decision would later provide fodder for the Court to initiate a change in its civil rights policy stances (e.g., *Brown v. Board of Education*).[28]

As Figure 5-5 indicates, the series is very dynamic, moving from zero percent to 50 percent or greater and then back again between several terms. It does not become stable and evince any significant degree of consistency until 1948. This dynamism in the series is due, in part, to the relative infrequency of these types of cases being brought to the Court for resolution prior to that time. The Fuller, White, and Taft Courts collectively hear 149 cases, which is slightly more than three cases on average per term year.

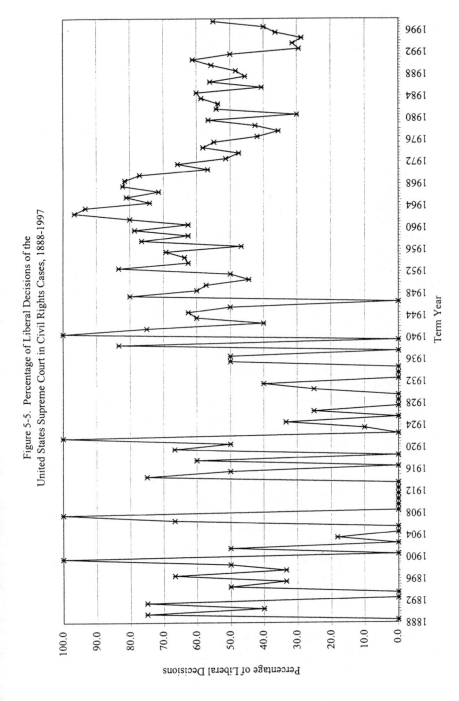

Figure 5-5. Percentage of Liberal Decisions of the
United States Supreme Court in Civil Rights Cases, 1888-1997

From 1888 to 1947 (sixty term years), the series overall exceeds 50 percent liberal twenty-four times. From 1948 to 1997, on the other hand, the series meets or exceeds the 50 percent mark thirty-five times during the fifty term years. Thus, about three-fifths of these later terms are associated with a relatively liberal period of Supreme Court decision-making for this issue area. After 1950, the series increases rather consistently through 1966. It reaches its historic high in 1962 (96.6 percent liberal), setting aside the 100 percent rates observed in the pre-1948 period because of a low number of decisions then. From then until 1979, the series begins to trend downward. However, the series then rebounds somewhat in the latter years of the series and begins to experience less change from one term year to the next. The post-1948 historic low is observed in 1994 when 28.6 percent of the civil rights decisions were liberal.

The chief justice court averages inform us about the change in the Court's perspective on matters of civil rights. The Fuller Court's average percentage of liberal decisions is 34.46 based upon seventy-one decisions across its twenty-two terms. The White Court's average is 27.43 based upon thirty-three decisions, indicating a slight decrease in the liberalism of the Court across these two chief justice courts. The Taft Court continued the trend toward decreased liberalism; its average is 24.04 in 45 decisions. Indeed, Figure 5-5 portrays that decline. There are many term years prior to 1921 whose scores are at or above the 40 percent mark, while there are none that exceed that mark during the Taft Court.

During the first years of the Hughes Court, the liberalism of these decisions continues to decrease. The average rate of liberalism from 1930 to 1935 is 23 percent. But in 1938, the Court's decisions become much more liberal. This increase in liberal policy preferences for decisions involving questions of civil rights may be due to the Court's liberal policy preferences in other issue areas. In fact, the Hughes Court's average liberalism rate is 43.54 percent, a 19 percent increase over that for the Taft Court. The Court under Stone's leadership similarly garners an average of 57.50 percent, representing an increase of 14 percent over the level reached during the Hughes Court. Hence, the Court's civil rights jurisprudence undergoes a drastic transformation over time. In particular, it moves toward an increased level of liberalism during the last forty-one years of the series when the Court decided this type of case.

FIRST AMENDMENT

Figure 5-6 plots the percentage of liberal decisions of the Supreme Court in First Amendment cases. The first finding that is apparent is that from 1888 to 1934 there are only five years with any liberal decisions. During the

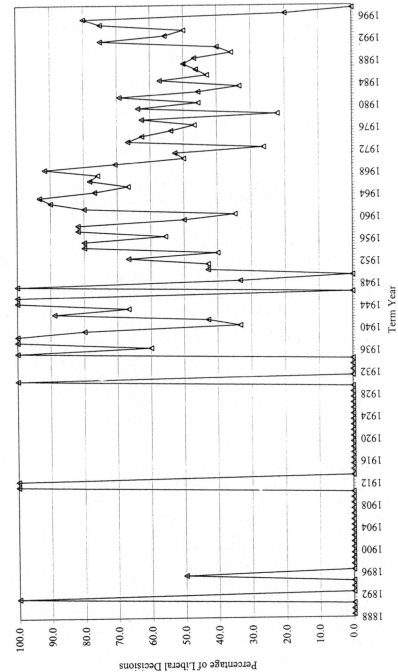

Figure 5-6. Percentage of Liberal Decisions of the
United States Supreme Court in First Amendment Cases

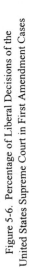

Fuller, White, and Taft Courts, only twenty-three First Amendment decisions are announced. When such decisions were announced by the Court
in the pre-1930 period, they are rather conservative, the series being on
average less than about 30 percent liberal across the Fuller, White, and Taft
Courts.

However, from the time of the United States's entry into World War I
in 1917 to the end of the war, there are no liberal decisions even though the
Court considered First Amendment questions in 1917, 1918, and 1920.
This finding confirms the historical analyses of Schwartz,[29] McCloskey,[30]
and Biskupic and Witt,[31] who suggest that the Court became much more
conservative when dealing with First Amendment issues surrounding the
war due to concerns about national security. Between 1934 and 1949, the
series becomes somewhat more stable, although there still remains a good
amount of movement from one term year to the next, which is perhaps due
in part to the low number of cases the Court considered dealing with these
issues. After 1949, the series' movement across term years is vastly reduced.
It increases from that point in the series until 1963, after which it begins to
trend downward until 1976 when it once again turns modestly upward.

The chief justice court averages summarize these changes in the Court's
decision-making in First Amendment cases during the pre-1946 period.
There is an increasing rate of liberalism, generally, across the four courts
considered in the present study. The Fuller Court average is 30 percent,
based on six cases in five term years (1891, 1895, 1896, 1899, and 1908).
The average rate of liberalism increases to 33 percent for the White Court,
based upon twelve decisions in six term years (1911, 1912, 1914, 1917,
1918, and 1920). This result comports with Schwartz's and McCloskey's
historical analyses of the Court that suggest that the Court's decision-making became somewhat more liberal during the White Court.

However, the series then declines to zero percent liberal during the
Taft Court, based upon five cases in three term years (1922, 1924, and
1928). This finding similarly supports Schwartz's and McCloskey's observations about the retrenched conservatism describing the Taft Court's decision-making. The series' average dramatically climbs to 81.90 percent
during the Hughes Court, based on eighteen decisions in seven term years
(1930, 1935, 1916, 1937, 1938, 1939, and 1940). The liberalism rate during the Stone Court declines slightly to 79.70 percent, based upon twenty-
five decisions in five term years (1941 to 1945). Pritchett finds that the Court
ruled liberally in 62 percent of its nonunanimous First Amendment decisions.[32] Hence, the Court's decision-making in matters of First Amendment
issues became more consistently liberal over time, most especially during
the period from 1930 to 1945.

This finding of increased liberalism is expected. Based on the observations and results of the existing literature examining the Court's decisions in related issue areas,[33] the Court is hypothesized to be relatively conservative in its perspective on First Amendment issues from the latter nineteenth century to well into the twentieth century.[34] The Court is found in this study to have been particularly restrictive of rights of free expression and free exercise of religion during the First World War, but it was, somewhat unexpectedly, relatively liberal during the Second World War. During that period, the Court does not revert to the lower levels of liberalism observed during the era of World War I that arose from concerns of national security due to the country's involvement in a global conflict. Only two term years of the World War II era are associated with rates of less than 50 percent.

Certainly, the personnel of the Court had changed in the interim between the wars: the Court during the 1940s and the entire war period was composed of nine Roosevelt appointees who were noted for their liberal policy orientations.[35] In fact, the Court in 1943 overruled its prior decision, requiring Jehovah's Witnesses to salute the flag even though such action violated their religious beliefs, in *West Virginia State Board of Education v. Barnette*.[36] Thus, the Court became more expansive during the 1930s and 1940s in its view of the civil liberties protections the Constitution required. These rulings would later serve as precursors to the increased liberalism of the Warren Court.

DUE PROCESS

Figure 5-7 shows the percentage of liberal decisions dealing with due process issues. As one can see, there is no apparent trend to the series. It moves abruptly from one term year to the next. However, the series does reach 100 percent many times during the period from 1933 to 1940. The other term years (1888–1932, and 1941–45) achieve percentages that are somewhat less liberal and somewhat more consistent than the rates observed during the last seven years of the Hughes Court (1933–40).

To provide some indication of the Court's liberalism over time, the chief justice court averages are discussed when dealing with this issue area surrounding the war. The Fuller Court average is low, 18.25 percent, based upon 112 decisions in twenty-one of the twenty-two term years during Fuller's tenure. The series increases somewhat during the White Court, whose average is 22.04 percent based upon ninety-seven decisions across the eleven term years of White's tenure. This result indicates that the Court became somewhat more liberal in the period from 1910 to 1921, again confirming the alleged growth in liberalism during the White Court. The Taft Court, on the other hand, is much more liberal than its predecessors, its average being 40.82, based upon fifty-four decisions, across these nine

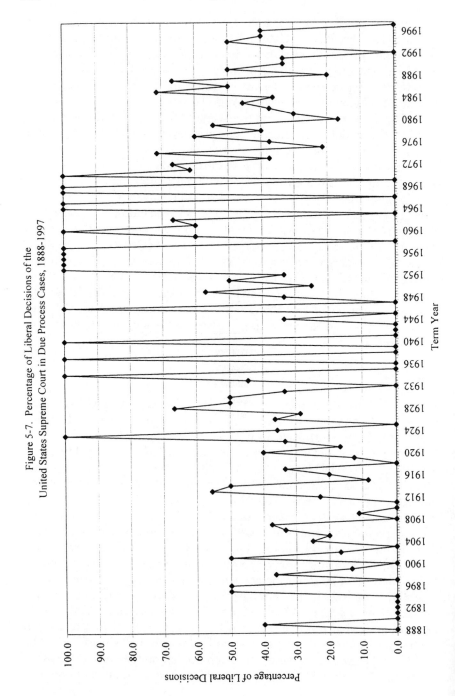

Figure 5-7. Percentage of Liberal Decisions of the
United States Supreme Court in Due Process Cases, 1888-1997

years of Taft's tenure. The Hughes Court is somewhat more liberal than is the Taft Court, with 47.52 percent of its due process decisions being liberal on average (based upon thirty-two decisions) across the eleven term years it comprises. The Stone Court becomes much more conservative in its due process decision-making, with an average liberal decision-making rate of 6.66. Hence, the Court's decisions in the area of due process are at first rather conservative, become much more liberal during the next thirty term years, and then ended up being more conservative, on average, than they initially were.

At the end of the series, the percentage of liberal decisions declines, beginning in 1971 and continuing through 1997. This drop perhaps reflects the effect of the leadership of Chief Justices Warren Burger and William Rehnquist, and the growing conservative policy perspectives that the justices on those Courts possessed. However, one should remember that the results for the pre-1945 period are based on relatively small numbers of decisions during each term year, although they do give some perspective on the liberalism of the Court's decisions during the period at hand.

PRIVACY

Figure 5-8 portrays the percentage of liberal privacy decisions that the Supreme Court issued across the period analyzed. As Pacelle indicates, the Court does not consider many decisions involving privacy issues prior to the 1960s and 1970s, largely because the Court had not specifically interpreted the Fourth Amendment as protecting against governmental intrusions.[37] However, in *Olmstead v. United States*, Justice Brandeis, in dissent, argued that evidence gathered as a result of a wiretap on a telephone violated the search and seizure provisions of the Fourth Amendment, a key part of the reasoning that would later become part of the Court's enunciation of privacy rights within the Constitution.[38] Indeed, prior to this time, the figure bears out Pacelle's findings because the Court considered the first privacy case in 1945, which it decided liberally. The Court also considered one privacy case in 1957 but ruled conservatively.

The records of the Burger and Rehnquist Courts are somewhat mixed. From 1969 to 1985 (the Burger Court years), the series exceeds 50 percent only five times. The remainder of the term years are most often found to attain liberalism rates of less than 30 percent, and oftentimes the series is observed to be zero percent. During the Rehnquist Court, the Court attains a rate of 100 percent in 1986, but falls to 50 percent the next term year and 25 percent in 1988. The series declines once again to zero percent in 1990. It then rebounds for a short time, but ultimately falls to zero percent in the final term year, 1997.

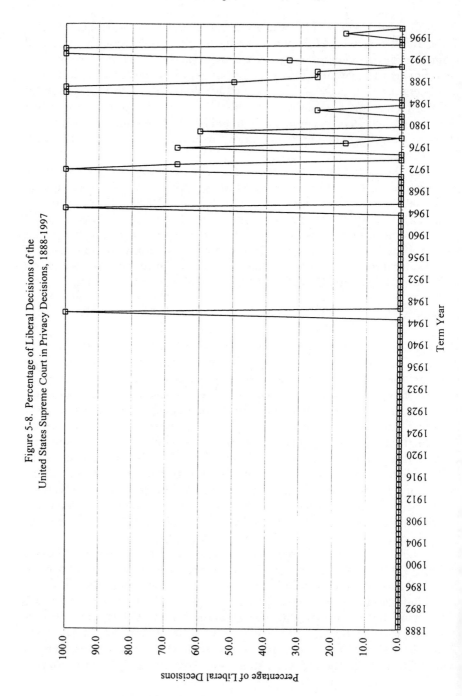

Figure 5-8. Percentage of Liberal Decisions of the
United States Supreme Court in Privacy Decisions, 1888-1997

FEDERALISM

The final issue that is discussed in this part of the study involves cases deciding issues of federalism; it is displayed in Figure 5-9. As with several other of
the series examined above, this series is quite volatile. There are several
term years, especially in the early part of the Court's history, that move
from zero to 100 percent rather abruptly. The series becomes less abrupt
briefly from 1933 to 1959.

The Fuller Court's average rate of liberal decisions is 59.80 percent,
based upon fifty decisions in twenty term years. Only two term years (1897
and 1898) contain no federalism decisions. This finding is somewhat surprising given the Fuller Court's purported policy perspective on questions
of regulatory power. However, the Fuller Court may have been ensuring
that the federal government was supreme over the powers of the states.
These rulings may have paved the way for the Court in later years to begin
to incorporate the protections of the Bill of Rights against the states through
the Due Process Clause of the Fourteenth Amendment.

The White Court's federalism decisions are more liberal, attaining an
average rate of 73.94 percent in sixty-seven decisions. Only one term year
(1912) has no federalism decisions. Moreover, as one can tell from the figure,
the series during this time becomes more consistent in that there is less
movement from one term year to the next. Hence, the Court's perspective
on issues of federalism may have begun to coalesce. By upholding federal
power vis-à-vis the states, the Court may have unwittingly created precedent that laid the groundwork necessary for the transformation in the Court's
outlook on the larger question of governmental power to remedy social and
economic problems that were to occur over the next twenty years and particularly during the Hughes Court.

The Court's decisions during the Taft and Hughes Courts bear out this
change. The Taft Court's average rate of liberal decisions is 66.64 percent
(based upon sixty-nine decisions). During the Hughes Court (and in particular after 1932), the series becomes much more stable, with movement
between term years limited to around 13 percent on average. The largest
change between term years is 30 percent, which occurred only once, between
1938 (80 percent) and 1939 (50 percent). The Court's average rate is 63.70
(in 172 decisions), although the series does move downward modestly.

This decline in liberalism continues during the Stone Court. Its average is 57.70 percent (in thirty-eight decisions), a decline of 6 percent from
the level observed during the Hughes Court. However, as the figure shows,
the series is rather stable during Stone's tenure. It neither increases nor
decreases appreciably. The Stone Court's decision-making in federalism
cases appears, thus, to be a rather quiet point positioned between the bitter

Figure 5-9. Percentage of Liberal Decisions of the
United States Supreme Court in Federalism Cases, 1888-1997

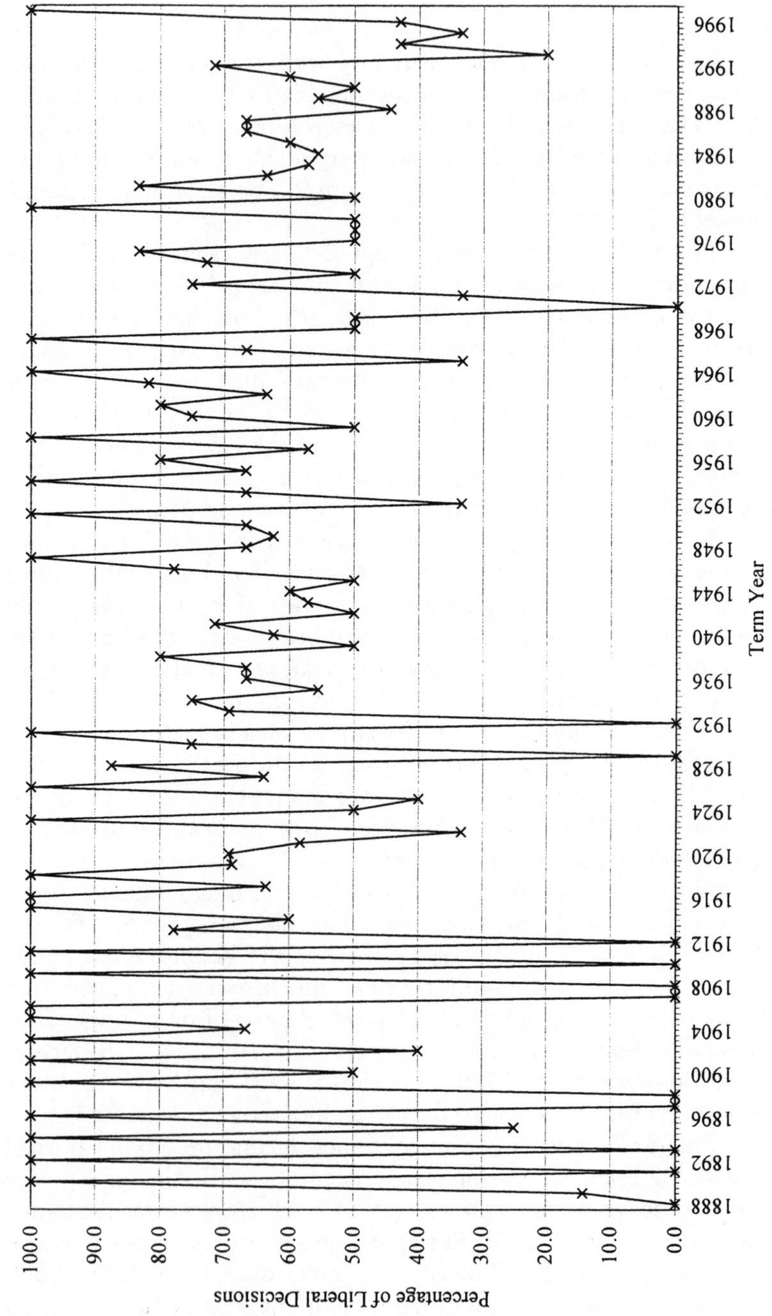

battles over federal power that characterized the decision-making of the Court during the New Deal and the coming battle that the Warren Court was to wage over federal and state power in the realm of civil liberties and civil rights.

Indeed, when one examines the figure for the 1960s, one finds that the series becomes much more dynamic than it had been during the latter part of the Hughes Court and the Stone Court. The change from one term year to the next is quite large for several years, even though the Court heard ninety-eight cases across Warren's tenure (1953–68). Overall, however, the series average for the Warren Court suggests that the Court's decisions are relatively liberal. Its average rate of liberal decisions is 60.17, thus indicating a swing back to an increased level of liberalism that was observed during the White Court. Thereafter, the series becomes somewhat less liberal. The averages for the Burger and the Rehnquist Courts are, respectively, 57.87 and 54.49. Thus, even during the putative conservative years of these Courts, more than one-half of the Supreme Court's decisions involving federalism issues are liberal.

ATTORNEYS

In addition to decisions involving issues of federalism, the Court during the period of study considers issues involving the regulation of attorneys. Figure 5-10 shows the percentage of decisions dealing with such issues that were decided liberally. As one can see, there is no clear trend to the series. The function line is quite dynamic, moving from zero to 100 percent and then back in several of the term years. Although there are increases surrounding the Great Depression, they are short-lived and do not portray a consistent pattern that depicts an underlying tendency of growth or decline in the liberalism of these decisions. Much of the movement in the series arises because of the relatively small number of cases on the Court's docket.

The Fuller Court hears this type of case during only nine of its twenty-two term years. These are 1890, 1891, 1893, 1895, 1896, 1906, 1907, 1908, and 1909. In the other fourteen terms, the Court does not consider any such cases. During the terms that the Fuller Court actually does hear at least one attorney case, the average percentage of liberal decisions is 31.48 percent. However, the Court considers only thirteen cases in total during these years for this issue area. The White Court's docket contains no attorney decisions in only three (1916, 1917, and 1920) of its eleven term years. During the years in which the Court does actually hear at least one such case, the liberalism rate is 50 percent. However, the number of decisions on which this rate is based is quite low, at nine cases across the entire period of the White Court.

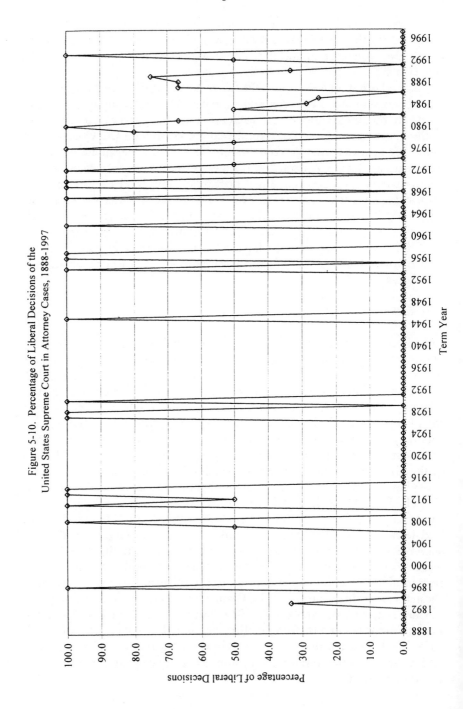

Figure 5-10. Percentage of Liberal Decisions of the
United States Supreme Court in Attorney Cases, 1888-1997

The Taft Court hears attorney cases in only four term years (1922, 1925, 1927, and 1928). During these years, the average liberal percentage is 25 percent. Yet, much like the prior Courts, the Taft Court only hears a total of five attorney cases across its ten term years.

The Court under Charles Evans Hughes hears only two cases. It hears one case each during the 1930 and 1931 term years. One is decided liberally; the other in the conservative direction. Thus, the Court's average liberal percentage for these cases is 50 percent. Similarly, the Stone Court only hears two cases during its five years: one each in 1944 (decided in the conservative direction) and in 1945 (decided in the liberal direction). Hence, the average liberal percentage for the Stone Court's decision-making in attorney cases is 50 percent.

UNIONS

Figure 5-11 shows the percentage of union decisions that are decided liberally. The historic high for the series is 100 percent, which is achieved in several term years. The historic low is zero percent, which is also observed in several term years. As with Figure 5-10 (dealing with matters of attorneys), the series displaying the liberalism of union decisions is quite dynamic, moving abruptly from one term year to the next, and displaying no clear trend, until 1954. This pattern is due to the relatively small number of union cases that the Court considered. This consistency in liberalism in these decisions that it does announce could be associated with the Court's perception of the need for legal protection of the interests of unions during the expansion of constitutional rights to other "underdogs."[39]

After 1954, the series' movement across term years drastically decreases and the series generally becomes somewhat more stable due, in part, to union cases being a consistent component of the Court's agenda, although there remains a large amount of movement across term years. The series also then begins to trend downward until 1961. This decline is a somewhat surprising trend given the Warren Court's liberalism in other issue areas (such as civil liberties) that have their genesis in regulatory areas, such as union decisions.[40] After 1971, the series changes course and begins to trend upward until 1981 when it again turns downward. This too is an interesting (and somewhat surprising) finding given the Burger Court's purported conservatism on economic issues. At the end of the series, the changes between term years appear to become more dramatic, with the series returning to the level of liberalism observed prior to 1954.

As has been done with the other series, the average percentages for each of the first four chief justice courts are calculated for this issue area.

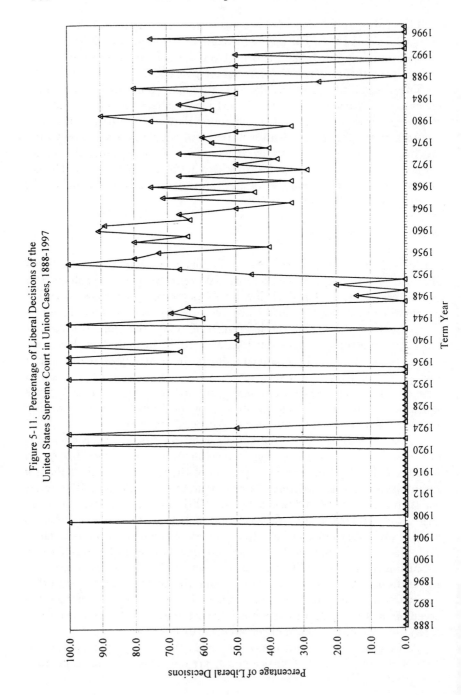

Figure 5-11. Percentage of Liberal Decisions of the
United States Supreme Court in Union Cases, 1888-1997

The Fuller Court's average is 50 percent, although this rate is based upon the decisions in only two term years (1907 and 1908). The White Court's average is zero percent, although it hears four union cases (cumulatively) in 1911, 1914, 1917, and 1920. The Taft Court's rate is 83.33 percent across three term years (1921, 1923, and 1924). However, this figure is also based upon a very small number of decisions: the Taft Court issues only four rulings involving questions of unions.

Union cases become much more frequent during the Hughes Court, attaining an average of 86.12 percent liberal outcomes. Although the Hughes Court rate is similar to that for the Taft Court, the figure for the Hughes Court is based on a much larger number of cases (twenty-seven, as opposed to only four). Thus, the results for the Court during Hughes's tenure may be a more accurate representation of the Court's policy preferences with respect to union cases than the rate for the Taft Court.

Finally, the Stone Court's decisions reflect an average rate of liberal decisions of 69.80 percent. In four of the Stone Court's five term years, thirty-seven union decisions are issued. Similarly, Pritchett finds that the Stone Court ruled in the liberal direction in nonunanimous decisions of this type 68 percent of the time.[41]

Hence, from the first year of the Taft Court (1921) to the last year of the Stone Court (1945), there appears to be a growing trend of consistent liberal policy outputs across the five chief justice courts examined here. The Fuller Court decides only one-half of its cases liberally. By the time of the Taft Court, the average liberal percentage grows to about 83 percent, and continues to grow during the Hughes Court (about 86 percent). However, the series declines moderately during the Stone Court (to 69.8 percent), although it remains at a relatively high level, despite the growing number of rulings that the Court issues during this period.

Liberalism in Aggregated Issue Areas

Next, the specific issue areas are aggregated into the more manageable four major issue dimensions—economics, civil rights–civil liberties, judicial power, and other—described earlier in chapter 3. The fourteen individual issue types are aggregated into four major categories, following the methodology of Pacelle and Schubert.[42]

THE CONTENT OF THE ISSUE AREAS

The fourteen individual issue areas used in the present investigation are aggregated as follows: decisions in criminal procedure, civil rights, First

Amendment, privacy, and due process cases are combined into an overall civil liberties–civil rights dimension; decisions in attorney, union, economics, and federal taxation cases are combined into an overall economics dimension; and decisions in judicial power cases are combined into a single dimension. Decisions in federalism, interstate relations, separation of powers, and miscellaneous cases are combined into a dimension labeled "other."

Table 5-2 gives the annual proportions of liberal decisions in each issue area. Figures 5-12 through 5-15 display the percentage of liberal Supreme Court decisions in each of the four major issue areas for term years 1888 to 1997.

Economics

Figure 5-12 shows the percentage of liberal economics decisions. This series' maximum point occurs in 1954 (82.5 percent); its minimum in 1892 (42.0 percent). Overall, the series is rather stable beginning in 1888 and extending through 1930. Thereafter, the series increases gradually through 1941, when it declines through 1952. It trends very strongly upward in 1953, the year in which Earl Warren succeeded Fred Vinson as chief justice. The Warren Court's decisions are consistently liberal, and well above the rate for the prior courts examined here. After Warren left the Court in 1969, the series declines, due to the growing conservatism of the Court under Burger and Rehnquist.

The series average during the Fuller Court is 54.68, which is a somewhat surprising finding given the Court's purported conservative bent in economics issues.[43] This study shows that the Court voted in the liberal direction in more than one-half of the economics cases that it heard. Hence, the picture that prior descriptive studies paint of an entrenched Court seemingly entirely unwilling to uphold even the smallest liberal policy is somewhat inaccurate. The average for the White Court increases somewhat to 59.67. This, too, is a surprising finding given the policy perspective that most historical analyses lend to the White Court, although Schwartz and McCloskey do state that the Court became moderately more liberal in its decisions, upholding some of the Progressive reforms it reviewed.[44] These results confirm the observations of Melvin I. Urofsky and Charles Warren that the purported conservatism of the Court in reviewing protective legislation is simply not an accurate characterization of the Court in the late nineteenth and early twentieth centuries.[45]

The slightly increased liberalism of the White Court is most likely due, at least in part, to the change in its membership. Louis D. Brandeis and John H. Clarke both arrived at the Court and brought with them their

Table 5-2. Percentage of Liberal Decisions of the United States Supreme Court in Aggregated Issue Dimensions, 1888-1997

TERM YEAR	ECONOMIC	CIVIL LIBERTIES-CIVIL RIGHTS	JUDICIAL POWER	OTHER
1888	45.4	40.0	26.2	0.0
1889	53.8	50.0	24.6	14.3
1890	45.6	29.6	17.5	75.0
1891	51.7	36.8	20.0	50.0
1892	42.0	20.0	7.5	100.0
1893	45.6	41.9	12.3	66.7
1894	52.6	30.3	23.6	60.0
1895	64.7	38.0	7.3	45.5
1896	58.2	50.0	13.3	100.0
1897	49.6	16.7	30.0	0.0
1898	56.6	48.0	17.1	66.7
1899	46.5	20.0	26.0	66.7
1900	62.0	6.7	16.7	54.5
1901	63.6	16.7	38.1	50.0
1902	64.3	20.0	22.4	40.0
1903	54.1	22.6	23.1	83.3
1904	54.0	20.0	25.0	55.6
1905	60.7	5.3	21.2	100.0
1906	56.4	34.2	15.6	100.0
1907	62.1	37.5	47.6	20.0
1908	62.5	33.3	9.3	50.0
1909	51.0	8.8	18.2	100.0
1910	70.5	7.4	21.7	25.0
1911	59.2	9.5	21.2	100.0
1912	46.2	20.3	14.7	50.0
1913	67.8	43.3	30.4	63.2
1914	59.2	29.6	25.7	33.3
1915	58.1	20.0	20.0	66.7
1916	65.7	17.6	23.3	100.0
1917	58.6	33.3	17.4	62.5
1918	54.9	8.6	20.8	72.7
1919	63.4	21.7	21.7	65.2
1920	52.8	26.9	17.6	72.0
1921	59.4	20.0	23.5	55.2
1922	53.5	25.9	20.0	60.0
1923	61.3	13.0	27.6	40.0
1924	53.5	25.7	51.1	63.3
1925	46.8	33.3	31.8	61.5
1926	52.5	31.9	31.3	46.7
1927	51.3	22.2	53.8	65.1
1928	53.4	13.3	80.0	72.7
1929	43.2	37.5	20.0	81.0
1930	55.3	52.2	50.0	55.2
1931	57.3	29.4	21.4	64.0
1932	74.7	28.6	61.1	82.5
1933	63.6	47.4	61.1	63.9

Table 5-2. Percentage of Liberal Decisions of the United States Supreme Court in Aggregated Issue Dimensions, 1888-1997

TERM YEAR	ECONOMIC	CIVIL LIBERTIES-CIVIL RIGHTS	JUDICIAL POWER	OTHER
1934	45.3	62.5	59.3	65.1
1935	68.9	83.3	36.4	40.9
1936	62.8	42.1	40.0	69.0
1937	74.4	64.3	50.0	75.6
1938	77.6	57.1	50.0	57.1
1939	79.7	64.3	33.3	75.0
1940	80.3	57.9	40.0	75.5
1941	73.8	51.9	33.3	71.4
1942	64.5	63.6	38.5	50.0
1943	71.8	37.0	40.0	57.1
1944	67.7	64.5	26.3	60.0
1945	69.0	60.6	60.0	50.0
1946	69.2	25.8	33.3	77.8
1947	75.5	61.2	50.0	100.0
1948	68.3	50.0	68.8	66.7
1949	67.5	28.6	37.5	62.5
1950	54.0	45.2	50.0	66.7
1951	50.0	47.5	58.3	100.0
1952	46.6	50.0	56.3	33.3
1953	52.4	50.0	33.3	71.4
1954	82.5	63.2	30.8	57.1
1955	78.7	61.8	53.3	25.0
1956	83.3	61.2	47.4	80.0

TERM YEAR	ECONOMIC	CIVIL LIBERTIES-CIVIL RIGHTS	JUDICIAL POWER	OTHER
1957	67.9	63.0	40.0	12.5
1958	72.6	59.6	60.0	100.0
1959	70.0	59.6	44.4	50.0
1960	70.0	54.2	60.0	60.0
1961	73.3	74.0	66.7	66.7
1962	81.0	86.8	58.3	63.6
1963	75.5	89.8	56.3	81.8
1964	71.1	70.5	42.9	100.0
1965	71.4	72.3	22.2	0.0
1966	74.3	70.2	66.7	66.7
1967	72.7	80.3	75.0	100.0
1968	77.8	76.8	42.9	50.0
1969	66.7	59.8	22.2	50.0
1970	66.7	48.3	0.0	50.0
1971	50.0	58.0	16.7	50.0
1972	67.4	41.8	33.3	75.0
1973	51.3	46.1	33.3	60.0
1974	57.5	53.8	61.5	87.5
1975	44.7	36.7	62.5	100.0
1976	48.4	38.6	40.0	57.1
1977	63.3	48.7	44.4	50.0
1978	43.6	41.8	40.0	33.3
1979	56.8	46.7	33.3	100.0

Table 5-2. Percentage of Liberal Decisions of the United States Supreme Court in Aggregated Issue Dimensions, 1888-1997

TERM YEAR	ECONOMIC	CIVIL LIBERTIES-CIVIL RIGHTS	JUDICIAL POWER	OTHER		TERM YEAR	ECONOMIC	CIVIL LIBERTIES-CIVIL RIGHTS	JUDICIAL POWER	OTHER
1980	57.1	34.2	25.0	28.6		1989	57.5	35.7	52.6	45.5
1981	63.6	41.8	31.0	46.2		1990	46.2	45.2	66.7	30.0
1982	54.3	36.8	44.4	46.7		1991	45.7	46.0	52.9	60.0
1983	45.0	34.9	23.5	40.0		1992	55.2	38.3	45.5	50.0
1984	46.8	43.0	41.7	38.5		1993	55.6	43.1	9.1	14.3
1985	46.7	37.6	33.3	46.2		1994	45.0	43.5	31.3	30.0
1986	47.2	45.3	20.0	53.3		1995	44.0	40.9	64.3	25.0
1987	55.0	48.7	40.0	50.0		1996	57.9	30.9	25.0	37.5
1988	50.0	36.8	36.8	28.6		1997	42.9	35.2	38.1	33.3

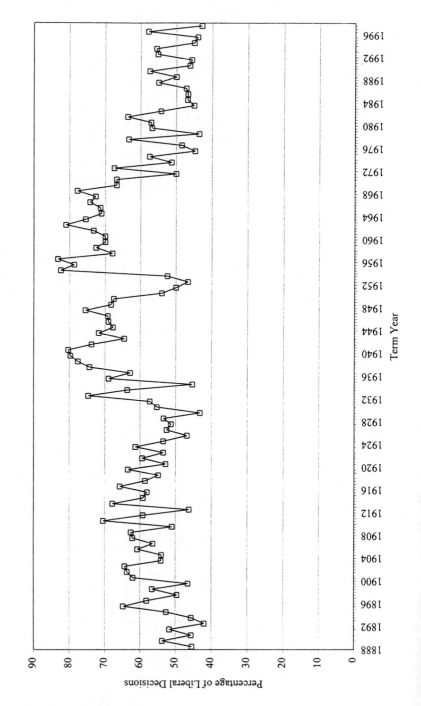

Figure 5-12. Percentage of Liberal Decisions of the
United States Supreme Court in Economics Dimension Cases, 1888-1997

Progressive ideals.[46] Moreover, James C. McReynolds had a reputation as a "trust-buster" prior to joining the high tribunal.[47] "Every era of history represents a period of transition for the Court, but for this period it was especially true, since the conservative hegemony in political and economic life was threatened by the early Wilsonian movement.... . [However,] the threat of a nonconservative Court majority faded with the return to 'normalcy' and the arrival of Chief Justice William Howard Taft."[48]

When Taft was appointed chief justice, the Court did become slightly more conservative on average than was the White Court. Willis Van Devanter and George Sutherland joined the Court, and formed, with Pierce Butler and James McReynolds, the "The Four Horsemen of the Apocalypse. " The series' average during Taft's tenure is 52.77, declining below the level observed during the Fuller Court. This result is not surprising given Taft's and his colleagues' common policy orientation towards economic regulation and governmental power.

When one examines the period surrounding the New Deal and the Great Depression, the figure demonstrates a fairly significant upsurge in the proportion of decisions that the Court decided liberally. Most of the term years surrounding 1937 (the year in which Roosevelt attempted his Court-packing scheme) in particular prove to be increases over the proportion of liberal decisions for the previous several terms. Indeed, the average rate of liberalism for these decisions during the Hughes Court is 67.26, a change of 15 percent over that seen during the Taft Court. The series begins to increase in 1930, declines temporarily in 1934, but then increases consistently reaching then-historic highs. The growth in the series continues through 1940, when it declines once again. The series average for the Stone Court is slightly elevated over the rate for the Hughes Court; the Court's average is 69.36. The series declines modestly beginning in 1941, lasting through 1953 when it begins to increase once again.

Thus, the Court's economic decisions are frequently liberal in the years prior to 1937, despite what Roosevelt, other political actors, and the public at large may have believed about the policy content of the Court's rulings. Indeed, the series dips below 50 percent liberal only once (1934, 45.3 percent) during Roosevelt's incumbency. These results are in marked contrast to the civil liberties–civil rights series, which exceeds 50 percent liberal only once up until 1935 (see Figure 5-13). However, the president's attack on the Court is associated with a slight increase in the Court's liberalism in decisions involving economic issues. The change may be due to the direct effect of the crisis of legitimacy that it allegedly suffered, but perhaps also due to a steady and gradual adoption of a supportive view of the social welfare policies with which the government and the nation as a whole was then

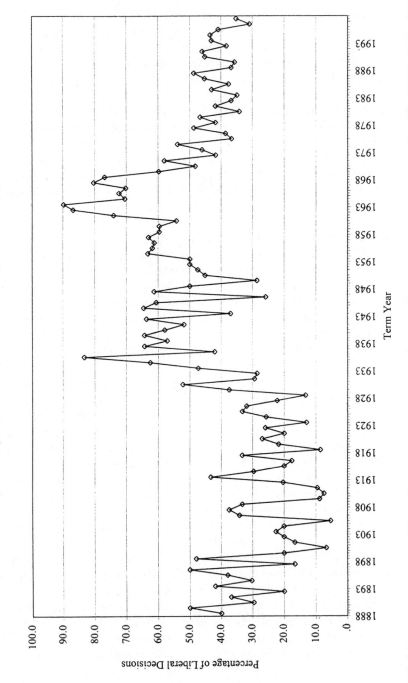

Figure 5-13. Percentage of Liberal Decisions of the
United States Supreme Court in Civil Liberties-Civil Rights Cases, 1888-1997

grappling, for the justices themselves were equally aware of the extant macro-economic problems that the nation faced. This result of increasing liberalism during the Hughes Court is thus associated with the liberal economic policy preferences that the justices brought to the Court. Indeed, Franklin Roosevelt nominated them to the Court, in part, for that very reason.[49]

Pritchett also examines the liberalism of the Court during the Stone Court. He finds that the Court decided liberally in 58 percent of the nonunanimous cases involving questions of federal regulation, the Interstate Commerce Commission, labor relations, monopolies, and state regulation.[50] This categorization of case types is quite similar to the economic dimension discussed immediately above, although there are differences in the issues included in each analysis. This study aggregates within the economic dimension decisions involving questions of general economic regulation, regulation of attorneys and unions, and the implementation of the federal income tax. The results of the present study indicate that the rate for all such cases (unanimous *and* nonunanimous) from 1937 to 1947 is slightly more than 69 percent (see Table 5-2). Haynie and Tate similarly examine nonunanimous decisions within this aggregated dimension and find a similar pattern of advancing and declining liberalism beginning in 1916 and extending through 1988.[51] Hence, the results for Pritchett's and Haynie and Tate's studies, and the present investigation are comparable, even though Pritchett's and Haynie and Tate's results are somewhat smaller in magnitude, which is most likely due to the slight difference in the issues both studies combine in this dimension and the type of data analyzed.

Throughout the Warren Court (1953–68), the series stays at or well above 50 percent liberal. Although the series declines slightly during Warren's tenure, the average percentage of liberal economic decisions is 73.83. Thus, nearly three-quarters of the Court's decisions are liberal. Also, the change in the series across term years is much less than that for prior courts. However, the series does decline below 50 percent when Chief Justice Burger's tenure begins. This trend of declining liberalism continues through the Rehnquist Court. This finding is not surprising due to the well-documented policy views of both these chief justices and the growing conservative viewpoint of the associate justices who served with them.[52] However, the decline in the series is not as dramatic as some observers of the Court might have otherwise expected.

Civil Liberties and Civil Rights

Figure 5-13 describes the time series of the rate of liberal decisions in the civil liberties–civil rights issue dimension. The series declines from 1888 to

1905; the series' historic low occurs in 1905 (5.3 percent). After 1905, it begins to increase. The overall average for the series during the Fuller Court is 28.47. This result confirms prior studies' findings of the Court's conservative outlook on matters of civil liberties during the period at hand.[53] The Court becomes even more conservative (or less liberal) during the White Court, whose average is 21.65, a relative change of 24 percent from the rate observed during the Fuller Court. However, the Taft Court becomes somewhat more liberal; its average rate is 24.76 percent, perhaps due to the Court's not making its decisions during times of war.

Beginning in 1928, the series increases quite dramatically until 1963, when it begins to decline. During the period of the Hughes Court (1930–40), the Court's average jumps dramatically up to 53.55, an increase of 29 percent from that observed during the Taft Court. As many other scholars have noted, the Court was beginning to become more supportive of expanded claims of civil liberties during the mid-1930s.[54] Hence, this increase in the series during the Hughes Court confirms these expectations, although the Court certainly is not as liberal as the Warren Court was to be some thirty years later. The series does not increase significantly during the Stone Court. The average for the Stone Court is 55.54, representing approximately a 2 percent change over the rate observed during the Hughes Court.

These findings support the results of Epstein, Walker, and Dixon,[55] Haynie and Tate,[56] and the historical observations of Schwartz[57] and McCloskey,[58] all of whom suggest that a decreased level of liberalism in civil liberties–civil rights decisions occurs during the period surrounding the two world wars. Haynie and Tate, in particular, empirically examine the liberalism of the Court from 1916 to 1988 in nonunanimous decisions. They find similar periods of growth and decline in the series, and observed levels of liberalism across the term years analyzed. However, they suggest that the series is much more dynamic when considering only nonunanimous decisions. For example, their study indicates a large and abrupt decline in the series from 100 percent in 1922 to zero percent in 1928, although the authors do note the small number of cases on which these results are based.[59] In this study, Figure 5-13 and Table 5-2 show that indeed the series declines, but only by 12.6 percent.

Furthermore, Pritchett examines the Stone Court's decision-making in issues of civil liberties and the rights of criminal defendants. He finds that the Court ruled in favor of these claims in 49 percent of such nonunanimous decisions.[60] Thus, the results of the present investigation generally are in line with all of these studies' findings, although there are slight differences in magnitude.

After 1948, the series begins to increase gradually in liberalism through 1960, when the change between term years increases dramatically. In only four term years (1960–63), the series increases from 53.5 percent to 89.6 percent, the historic high. In no year during the Warren Court does the series decline below 50 percent liberal. This finding corresponds with other conceptions of Warren Court decision-making in this aggregated issue dimension.[61] During the Burger and Rehnquist Courts, however, the series begins to decline in liberalism, and does so rapidly reaching a point in the term year 1997 of 35.2 percent liberal decisions. Again, this finding confirms the findings of prior studies of the Court's policy orientations during these years.[62]

Judicial Power

Figure 5-14 shows the proportion of judicial power cases the Court decided liberally.[63] Overall, the series is rather volatile throughout the period of analysis. The historic low occurs in 1895 (7.3 percent). From 1924 to 1949, it fluctuates rather wildly, changing from its historic high of 80 percent in 1927 to only 20 percent in the very next year, 1928. From 1951 to 1970, the series declines modestly, but then begins to trend upward yet again in 1971. However, some of this volatility is due to the comparably small number of cases that the Court considered in this issue area.

Other

Figure 5-15 shows the series for the proportions of liberal decisions in the "other" issue area. Because of the small number of cases involved in this area, the series is quite volatile. It experiences three years in which the Court issued no liberal decisions, and it experiences fourteen years in which 100 percent of its decisions in this issue were liberal. Sometimes these disparate scores immediately follow each other, such as in 1896 and 1897. However, there is a period of less dynamism from 1917 to 1945, although no clear trend can be discerned from these years' scores. Thus, it is evident that this series is mostly noise due to small N's, and it therefore resists accurate analysis.

To provide some indication of the direction and magnitude of the series, the average rates of liberal decisions during each of the chief justice courts are presented for this issue area. During the Fuller Court, the rate is 59.01 percent. The average remains about the same during the White Court, 59.15. It increases very slightly to 60.61 percent during the Taft Court and then to 66.71 percent during the Hughes Court. However, during the Stone Court, the series average declines to 57.70 percent. Hence, even this amal-

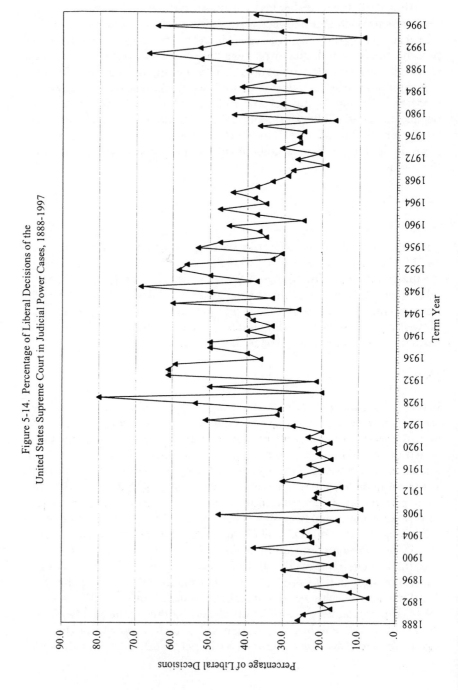

Figure 5-14. Percentage of Liberal Decisions of the
United States Supreme Court in Judicial Power Cases, 1888-1997

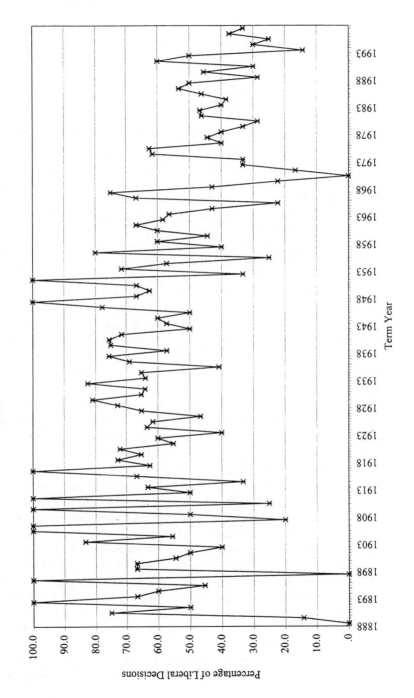

Figure 5-15. Percentage of Liberal Decisions of the
United States Supreme Court in Other Cases, 1888-1997

gamation of decisions portrays a general trend toward increasing liberalism across the four chief justice courts and the fifty-eight term years primarily analyzed here.

CHAPTER SUMMARY

This chapter examines the liberalism of the decision-making of the United States Supreme Court during the period from 1888 to 1997 across several issue areas. It finds that decisions involving economic issues (economics, attorneys, unions, and federal taxation) were initially relatively conservative during the Fuller, White, and Taft Courts, although not as conservative as we might expect based upon many prior descriptions of the Court during this period. These three Courts maintained a rate of about 50 percent liberal across the forty-two term years that they comprise. However, with the advent of the Hughes Court, these decisions become progressively more liberal. The trend toward increasing levels of liberalism continues in the Stone Court. Moreover, the rates of liberalism overall become much more consistent and less volatile beginning most notably with the Hughes Court. The Warren Court's decision-making is predictably liberal as well, but the series begins to decline during the latter Courts. These results affirm the findings of Haynie and Tate, and the observations of McCloskey, Schwartz, and other scholars that the Court then held a conservative policy perspective in economic matters.[64]

In the realm of civil liberties and civil rights, the Court is predictably conservative during the first three chief justice courts examined herein, attaining a rate of about 25 percent across these Courts. The Fuller Court's decisions become even more conservative surrounding the period of World War I, ruling against the majority of claims of civil liberties generally. The White and Taft Courts continue that trend of conservative decisions in these issue areas. Mirroring the changes in the level of liberalism for the economic series, the Court becomes more liberal over time for decisions involving questions of civil liberties and civil rights. Once again, the Hughes Court's decision-making proves to be a turning point in the policy perspective of the Court. The Hughes and the Stone Courts issue more consistently liberal decisions in these issue areas. Their combined average is 54.17, more than double that of the prior three Courts. However, the Stone Court's rulings during the World War II period become less liberal than the Court had been previously, although the decline is less than that observed for the Fuller Court's decisions in the era of the First World War. Predictably, the Warren Court's jurisprudence is found to have been very liberal. The series falls off during the Burger and Rehnquist Courts. Thus, these results dem-

onstrate the growth in the liberalism of the Court's decisions that has occurred in the United States Supreme Court's decision-making across more
than a century of American jurisprudence. Perhaps more importantly, they
also demonstrate that the Court began to assume a much larger responsibility for resolving particular issues of civil liberties and civil rights, as Pacelle
finds.[65]

6

The Long-Run Relationship between the United States Supreme Court's Decision-Making Environment and Its Liberalism, 1888–1997

> Every Court prior to the Roosevelt Court has enjoyed the protection of perhaps the most potent myth in American life—the myth that the Court is a non-political body, a sacred institution on which politics must not lay its profane hands.
>
> —C. Herman Pritchett, *The Roosevelt Court*[1]

THIS CHAPTER UNDERTAKES TIME SERIES ANALYSES OF THE LIBERALISM OF THE United States Supreme Court's decisions in three aggregated issue dimensions—economics, civil liberties–civil rights, and judicial power—so as to determine whether there is a long-run equilibrium underlying the Court's policy-making. To that end, several considerations dealing with Supreme Court data are discussed. Models for each policy domain are also estimated to assess the effects of institutional and environmental influences in order to explain the Court's institutional decision-making across over a century of Supreme Court jurisprudence that includes the Panic of 1893, the Spanish-American War, the rise of Progressivism, two world wars, the Great Depression, and a president's bid to pack the Court. During this period, the Court begins to issue consistently liberal decisions, especially when it reviewed the constitutionality of New Deal legislation in the mid- to late 1930s.[2] There are significant changes in the percentage of liberal decisions across issue areas, but the policy output is quite dynamic as the political and legal battles fought within and without its walls transform the Court as an institution.

By undertaking time series analyses of Supreme Court decision-making, we obtain a better understanding of these dynamics in the level of liberalism expressed in the Court's decisions, and in particular the influence

176

of various factors on those public policy outcomes that its decisions represent within the American political system. Because the Court has come to
be a significant force within the American system, especially in this century,
detailed analysis of its decision-making across time is indeed appropriate.

THEORETICAL FOUNDATION FOR
SUPREME COURT DECISION-MAKING

The basic theoretical foundation on which the analyses completed in this
chapter rest (in addition to the conceptual analyses reviewed in chapter 1)
is that political outcomes result from individual, goal-oriented behavior that
is determined by the limitations and opportunities that institutions afford
the political actors who function within them.[3] Murphy first articulates the
general hypothesis that justices heed the preferences of external actors and
the constraints of the institution within which they are acting, in addition to
seeking primarily to infuse policy with their own views.[4] Murphy espouses
a paradigm that is now commonly referred to as "rational choice."[5] Epstein
and Knight clearly articulate the propositions associated with this theoretic
conception: (1) political and social actors choose to attain certain goals; (2)
they behave strategically in that their behavior is dependent on the choices
that they expect other actors to make; and, (3) their choices are constrained
by the institutional structure within which these choices are made.[6] Under
this conception, a justice is presumed to choose that course of behavior that
will ultimately come closest to satisfying his or her goal set. A justice is
similarly presumed to compare the relative outcomes of each of the alternative courses of action and then rank them according to how closely each
produces the result that the justice desires to effectuate and ultimately choose
the alternative that will result in the greatest utility with respect to his or her
specific goals.[7]

Each of the elements of the strategic view bears further explanation.
First, perhaps the primary goal of all justices is to write their policy views
into the law of the land.[8] They are also presumed accordingly to want to
influence external political institutions and actors.[9] However, there are many
factors that influence a justice's ability to achieve these goals. He must, for
example, be concerned with the legitimacy that the Court enjoys in the
eyes of the public and of public officials. While he may simply vote his
policy preferences, he must also be ever aware of the reputation of the Court,
since it is structurally unable to enforce its own decisions and its members
are unelected.[10] The Court has twice in its history come dangerously close
to squandering its structurally limited store of institutional credibility: first,
as a result of its ruling in *Scott v. Sanford*[11] and, later, as a result of its ardent

laissez-faire perspective in reviewing New Deal legislation during the mid-1930s.[12]

Second, justices are, under rational choice theory, hypothesized to act "strategically." This term is simply used to mean that a justice's choice is, in part, dependent on how he or she believes that other relevant persons will act; thus, his or her behavior is accordingly modified because he or she realizes that the efficacy of his or her choice is contingent on the goals and respective behavior of other actors. The other actors the behavior of whom a justice must anticipate include not only colleagues (most certainly), but also political elites such as the president or members of Congress, as well as members of the public to some extent.[13] The justices are expected to be cognizant of the structural limitations on the Court's decision-making power, because it is presumed that justices highly value the policy-making power of the Court and, thus, jealously guard its attendant institutional credibility that could be diminished by any of the external actors who may choose to modify the effect of the ruling of the Court or simply ignore its order.[14] Hence, the justices' behavior is strategic in that they anticipate the reaction of others beyond the Court's walls to its pronouncements. As a result, they may choose to moderate their policy views (and, hence, move away from their most preferred policy position) so as to most efficiently achieve their goals.

Further, the Court's members are political veterans, having been involved in politics and known politicos for most of their adult lives. Many of them have served in key governmental positions prior to their nominations, having been governors, prosecutors, attorneys general, senators, and even (in one case) president.[15] Having served in such roles gives them the exposure necessary to gain the president's attention and the experience to make them more politically astute. Indeed, several have been personal friends of the nominating president prior to ascending to the bench.[16] They are, thus, keenly aware of the political dynamics that surround the Court and its role within the American governmental structure. This awareness is hypothesized to condition the expected utility of achieving their goal that the Court retains its institutional legitimacy in the eyes of governmental officials and the public alike.[17]

Justices must consider not only their own goals and those of others, but they must also be aware of the institutional constraints within which they act. Institutions can be conceptualized as "shared expectations about appropriate behavior" that serve to structure interaction among particular individuals in certain ways.[18] More specifically, institutional structures determine, in part, the aggregation of individual policy preferences within a decision-making body.[19] These institutions can be formal (e.g., laws) or informal (e.g., norms and customs).[20] For example, Article 3 of the Constitution requires that the Court hear only "cases and controversies"; it cannot hear hypothetical questions, thereby restricting the kinds of questions it is asked to resolve. Also, under the customs of the Court, the most senior justice who is part of the majority coalition assigns the opinion-writing responsibility, a choice that can drastically impact the tone and breadth of the Court's policy statement.[21] "'The fundamental equation' [of this conception] is that political outcomes are the result of the interplay of actors as they seek to realize their goals, of the institutional setting in which they act and which they may help to shape, and the historical context in which their decisions are set."[22] Thus, the justices' behavior is to some extent circumscribed by the environmental constraints that impinge on their decision-making.

MODELS OF SUPREME COURT LIBERALISM ACROSS TIME

Based on the categories of influences on the Court's decision-making that the literature finds, three separate models of the Court's liberalism over time are identified, specified, and estimated. Each of the models explains the Court's liberalism in one aggregated issue dimension across the 110 term years examined in this study.

Case Selection

Consistent with the analyses in prior chapters, all decisions of the Court are considered in this modeling endeavor. While some studies select only the nonunanimous decisions of the Court when examining its liberalism over time, many of those studies are conducted at the individual level of analysis.[23] They do so because they seek to understand the limits of the individual justices' agreement on important questions of public policy, which is most appropriately investigated in nonunanimous decisions. This inquiry, on the other hand, investigates the institutional liberalism of the Court. Hence, to obtain a more complete explanation of its policy preferences over time, it uses all of the Court's decisions, whether they be unanimous or nonunanimous. Additionally, to select only the nonunanimous cases for analysis would have greatly restricted the number of cases upon which the data on the Court's liberalism are based because of the quite small number of such opinions prior to 1945, thereby limiting the confidence we have in the results obtained.

Aggregated Issue Dimensions

As demonstrated in the previous chapter, the decisions of the Supreme Court can be aggregated into four issue dimensions. Only three of these (economic, civil liberties–civil rights, and judicial power) are separately examined here; they represent the dependent variables in the analyses conducted below. The fourth issue dimension, "other," is not considered because of the divergent types of decisions that comprise that dimension, making the modeling process extremely difficult and, consequently, drawing any inferences based upon the results may lead to invalid conclusions. Moreover, these three issue dimensions comprise the bulk of decisions the Court has announced from 1888 to 1997 and are, thus, central to understanding the level of the Court's institutional liberalism and its dynamics.[24]

Individually considering each of the three dimensions that comprise the aggregate function of the Court's liberalism allows one to more clearly determine the influence of the continuity and change in the Court's agenda over time on its resulting decisional trends. That is, when the Court began to consider fewer economics decisions beginning in the 1940s,[25] the influence on its policy-making may also have changed. This methodology is particularly appropriate for the period of analysis in the present study, since their relative share of the Court's agenda has dramatically changed from a time in which economic decisions dominated the Court's agenda to a more contemporary period in which the Court, along with the remainder of the American political system, has turned its attention to issues of civil liberties and civil rights.[26]

Economic Liberalism

Following Spaeth,[27] the measure of the Court's economic liberalism is composed of decisions involving questions of economics, attorney regulation, union-labor relations, and federal taxation. Recall that this variable is measured from zero, representing entirely conservative decisions, to one hundred, representing entirely liberal decisions. The variable is separately calculated for each of the 110 term years investigated.

POLICY VIEWS OF THE JUSTICES

The continuous variables described below serve to measure the influences on economic policy preferences that the literature has examined. They serve as proxies for the justices' values, which are difficult to directly measure given the cloistered nature of the Court. It is also well nigh impossible to obtain accurate data from justices who served long ago. Although there are many variables that theoretically could be included in the model, those variables that are thought to be most closely associated with the Court's institutional liberalism across the period at hand are included.

Political Factors

Most of the persons who become justices of the Supreme Court are beyond their mid-forties. They, thus, bring to the bench a well-formed and cohesive macropolitical worldview and attitudinal structure.[28] It is therefore reasonable to theorize that their policy preferences, based on their attitudes, affect their voting behavior. This is main tenet of the attitudinal model, the current dominant paradigm in explaining the judicial behavior of the members of the United States Supreme Court.[29] Moreover, most of the justices' decision-making remain stable over time.[30] Hence, their attitudes are also most likely stable. While Segal and Cover scores have been widely used as proxies of the justices' attitudes,[31] recent scholarship questions whether this protocol is valid prior to 1945.[32] Indeed, Epstein and Mershon conclude that such scores should not be used outside the policy domain for which they were originally developed (i.e., civil liberties–civil rights).[33] Thus, other proxies of the justices attitudes arising from their social backgrounds are instead employed.

Therefore, the dynamics of the liberalism of the Court's decisions over time are largely influenced by the change in its membership. Since the justices' attitudes affect their decision-making, any change in who those justices are (and, hence, what attitudes they possess) will affect the institutional liberalism of the Court's policy outputs.[34] Hence, the president can exert tremendous influence on the Court's policy-making by nominating fellow ideologues or partisans. However, Baum notes that the impact of membership change should not be exaggerated since the Court during the 1970s and 1980s, when there were a number of alleged conservatives on the Court, did not engineer as a large-scale policy shift as some Court observers expected by solely looking to the policy preferences of the individual justices.[35]

Party Identification. One indicator of the justices' political values or attitudes is their respective political party affiliations. The party identification of each of the justices who served on the Court during a particular term year is assessed. Following Tate, Tate and Handberg, and Haynie and Tate, this variable is scored with zero (0) representing justices who considered themselves to be Republicans, one (1) for justices who were independents, and two (2) for justices who were Democrats.[36] Based on this scoring metric, a mean is calculated for each term year. At the institutional level of analysis, Haynie and Tate find that the justices' partisanship is marginally significant and positively associated with the Court's economic liberalism indicating that as the variable's mean increases, the Court's liberal policy-outputs increase as well.[37] Although some studies simply look to which party claimed a majority of seats on the Court,[38] the partisan composition is herein alternatively captured by examining the party identification of all the justices so as to indicate the prevailing partisan balance on the Court. The data used in the construction of this variable come from *The Supreme Court Compendium*.[39] Only those justices who served a majority of the term year are considered in the calculation of this and all the other independent variables.

Because Democrats tend to support economic liberalism more strongly than do Republicans during the period analyzed, a positive relationship is hypothesized to exist between this measure of political party identification and the Court's decision-making in economic matters. Hence,

H_1: As the mean score of the justices' partisan affiliations increase, the level of the United States Supreme Court's institutional economic liberalism increases.

Presidential Intentions. Another indicator of a justice's attitudinal content may theoretically be represented by the policy intentions of the president who nominated the justice to the Court originally. That is, if a president is known to be ideologically conscious (either in a liberal or a conservative direction) in his Supreme Court nominations, then such motivations may evidence the justice's policy preferences. The president's intentions may reflect changes in elite opinion as well.[40] Prior studies have discussed the policy intentions of all the presidents who have nominated justices who served during the period of analysis of this study and provide solid historical evidence that allows one to discern the policy intentions of presidents.[41] Hence, their policy intentions with regard to Supreme Court nominees are relatively clear and can be discerned without undue effort.

In this study, justices who were nominated by a conservative-conscious president are scored negative one (–1); those who were nominated by presidents with moderate or no ideological intentions are scored zero (0); and, those who were nominated by liberal conscious presidents are scored one (1). Many presidents expressly seek to influence the Court's decision-making by appointing justices who share their policy preferences. Conservative presidents may try to influence the Court by nominating conservative justices; liberal presidents may attempt the same maneuver by nominating judges whom they perceive to hold liberal policy perspectives. Ideologically conscious presidents, thus, may search for nominees who have a common ideology and who will, once nominated and confirmed, advance the views of the president on various issues. If chief executives do have these strong views in mind when nominating justices to the Court, the president is scored as being conscious of the nominee's policy views. Because the president himself selects the nominee based upon a relatively common set of policy preferences, the attitudes of the justice are inferred from his selection. Other less ideologically concerned presidents may simply have no interest in the policy view of their nominees to the Court, or a president may be moderate in his policy views, as opposed to holding ardent stances on various issues.

This coding scheme in the present study adopts the operationalizations of Tate and Handberg.[42] These authors, based on Abraham's study and other studies, classify Taft, Harding, Nixon, and Reagan as conservative-conscious presidents.[43] They classify Woodrow Wilson, Franklin Roosevelt, and Lyndon Johnson as liberal-conscious presidents.[44] The present study follows Tate and Handberg's coding protocol and additionally identifies Grover Cleveland, Ulysses Grant, and Benjamin Harrison as conservative-conscious presidents. Theodore Roosevelt and Abraham Lincoln are similarly identified as additional liberal-conscious presidents. All other presidents are scored as moderates or having no conscious ideological goals in nominating a Supreme Court justice. Thus,

> H_2: As the mean of presidential policy intentions increases, the level of the United States Supreme Court's institutional economic liberalism increases.

Cleavages

Seymour M. Lipset and Stein Rokkan show that social cleavages that affect the development of partisanship in Western nations in turn influence mass voting behavior.[45] This study investigates the effects of these divisions by examining the influence of the justices' religious preferences, urban/rural origins, and Southern regional origins as proxies of their political attitudes.

Non-Protestants. One variable that taps into the differing socialization processes through which the justices have gone is their religious preference.[46] Non-Protestants are typically more liberal in their policy preferences than Protestants because of the content of their religious traditions.[47] In the present study, a justice whose religious affiliation is non-Protestant is scored one (1), while Protestant justices are scored zero (0). The data for this variable come from *The Supreme Court Compendium*.[48] Thus,

> H_3: As the mean of the justices' religious affiliations increases, the level of the United States Supreme Court's institutional economic liberalism will increase as well.

Agricultural Origins. As discussed above, one of the principal cleavages that has affected mass political behavior in Western industrialized nations is the urban/rural division. In the last 150 years, the United States has become much more industrialized. Tate and Handberg suggest the process of industrialization and the growth of urban areas influenced the public's attitudes about the legitimacy of the government's efforts to regulate the economy so as to control the deleterious effects that growing industrialism had on the populace.[49] Following Tate and Handberg's operationalization, justices are considered to have agricultural origins if their fathers were farmers. The data for this variable come from *The Supreme Court Compendium*.[50] Thus,

> H$_4$: As the mean of justices with agricultural origins increases, the level of the Court's economic liberalism decreases.

Southern Regional Origins. One of the factors that clearly distinguishes political attitudes in the United States is American geographic origins. In particular, the South, with its unique history and culture, tends to produce attitudes in its residents that are more conservative than those of persons who were socialized in other areas of the nation. Accordingly, Southern Supreme Court justices are most likely more conservative in their economic decision-making than are those justices who hail from other regions of the country.[51] The data for this variable of Southern regional origin come from *The Supreme Court Compendium*'s listing of the justices' home states.[52] As with the other independent variables, a proportion of the justices with Southern regional backgrounds is calculated for each term year. Based on Key's study, the South includes the eleven states of the Old Confederacy plus two border states, Kentucky and Oklahoma.[53] Thus,

> H$_5$: As the mean of justices with Southern regional origins increases, the Court's level of economic liberalism decreases.

Career Experiences

In addition to the larger social context in which Supreme Court justices were raised, their preappointment career experiences may serve to influence attitudes and, in turn, the Court's economic decision-making.

Judicial Experience. The associations that prior studies find between a justice's preappointment judicial experience and their economic decision-making are mixed. Richard Johnston asserts, based in part on research that John R. Schmidhauser conducted, that there is a negative relationship between the two constructs because individuals with such experience are more likely to have been inculcated with the norms of judicial restraint and, hence, would make decisions more closely based upon law and precedent "than upon their perspective of the political, social, and economic needs of the moment."[54] Indeed, Walker, Epstein, and Dixon suggest that the Stone Court may have experienced elevated levels of dissent because many of the justices had "almost no exposure to the 'no dissent' traditions common to appellate tribunals."[55] Their prior career experiences do not develop in them the value of deferring to the views of others. Stone, Frankfurter, Douglas, and Rutledge, for example, each came from academia, where individuals are encouraged to articulate their own theories of the law under the prevailing reward structure. Similarly, Black, Burton, and Byrnes joined the Court after serving in the Senate, where spirited debate is promoted.[56] However, Tate and Handberg find a positive association between judicial experience and economic voting behavior.[57] Because of the mixed results the literature finds for this concept, this study adopts the theoretical justification that Johnston offers, based upon Schmidhauser's prior research.[58]

Following the scoring methodology of Haynie and Tate, and Tate and Handberg,[59] a justice's judicial experience is scored in the following manner: two (2) if he or she has five or more years of preappointment experience; one (1) if he or she has some but less than five years experience; and, zero (0) if he or she has no judicial experience. An index of judicial experience is used rather than the absolute number of years of experience because the latter is skewed strongly to the left since a large number of Supreme Court justices have no such experience.[60] The data are obtained from *The Supreme Court Compendium*.[61] Thus,

H_6: As the extent of the justices' judicial experience increases, the level of economic liberalism decreases.

THE COURT'S EXTERNAL ENVIRONMENT

Although the Court has been described as a "marble temple"[62] and a "monastery,"[63] the Court operates within a highly charged political environment. Its decision-making is, thus, oftentimes influenced by discrete events that occur at one point in time and affect the justices' voting behavior for only that limited period. To properly construct explanatory models of the long-term institutional liberalism of the Court, one must specify and estimate the effects of events that may impact its rulings that may occur beyond the marble walls of the Court building but yet within the purview of its goal-driven members.

The Panic of 1893

Although lesser in scope and magnitude than the Great Depression, the Panic of 1893 may have impacted the Supreme Court's economic policy-making. The stock market failed shortly after Grover Cleveland assumed the presidency in 1893. As a result, many banks called in their loans and diminished the amount of credit that they would extend to their customers.[64] Before the end of the year, five hundred banks and nearly sixteen thousand business had declared bankruptcy. No sector of the economy escaped the effects of the Panic. "Everywhere mills, factories, furnaces, and mines closed down in large numbers, and hundreds of thousands of workers lost their jobs. . . . The panic developed into a major depression."[65] Thus, the Panic of 1893 was a significant economic event in the pre–twentieth–century Court's environment whose effect should be empirically investigated.

The Panic's occurrence is hypothesized to increase the Court's economic liberalism for reasons similar to those that have been proffered for the Great Depression: the Court as the last court of resort within the U.S. judicial system must resolve the issues causing concern in the courts below.[66] The lower courts of the day were most likely struggling with issues of how to deal with the economic and labor demands that were associated with the Panic of 1893, as they will do nearly forty years later. Moreover, the Panic is important in terms of partisan politics because it led, in part, to the critical election of 1896 resulting in a subsequent partisan realignment.[67] The intervention modeling the Panic of 1893 is scored zero (0) up until 1893 and one (1) through 1897. Thus,

> H$_7$: The Panic of 1893 is associated with an increase in the liberalism of the Supreme Court's economic decision-making.

Election of Theodore Roosevelt

Theodore Roosevelt has a reputation as being a trust-buster and a reformer, seeking to propose policies that would protect the consumer, increase the level of regulation of business activity, prevent monopolies, and reduce the level of corruption in government.[68] Although he served as vice president under President William McKinley and assumed the presidency when McKinley was assassinated in 1901, the electorate did not have the opportunity to vote on him as president until 1904. Even though Roosevelt later ran as the Bull Moose Party Candidate, he developed a reputation as a reformer while he served as president from 1901 to 1904.[69] His election may have signaled a rise in popular support for Progressive reforms. This event may, thus, have influenced the Court to become more liberal in its economic decision-making because of the perceived change in public opinion on issues of reform that Roosevelt's election represented.

Thus, the election of Roosevelt is scored zero (0) through 1903 and one (1) beginning in 1904. The variable is hypothesized to be a continuous influence because Roosevelt's efforts to enact reform policies, in part, helped to energize the Progressive movement that permanently transformed the complexion of American politics. The U.S. has, for example, not repealed the antitrust laws that bind economic interests. Hence,

H_8: The election of Theodore Roosevelt as President of the United States in 1904 is associated with an increase in the level of the Court's economic liberalism.

Great Depression

Perhaps the single most important macroeconomic event to occur in United States history is the Great Depression. It transformed the political system from one that was dominated by a laissez-faire, noninterventionist attitude toward one that adopted a progressive social welfare system. "It was an emergency, as Justice Brandeis remarked 'more serious than war.'"[70] As a result of the Depression, the federal government began to provide more and more services to residents and to delve deeper into regulation of many aspects of the economy. Historical accounts suggest that the Supreme Court was at first an unwilling conspirator in this transformation, "maintaining a position on the margin of the political arena."[71] But in 1937, it became a full-fledged partner in the effort to respond to the enormous challenges facing the government, the economy, and the nation as a whole as a result of the Great Depression. It did so by supporting greater economic liberalism.[72]

Since the Supreme Court is located at the apex of the judicial system, it is likely that the Court's economic decision-making may be impacted by such a large-scale event. Haynie and Tate find the occurrence of the Great Depression is statistically significantly associated with an increase in the liberalism of the Court's economic decisions.[73] Indeed, it seems very unlikely that the Court's rulings would *not* be affected by this event. Because it was a discrete occurrence, it is modeled as an intervention affecting the Court's economic policy-making. Accordingly, this variable is scored as taking on the value of zero (0) up to 1928 and one (1) beginning in 1929. Thus,

H_9: The advent of the Great Depression is associated with an increased level of liberalism in the economic decision-making of the Supreme Court.

Franklin Roosevelt's Court-Packing Plan

Many scholars note the Supreme Court's abrupt turnabout in its economic decision-making to become more supportive of New Deal legislation and the government's efforts to regulate the economy and business activity after Franklin D. Roosevelt announced his Court-packing plan in 1937.[74] The Court had struck down as unconstitutional a string of laws the Congress had passed to ameliorate the tremendous demands of the Depression, thereby continuing the Court's laissez-faire perspective that dominated its institutional decision-making for the prior fifty years or more.[75] Notable among this legislation were parts of the National Industrial Recovery Act, the cornerstone of the New Deal program. "At a moment when the political pressure for economic legislation was greater than ever before, the Court had chosen to call a halt; at a moment when the Constitution's famous flexibility was most required, the Court had chosen to regard judicial review as the automatic application of static principles. The depression, and the New Deal which was its reflex, were forces too cosmic for those Canutes to withstand."[76] Labor relations had also grown violent, graphically illustrating the "grim fact that the national economic dilemma was still very acute."[77]

In response to the Court's recalcitrance, President Roosevelt proposed in February 1937 that the Court's membership be expanded; he, having been reelected in 1936 by a landslide, claimed a popular mandate.[78] He suggested that for every justice who was older than seventy years of age who failed to retire, he have the opportunity to nominate an additional justice. Roosevelt argued that these additional justices were needed in order to lighten the Court's burgeoning workload because the Court's septuagenarians allegedly were not efficient and timely in fulfilling their judicial responsibilities.[79] Roosevelt's plan, had it been enacted, would have allowed him to nominate six new justices and thereby insure the approval of the New Deal program.[80]

As McCloskey notes, the Court cannot lag too far behind the nation if the institution is to survive. Roosevelt's proposal brought that stark reality home for the justices, who had previously sought to disassociate the Court as an institution from what the justices considered to be the distasteful and unseemly ordinary political process of the day. The bill's

> passage would set a precedent from which the institution of judicial review might never recover. It is not too much to say that the ambiguous and delicately balanced American tradition of limited government was mortally endangered by this bill. And it was offered by a President who had just received an overwhelming popular vote of confidence and who had not yet been denied in Congress any of his important demands. Even the five or six judges who had provoked this threat must have slept rather uneasily for a few months.[81]

The president's plan may have, thus, affected, if only subconsciously, the justices' voting behavior. "No one, perhaps not even Justice Roberts [one of the swing justices], could say which of these circumstances was decisive for him; but it is hard to doubt that they played a part in the new tone of judicial decision that began to be sounded in the early months of the year."[82] Hence, Roosevelt's attack on the legitimacy of the Court's decision-making and a thinly veiled attempt to restructure its membership served to demonstrate the boundary of the Court's authority and power within the U.S. political system.

While the proposal of Roosevelt's Court-packing plan is certainly an historically and politically significant event in Supreme Court history, only Schubert investigates empirically whether the plan is in fact associated with the Court becoming more liberal in its overall economic decision-making.[83] Schubert notes that the Court during the 1936 term (during which Roosevelt announced his plan) was composed of three voting coalitions: liberal (Cardozo, Brandeis, and Stone), right (Van Devanter, McReynolds, Sutherland, and Butler), and moderate (Hughes and Roberts).[84] Before Roosevelt announced his plan, Schubert finds that Hughes and Roberts voted with the right coalition more frequently than with the left. After the plan was announced, however, the moderates joined the left bloc at a much higher rate than they joined the right, presumably to move closer to the policy preferences of the president and, thus, to reduce the conflict with him.[85] Constructing strategies and incentives, Schubert adopts a game theoretic model ("the Hughbert Game") of the voting coalitions during the 1936 term year that would maximize the amount of power of each of the blocs, based upon the structural imperative of a minimum five-member majority coalition.[86] He finds that the actual voting behavior closely resembled the voting coalitions that his model predicted, thereby demonstrating the justices' strategic calculations. The Court's first alternative was to build a unanimous decision so as to show a united front to other political actors, notably the president and the Congress. If that alternative was not possible, then Hughes and Roberts's optimum strategy (as swing votes) was to align themselves with the liberal coalition because of the greater influence they gained as a result of forging a majority and because of the justices' perceived desire to move the Court's policy announcements closer to the president's preferred position.[87] Thus, Schubert implicitly asserts Roosevelt's plan increased the level of liberalism of the Court's decision-making.

Therefore, a variable measuring the effect of Roosevelt's Court-packing plan is estimated, along with the other variables discussed above. Since it is a discrete event, it is modeled as an intervention, taking the value zero (0) through the 1936 term year, and one (1) through 1945. Although Roosevelt's plan was sent to Congress in February of 1937, the intervention is not specified to begin to be effective until the following full term-year (1937) because there were several months during the previous period in which the intervention was not theoretically influential since Roosevelt had not yet proposed it. Thus,

H_{10}: President Franklin D. Roosevelt's Court-packing plan of 1937 is associated with an increase in the level of economic liberalism in the Court's decision-making.

Civil Liberties–Civil Rights Liberalism

An explanation of the Court's civil liberties–civil rights liberalism is also constructed. While this second aggregated issue area is a large part of the Court's current agenda, it is not a dominant portion of the docket prior to the 1950s, when economic concerns comprised the lion's share of the Court's rulings.[88] Nevertheless, to understand accurately the Court's decisional processes throughout the period from 1888 to 1997, one must examine the specific influences on this second type of institutional policy-making. Once again, recall that this aggregated issue dimension is its liberalism rate across the period from 1888 to 1997 for the individual issues contained within it. Following Spaeth,[89] this dimension includes criminal procedure, civil rights, First Amendment, privacy, and due process cases. The variable, as discussed in prior chapters, is calculated as a percentage. As with economic liberalism, a mean is calculated for each term year.

POLICY VIEWS OF THE JUSTICES

There are several influences on the Court's civil liberties–civil rights decision-making that could be included in a model. In this analysis, however, a select few of these are included due, in part, to concerns of parsimony. Two of the independent variables that are used in this specification of civil liberties–civil rights liberalism (party identification and agricultural origins) are also used above in the development of an explanation of the Court's economic liberalism. A brief discussion of their relationship to civil rights–liberties policy views is thus in order.

Agricultural Origins

The process of industrialization and urbanization tend to engender liberal attitudes among urban residents. Those persons who were socialized in agrarian areas tend to develop conservative attitudes toward these issues. Hence the association of the justices' agricultural origins' relationship with the Court's decision-making is expected to be negative. Thus,

H_{11}: As the mean of the number of justices with agricultural origins increases, the liberalism of the Court in civil liberties–civil rights matters decreases.

Party Identification

The direction of the hypothetical association of the proportion of the justices' party identification, however, changes in direction in the context of developing an explanation of the Court's institutional civil liberties decision-making.[90] Whereas the Democrats are during the pre-1945 period of analysis generally thought to be more supportive of economic liberalism than were Republicans, the opposite is true in the civil liberties context. "There is a seeming paradox in the liberal's attitude toward the state, for he welcomes its intervention in economic affairs, but seeks to limit very severely its restrictions on individual expression of intellectual and physical freedom. In the former area, liberalism is typically pro-state; in the latter, its fundamental bias is anti-statist."[91] The opposite is true in the civil liberties juridical context. Accordingly,

H_{12}: As the mean of the justices' party identifications increases, the Court's institutional civil liberties liberalism increases.

Prosecutorial-Judicial Experience

The third variable in this specification of the Court's civil liberties decision-making is the justices' preappointment prosecutorial and judicial experience. Like judicial experience alone, a justice's experience as a prosecutor can serve to shape his or her attitudes and policy preferences, especially those relating to civil liberties. These experiences alternatively may demonstrate that the justices hold conservative policy views. As a prosecutor, the justice advocated the government's position, arguing in a court of law against granting a dissident or civil liberties claimant some freedom or granting a criminal defendant some protection or procedural right.[92] These prior career experiences may influence the justice to hold attitudes that are generally not supportive of expanded civil liberties. These attitudes bring the justice into conflict with liberal civil liberties policy preferences. Tate and Handberg suggest that a justice's prior prosecutorial experience is best modeled as an interaction with any prior judicial experience that he or she may have.[93] They argue that judicial experience may moderate the much more conservative influence of prior prosecutorial service. Indeed, at the individual level of analysis, they find that there is a negative relationship with civil liberties liberalism, while an index measuring only the justices' prior judicial experiences is not significantly associated with their voting behavior.[94] Justices who have been prosecutors, but have not held judicial office, are less liberal than those who have been prosecutors and judges, who are in turn less liberal than those justices who have held neither office.[95]

Haynie and Tate also examine the effect of a justice's combined prosecutorial and judicial experience at the institutional level of analysis. They find that the coefficient for this variable is negatively signed and marginally significant.[96] Following these authors' protocol, the variable is scored in this manner: two (2) for justices with no prosecutorial or judicial experience; one (1) for justices with both prior prosecutorial and judicial experience, or with judicial experience only; and, zero (0) for those justices who had only experience as a prosecutor. An index is specified here, as with judicial experience in the analysis of economic decision-making, because a large number of the justices had no prior judicial experience. Thus,

H_{13}: As the mean of the justices' prosecutorial-judicial experience increases, the Court's institutional civil liberties liberalism increases.

COURT'S EXTERNAL ENVIRONMENT

Wars

Perhaps the most influential events that influence the Court's civil liberties policy-making are wars in which the United States is a participant. Because of the perceived threat that political dissidents or protestors represent to national security, the Court has historically been less receptive to civil liberties claims during times of war. "As Justice Holmes wrote, '[w]hen a nation is at war many things that might be said in times of peace are such a hindrance to its effort that their utterance will not be endured so long as men fight.'"[97] Three of the wars in which the U.S. has been involved are considered here.[98]

They are modeled as interventions or shocks to the Court's civil liberties liberalism, since they theoretically affect the Court's decision-making only at discrete times. These are the Spanish-American War (1898), World War I (1914–19), and World War II (1939–45). They are hypothesized to be initially associated with a decline in the Court's liberalism because of the extant threat to the nation's security. Thus,

H_{14}: The occurrence of the Spanish-American War (1898) is associated with a decrease in the Court's civil liberties liberalism.

H_{15}: The occurrence of World War I (1914–19) is associated with a decrease in the Court's civil liberties liberalism.

H_{16}: The occurrence of World War II (1939–45) is associated with a decrease in the Court's civil liberties liberalism.

Judicial Power Liberalism

While economics and civil liberties decisions comprise the bulk of the Court's decision-making across the 110 term years analyzed in this study, the Court also considered a large number of cases that involved issues of judicial power.[99] Indeed, an investigation of the influence on the Court's decisional processes for this issue area is an appropriate inquiry because since the 1930s, the government has become more involved in the economic and social order of the nation. Because the courts are a significant element of the American political structure, the Supreme Court's policy preferences in decisions involving issues of judicial power empirically demonstrate the contours of its liberalism, beyond the large scale effects that arise from its economics and civil liberties-policy-making. The measure of the Court's liberalism in judicial power decisions is, similar to the decisional measures for economics and civil liberties, a percentage.

POLICY VIEWS OF THE JUSTICES

There are four continuous variables that are modeled in this analysis of judicial power liberalism. They are: the justices' party identifications, their religious affiliations, their agricultural origins, and their preappointment judicial experience. The first two variables (justices' partisan affiliations and religious preferences) are all hypothesized to be positively associated with the dependent variable because of the generally increasing liberalism with which they are associated in other decisional contexts (see the above analysis of the Court's economic liberalism). Hence,

H_{17}: As the proportion of the Democrats on the Supreme Court increases, the Court's judicial power liberalism increases.

H_{18}: As the proportion of non-Protestants on the Supreme Court increases, the Court's judicial power liberalism increases.

The latter two variables (the justices' agricultural backgrounds and their extent of prior judicial experience) are hypothesized to be negatively associated with the dependent variable. The agrarian context in which a justice spends his or her formative years is associated with a conservative tendency in political attitudes, and, in turn, in Supreme Court voting behavior.[100]

Hence,

H_{19}: As the mean number of justices with agricultural origins increases, the Court's judicial power liberalism decreases.

The prior career experience of judicial service is mixed in its effect. Some studies find that it is positively associated with liberal economics and civil liberties decision-making.[101] Other studies assert a negative relationship with voting behavior.[102] In the context of judicial power decision-making, however, this study proposes that greater judicial experience on lower courts serves to educate judges about the limits of the judiciary's authority and the restrictions of the process on the injection of their partisan attitudes into their decision-making. Hence,

H_{20}: As the prior judicial experience of the justices of the Supreme Court increases, the Court's liberalism in judicial power cases decreases.

COURT'S EXTERNAL ENVIRONMENT

Jurisdictional Changes

The Congress should theoretically exert some degree of influence on the Court's decision-making. Under the Constitution, the Congress has the power to restrict the Court's jurisdiction. The federal legislature has, in fact, transformed it over time as we have seen. Congress can also determine how much the justices' salaries will be raised and how many Court members there are. The justices, thus, have several incentives to avoid conflict with Congress.[103] Hence, Congress may influence the Court's decision-making.

The single intervention hypothesized to represent the influence of Congress on the Court's judicial power liberalism policy-making during the period at hand is the promulgation of the Judges' Bill. The passage of the act may have signaled the Court that courts generally should be involved in more matters and be given more power of administration than they had in prior years. Halpern and Vines conclude that "[a]n enlarged discretionary jurisdiction broadened the Court's opportunities to provide cues to litigants, encouraging the appeal of certain issues while discouraging others. In these ways, the Judges' Bill enhanced the opportunities of the justices to pursue a variety of judicial strategies to advance goals consonant with their values and to make the high tribunal a more 'activist' institution."[104] Hence,

$H_{21:}$ After the enactment of the Judiciary Act of 1925,[105] the Court's judicial power liberalism increases.

FRACTIONAL INTEGRATION, NONSTATIONARITY, AND COINTEGRATION

The models of Supreme Court liberalism are estimated using fractional cointegration and error-correction models. Accordingly, a brief review of these methods is in order. When working with time serial data, the analyst must first insure that the series in question are stationary; otherwise spurious regressions may result.[106] Traditionally, analysts have dealt with this problem by taking the first differences of the data.[107] Long-memoried series that can be made into stationary, or short-term, series by taking the first differences of the series are said to be integrated of order one, denoted $I(1)$. They are therefore described as having a unit root.[108] More generally, a series is referred to being integrated to the order of d ($I(d)$), where d is the number of differences needed to make the series stationary. This general form implies that the value of the differencing parameter need not be constrained to integers (e.g., 0 *or* 1). That is, a series' d value may take on noninteger values (e.g., $0 < d < 1$). If so, then the series is referred to as being *fractionally integrated*.[109]

These characteristics have profound implications for researchers who seek to accurately model their underlying data-generating process. First, by fractionally differencing variables, researchers are able to more accurately capture the data-generating process underlying their data.[110] Imposing the restriction that their data exhibit the perfect memory of a unit root, or no memory entirely, implies a profound implication about the nature of one's data, which can be avoided if one is open to the potential for the fractional structure of the data.[111] Second, if researchers were to take the first difference of a data series when in fact the series is fractionally integrated, that transformation may serve to create patterns in the data that are not naturally present.[112] By measuring the degree of a series's fractional integration, researchers can avoid the "knife-edge" decision that they otherwise would have had to make as whether there data were stationary ($I(0)$) or described by a unit root ($I(1)$) and, thus, have greater confidence in the results obtained with a fractionally differenced variable.[113] Third, an understanding of the origin of fractional dynamics may assist researchers in identifying the proper degree of differencing for a series. Granger asserts that when heterogeneous individual-level data are aggregated, fractional dynamics result in the time series since the aggregate series is produced by different autoregressive and/or moving average components that describe the individuals' behavior that is being combined.[114] In more formal terms, a series composed of other micro-level series that are described by AR(p) processes where p (the degree of autoregressiveness) varies among the different individuals will be fractionally integrated.[115] For the purposes of this study, it is quite likely that the series measuring the Court's decision-making are fractionally integrated because they are the aggregate of the individual justices' voting behavior and social attributes. This data structure may also be present because the justices will exhibit differential levels of adherence to the notion of a restraintist judicial role.[116]

Tests of Fractional Integration

Accordingly, we first test each of the present variables to determine whether they are fractionally integrated. To do so, we employ Robinson's Gaussian semiparametric estimation procedure.[117] When implementing this procedure, one must difference the data first to avoid the estimation of the "troublesome intercept parameter."[118] Hence, Robinson's test statistic arises from the estimates of $(0,1+d,0)$ on first-differenced data due to the constrained parameter space (i.e., $-1.5 < d < .5$) and to ensure that the data are stationary.[119] Thus, to determine the order of integration of the level-form data, one must add 1.0 to the estimate of d.

Table 6-1 presents the results of these tests. As one can see, all three liberalism series are fractionally integrated, with estimates for economic and civil liberties–civil rights liberalism midway between zero and one, and that of judicial power liberalism closer to zero than one. The political values variables, on the other hand, are much more proximal to one and are, thus, known as "near-integrated data."[120] As such, if one were to have wholly differenced all the variables, one most likely would have obtained spurious results. With these more precise estimates, the variables can individually be made stationary $(I(0))$ based on their own respective data structures. Hence, more accurate and valid estimates of their relationships to the other variables in the model can be obtained.

Unit Root Tests

Traditionally, the well-known Dickey-Fuller (DF) and Augmented Dickey-Fuller (ADF) tests have been widely used to determine if a series is stationary.[121] The results from these unit root tests are presented in Table 6-2. While some of the series reject the null hypothesis of the presence of a unit root under the DF test, the results of the ADF tests demonstrate that the series are most likely nonstationary. All the series (except judicial power) fail

TABLE 6-1. POINT ESTIMATES OF THE ORDER OF INTEGRATION (D) OF THE
ECONOMIC, CIVIL RIGHTS/LIBERTIES AND JUDICIAL POWER LIBERALISM
AND POLITICAL VALUES VARIABLES FOR THE UNITED STATES
SUPREME COURT, 1888-1997

Series	Robinson's (1995) Gaussian Semiparametric Estimate of d[1]	H_o: $d=0^2$	H_o: $d=1^2$
Economic Liberalism	0.51 (0.068)	-7.13	7.42
Civil Rights/Liberties Liberalism	0.55 (0.068)	-6.55	8.08
Judicial Power Liberalism	0.33 (0.068)	-9.75	4.80
Presidential Intentions	1.16 (0.068)	2.32	16.88
Religious Affiliation	0.97 (0.068)	-0.43	14.12
Prosecutorial-Judicial Experience	1.01 (0.068)	0.14	14.70
Judicial Experience Index	1.02 (0.068)	0.29	14.85
Party Affiliation	1.01 (0.068)	0.14	14.70
Agricultural Origins	0.85 (0.068)	-2.18	12.37
Southern Region	0.91 (0.068)	-1.31	13.24

[1]The numbers in parentheses are the standard error of the estimate of d. The estimates are for level-form data.
[2]These are the t-ratios of the null hypothesis that $d=0$ and $d=1$.

to reject the null in the ADF models with a constant and a trend term. Thus, we can conclude that the series are characterized by some nonstationarity.

However, the DF and ADF tests have limited power in the presence of fractional alternatives. The Kwiatkowski, Phillips, Schmidt, and Shinn (KPSS) test is more robust to fractionally integrated series than are the DF or ADF tests.[122] The test statistic's null hypothesis is that the series is stationary. KPSS discuss the appropriate lag length that one should use in calculating the test statistic. Based on that discussion and the size of the samples we examine here, we use a lag of four as the preferred lag at which to determine if the series tested herein are stationary. Table 6-3 reports these results. The series all reject the null hypothesis of stationarity at conventional levels of statistical significance on one or both of the test measures. Further, results of variance ratio tests suggest that the series are nonstationary.[123] Taken together, these findings allow one to provisionally conclude

TABLE 6-2. RESULTS OF DICKEY-FULLER AND AUGMENTED DICKEY-FULLER
UNIT ROOT TESTS ON ECONOMIC, CIVIL RIGHTS/LIBERTIES AND
JUDICIAL POWER LIBERALISM AND POLITICAL VALUES
VARIABLES FOR THE UNITED STATES
SUPREME COURT, 1888-1997

Series	Dickey-Fuller Tests[1]	Augmented Dickey-Fuller Tests		Number of Lags[2]
	Constant, No Trend	Constant, No Trend	Constant and Trend	
Policy Preferences				
Economic Liberalism	-5.078	-3.322	-3.283	(1)
Civil Rights/Liberties				
Liberalism	-4.288	-3.071	-3.381	(2)
Judicial Power Liberalism	-7.022	-8.824	-8.870	(1)
Political Values				
Presidential Intentions	-1.240	-1.760	-1.635	(3)
Religious Affiliation	-1.727	-1.692	-1.704	(4)
Prosecutorial-Judicial Exp.	-2.787	-3.214	-2.976	(3)
Judicial Experience Index	-0.721	-0.482	-0.011	(4)
Party Affiliation	-1.534	-1.593	-1.337	(3)
Agricultural Origins	-3.090	-1.904	-1.931	(4)
Southern Region	-2.385	-2.239	-2.789	(3)
Critical Values (p<.05)	-2.88	-2.88	-3.45	--

[1]The Dickey-Fuller tests are t-tests to determine whether $\rho = 1$ or $(\rho - 1) = 0$. MacKinnon provides the critical values. James C. MacKinnon, "Critical Values for Cointegration Tests," in *Long-Run Economic Relationships: Readings in Cointegration*, eds. Robert F. Engle and Clive W. J. Granger (New York: Oxford University Press, 1991).

[2]The number of lags for the ADF tests were selected based on a minimization of the Schawrz Information Criterion.

that not only are the series in question nonstationary, but they are also most likely fractionally integrated.

Cointegration: Estimating the Long-Run Relationship

Engle and Granger argue that differencing series that one is investigating eliminates the long-run relationship among the series and limits the analyst to examining only the short-run relationship between them; while if the data are left in their level, undifferenced form spurious results may be obtained.[124] Engle and Granger propose a solution to this conundrum. Their "two-step process" is well-known in the econometric literature and has recently begun to be used by political scientists within many subfields.[125]

If the series are nonstationary,[126] then the researcher interested in testing for the presence of cointegration regresses the dependent variable of interest on the exogenous variable in their respective level, undifferenced forms; the residuals from that regression are themselves tested for stationarity. If the residuals from this initial regression are stationary, then under the

TABLE 6-3. RESULTS OF KWIATKOWSKI ET. AL (KPSS) (1992) UNIT ROOT TESTS

Series	Lag Truncation Parameter (l)				
	$l=0$	$l=2$	$l=4$	$l=6$	$l=8$
Economic Liberalism					
Constant, No Trend (η_μ)	1.044	0.484	0.339	0.268	0.225
Constant and Trend (η_τ)	1.022	0.475	0.332	0.263	0.221
Civil Rights/Liberties Liberalism					
Constant, No Trend (η_μ)	3.402	1.434	0.927	0.691	0.561
Constant and Trend (η_τ)	0.912	0.416	0.279	0.213	0.177
Judicial Power Liberalism					
Constant, No Trend (η_μ)	1.888	1.080	0.749	0.600	0.483
Constant and Trend (η_τ)	0.654	0.417	0.300	0.237	0.201
Presidential Policy Intentions					
Constant, No Trend (η_μ)	2.234	0.773	0.482	0.359	0.292
Constant and Trend (η_τ)	2.059	0.713	0.445	0.332	0.270
Religious Affiliation					
Constant, No Trend (η_μ)	0.865	0.331	0.224	0.180	0.158
Constant and Trend (η_τ)	0.754	0.286	0.191	0.152	0.132
Prosecutorial-Judicial Experience					
Constant, No Trend (η_μ)	2.824	1.043	0.687	0.542	0.467
Constant and Trend (η_τ)	0.712	0.270	0.182	0.148	0.133
Judicial Experience Index					
Constant, No Trend (η_μ)	2.347	0.817	0.508	0.376	0.301
Constant and Trend (η_τ)	2.163	0.755	0.471	0.349	0.280
Party Affiliation					
Constant, No Trend (η_μ)	1.763	0.621	0.390	0.292	0.240
Constant and Trend (η_τ)	1.322	0.467	0.294	0.221	0.182
Agricultural Origins					
Constant, No Trend (η_μ)	2.070	0.801	0.539	0.415	0.340
Constant and Trend (η_τ)	0.894	0.352	0.240	0.187	0.154
Southern Region					
Constant, No Trend (η_μ)	1.710	0.633	0.414	0.321	0.269
Constant and Trend (η_τ)	1.108	0.413	0.272	0.212	0.179

Note: Critical values for KPSS tests come from Kwiatkowski *et al.* (1992). The critical values ($p<.05$) for (η_μ) and (η_τ) are 0.463 and 0.146, respectively. The KPSS test proposes a null hypothesis that the series is characterized by a strong mixing process and thus stationary. The recommended lag truncation (l) is given by KPSS (1992: 169-73): l=integer[4(T/100)$^{.25}$] = 4 for these series.

Granger Representation Theorem,[127] the series are said to cointegrate because, while the individual series are nonstationary, a linear combination of them (as captured in the residuals of their regression) is stationary.[128] Thus,

$$Y_t = \beta X_t + \hat{\varepsilon}_t \text{ where } \hat{\varepsilon}_t = \rho\hat{\varepsilon}_{t-1} + \upsilon_t \text{ and } \upsilon_t \sim N(0, \sigma^2) \quad (1)$$

In Equation 1 if ρ is stationary (i.e., I(0)), then the series are cointegrated. An analyst can then conclude that the series exhibit a long-run relationship that will trend toward an equilibrium. Table 6-4 presents the results of the initial cointegrating regressions of policy preferences and political values of the Court. Overall, the findings suggest that each of the series are cointegrated. In both the economic and civil liberties–civil rights models, three of the five exogenous variables are statistically significant, even at stringent levels. The coefficient estimates for presidential intentions, party affiliation, judicial experience and agricultural origins are all quite robust. For judicial power, however, only the index of judicial experience is significant, which is not unexpected for this series that taps into the justices' policy views of the exercise of political influence. Also, the models are each characterized by relatively high R^2 and relatively low Durbin-Watson (d) statistics, which are features of cointegrating relationships.

Table 6-5 presents the results of the unit root tests on the residuals of the cointegrating regressions presented in Table 6-4. The tests generally indicate that the residuals of all three models are stationary, even at high levels of statistical significance. The KPSS tests also indicate that the residuals are stationary[129] and, thus, integrated of order zero (I(0)). Hence, based on the results presented in Tables 6-4 and 6-5, following the Granger Representation Theorem, we can provisionally conclude that economic, civil liberties–civil rights and judicial power policy views are each related in the long run to those proxies of the justices' political values.

FRACTIONAL COINTEGRATION

In the same manner as the degree of fractional integration of the liberalism and political values series are estimated, we estimate the degree of integration of the residuals of the initial cointegrating regressions, which are the empirical manifestations of the long-run relationship between the series (denoted as an ECM). Traditionally, cointegration analysts have assumed that the ECM terms (the residuals of the initial specifications) were integrated of the order of zero (I(0)). Recently, however, some practitioners have chosen to not make that assumption, since the Granger Representation Theorem only requires that the cointegrating vector be stationary; one need not require it to be an I(0) process.[130] This is a theoretically important assumption about the underlying data-generating process: "[f]inding fractional cointegration between two variables gives us insight into how the equilibrium relationship between the two variables reacts to exogenous shocks. Just as fractional cointegration methods avoid the knife-edged distinction between a series being I(0) and I(1), fractional cointegration methods avoid making the same claim about the residual series of a cointegrating regression."[131] Estimating the fractional structure of the ECM term provides analysts with a more precise understanding of the dynamic process

TABLE 6-4. COINTEGRATING REGRESSIONS OF ECONOMIC, CIVIL RIGHTS/LIBERTIES
AND JUDICIAL POWER POLICY PREFERENCES AND POLITICAL VALUES
OF THE UNITED STATES SUPREME COURT, 1888-1997

Regressors	Economic Liberalism[1]	Civil Rights/Liberties Liberalism[2]	Judicial Power Liberalism[3]
Presidential Intentions	8.08 (2.52)[4]	13.30 (2.33)	-2.39 (-0.41)
Judicial Experience Index	-9.64 (-3.05)	-----	-19.31 (-3.68)
Prosecutorial/Judicial Exp.	-----	-17.63 (-1.40)	-----
Party Affiliation	-3.11 (-0.93)	15.46 (2.48)	0.10 (0.02)
Agricultural Origins	-28.70 (-2.99)	-9.76 (-0.54)	-3.51 (-0.22)
Southern Region	21.72 (2.58)	-18.14 (-1.04)	-10.53 (-0.76)
Constant	73.99	53.03	45.61

[1]R^2=0.485, Durbin-Watson=1.42, SEE=7.95
[2]R^2=0.319, Durbin-Watson=0.87, SEE=15.73
[3]R^2=0.271, Durbin-Watson=1.74, SEE=13.02
[4]Numbers in parentheses are t-scores.

TABLE 6-5. UNIT ROOT TESTS ON RESIDUALS OF COINTEGRATION REGRESSIONS

Test	Economic Liberalism Residuals	Civil Rights/Liberties Liberalism Residuals	Judicial Power Liberalism Residuals	Critical Value (p<.05)
Dickey-Fuller Test				
Constant, No Trend	-7.82[1]	-5.50	-9.11	-2.88
Augmented Dickey-Fuller Test				
Constant, No Trend	-5.53	-3.87	-6.09	-3.45
KPSS Tests				
l=0	0.12[2]	1.48	0.65	0.46
l=2	0.08	0.72	0.52	0.46
l=4	0.07	0.50	0.43	0.46
l=6	0.06	0.37	0.38	0.46
l=8	0.06	0.34	0.35	0.46
l=0	0.06[3]	0.27	0.07	0.14
l=2	0.04	0.14	0.06	0.14
l=4	0.03	0.11	0.06	0.14
l=6	0.03	0.08	0.05	0.14
l=8	0.03	0.07	0.05	0.14

[1]Results from the ADF Test for the residuals for all three models demonstrate that the DF tests have lower Schwarz Information Criteria and thus are preferred in this context. The ADF test results are reported for comparative purposes.

[2]This first set of results are (η_μ) statistics.

[3]This second set of results are (η_τ) statistics.

describing the relationship between the cointegrating variables. Thus, allowing the ECM to take on noninteger values suggests that shocks to the system decay more slowly than the exponential rate of dissipation that describes ARIMA processes. Therefore, an analyst must ensure that the order of integration of the ECM term and the parent series be accurately estimated. For a series to be fractionally cointegrated, the cointegrating residuals (d') need only be integrated of a lower order than are the respective parent series (d). Hence, if $d' < d$, then the series are fractionally cointegrated.[132] Just as with the parent series, the analyst must fractionally difference the ECM term to avoid the problems of spuriousness, using its estimated order of integration (d') to reduce it to $I = 0$. This study once again employs Robinson's protocol to obtain those estimates.[133]

Table 6-6 displays the point estimates of the order of integration of each of the ECM terms for the three models of liberalism. The results show that each of the ECM terms is fractionally integrated because they are integrated of a lower order than are the corresponding parent series. In addition, because the estimates are less than 0.5, they possess characteristics more akin to a stationary series and, thus, they are mean-reverting and have finite variance. The t-statistics for the ECM terms allow us to reject the hypotheses that the order of integration is at either extreme; because they significantly differ from zero, the series are long memoried. These findings imply that a shock to one of the variables in the system will persist longer than a geometric decay may suggest, but that the shock will eventually dissipate as the variables return to an equilibrium.[134] Hence, had I treated

TABLE 6-6. SEMIPARAMETRIC ESTIMATES OF THE ORDER OF INTEGRATION (d') OF THE ERROR CORRECTION MECHANISM FOR THREE COINTEGRATING REGRESSIONS OF ECONOMIC, CIVIL RIGHTS/LIBERTIES AND JUDICIAL POWER LIBERALISM OF THE UNITED STATES SUPREME COURT, 1888-1997

Series	Robinson's Gaussian Semiparametric Estimate of d'[1]	H_o: $d' = 0$[2]	H_o: $d' = 1$[2]
Economic Liberalism ECM	0.46	-7.86	6.70
Civil Rights/Liberties Liberalism ECM	0.49	-7.42	7.13
Judicial Power Liberalism ECM	0.29	-10.34	4.22

[1]Because of the constrained parameter space (*i.e.*, -1.5<d'<.5), estimates were completed on first-differenced data (0,d'+1,0). Thus, the reported results actually reflect the estimates of d'+1. The numbers in parentheses are the standard error of the estimate of d'.

[2]These are the t-ratios for the null hypothesis that d'=0 and d'=1.

these ECMs as wholly stationary, I may have obtained invalid results. Thus, these empirical manifestations of the long-run relationship between the justices' political values and their decision-making in these specific three aggregated issue areas have some characteristics of both unit root and stationary series. These fractional residuals are employed in the subsequent phases of the modeling endeavor herein.

The Long-Run Relationship between the Justices' Policy Preferences and Political Values

Two cointegrating series may be expressed in what is termed an "error-correction model."[135] Thus,

$$\Delta X_t = \alpha_1 + \beta_1 (Y_{t-1} - \gamma_0 - \gamma_1 X_{t-1}) + \text{lags of } \Delta X, \Delta Y + \hat{\epsilon}_{1t} \quad (2)$$

$$\Delta Y_t = \alpha_2 + \beta_2 (Y_{t-1} - \gamma_0 - \gamma_2 X_{t-1}) + \text{lags of } \Delta X, \Delta Y + \hat{\epsilon}_{2t} \quad (3)$$

Equations (2) and (3) represent the long-term and short-term effects of the cointegrating variables on the level of the dependent variable.[136] The long-term effect is expressed by the error correction term, which is the residuals of the original cointegrating regression of X and Y (denoted by the β terms), in level form. Thus, an error-correction model may be generally expressed:

$$\Delta Y_t = \alpha + \beta Z_{n-1} + \text{lags of } \Delta X, \Delta Y + \hat{\epsilon}_t \quad (4)$$

in which Z_{n-1} is the error-correction mechanism. The degree to which the series returns to its pre-shock level is captured by the coefficient of the error correction term. The coefficient of the error correction term should range between zero (0) and negative one (-1), indicating the extent to which the series returns to a long-run equilibrium. For example, if the estimated value of the ECM coefficient is -0.55, then 45 percent of the impact of the shock to the system carries over to the second period and so forth for each successive period.[137] Thus, by the use of an error correction model, a researcher is able to test both for the long-run changes in policy preferences (as expressed by the ECM term), and any short-term changes (expressed in part by the differenced forms of the justices' social attributes). Hence, one can determine how quickly the functional system returns to an equilibrium after it experiences a shock. Similarly, short-term effects may be associated with historic events or incidents (such as wars) that occurred within the Court's external environment.

Table 6-7 presents the estimated coefficients of error correction models for Economic Liberalism, Civil Rights/Liberties Liberalism and Judicial Power Liberalism. The continuous independent variables and the error correction terms are fractionally differenced based on the respective estimates of d or d' reported above. The dummy variables are each lagged one period. The first finding the table displays is that each of the error-correction terms (Z_{t-1}) are significant and signed between 0 and -1, consistent with our hypothesis that there is a cointegrating relationship between the variables. For "Economic Liberalism" in particular, the estimated coefficient is -0.27, indicating that 73 percent of exogenous shocks to the system remain in second period following the shock, about 53 percent in the third period, and so forth. In the "Civil Rights/Liberties" model, the estimated coefficient is -0.18, suggesting that 82 percent of exogenous shocks to the system remain in the second period and 67 percent in the following period. For the "Judicial Power" model, the estimated coefficient for the ECM term is -0.28, similar in magnitude to that for the economic liberalism model, implying that 71 percent of the shock remains in the second subsequent period. These findings together demonstrate that shocks in the Court's decision-making environment tend to affect the Court for several periods after the shock occurred.

Specifically, looking at the interventions modeled for each series, we see that the Great Depression is associated with an increase in the level of the Court's economic liberalism. Yet, FDR's Court-packing plan of 1937 does not serve to make the Court significantly more liberal. Indeed, Schwartz reports that the Court had already come to its fateful decision in *NLRB v. Jones-Laughlin Steel* (although the ruling had not yet been publicly announced) when the president proposed his restructuring of the Court.[138] Although the estimate of the Spanish-American War is negatively signed consistent with our hypotheses, it does not reach conventional levels of statistical significance. Yet, World War I is associated with a decreased level of liberalism in the Court's civil liberties–civil rights rulings. This finding is consistent with theoretical expectations, given the observations of historical analyses that have found that the Court's civil liberties jurisprudence (particularly, free speech decisions) became less liberal during that time.[139]

However, the conservative effect of World War II on the Court's policy preferences is not borne out by these analyses, which is contrary to Haynie and Tate's finding.[140] But, those authors analyze only nonunanimous decisions. At first blush, the statistical insignificance of the occurrence of World War II may be cause for concern. Yet, Pritchett suggests that the Court may have understood that it need not be as restrictive in its decision-making as it was during the World War I era, because the fears and concerns for national security were simply exaggerated then;[141] there are, of course,

TABLE 6-7. ERROR-CORRECTION MODELS OF ECONOMIC, CIVIL RIGHTS/LIBERTIES AND JUDICIAL LIBERALISM OF THE UNITED STATES SUPREME COURT, 1888-1997

Regressors	Economic Liberalism Model[1]	Civil Rights/Liberties Liberalism Model[2]	Judicial Power Liberalism Model[3]
$\Delta^5 Z_{t-1}$ (ECM Term)	-0.27 (-2.67)[4]	-0.18 (-1.92)	-0.28 (-2.77)
Δ_f Presidential Intentions	9.19 (1.29)	28.88 (2.63)	4.14 (0.38)
Δ_f Judicial Experience Index	5.49 (0.76)	-----	-10.68 (-0.93)
Δ_f Prosecutorial/Judicial Exp.	-----	30.21 (1.30)	-----
Δ_f Party Affiliation	4.04 (0.56)	-6.82 (-0.61)	-8.72 (-0.74)
Δ_f Agricultural Origins	-15.93 (-1.00)	17.99 (0.77)	-6.72 (-0.26)
Δ_f Southern Region	9.84 (0.63)	-18.81 (-0.77)	29.91 (1.18)
Great Depression$_{t-1}$	6.69 (2.42)	-----	-----
Court-Packing Plan$_{t-1}$	0.51 (0.17)	-----	-----
Election of T. Roosevelt$_{t-1}$	-1.41 (-0.55)	-----	-----
Panic of 1893$_{t-1}$	4.77 (1.02)	-----	-----
Spanish-American War$_{t-1}$	-----	-18.30 (-1.48)	-----
World War I$_{t-1}$	-----	-11.15 (-2.00)	-----
World War II$_{t-1}$	-----	-6.57 (-1.30)	-----
Judiciary Act of 1925$_{t-1}$	-----	-----	4.59 (1.75)
Constant	1.80	1.34	-1.21

[1] R^2=0.19, Adj. R^2=.10, Durbin-Watson=1.80, SEE=7.88
[2] R^2=0.14, Adj. R^2=.06, Durbin-Watson=1.99, SEE=12.11
[3] R^2=0.10, Adj. R^2=.04, Durbin-Watson=2.00, SEE=12.79
[4] Numbers in parentheses are t-scores.
[5] Δ_f denotes that the associated variables are fractionally differenced.

notable exceptions in the Court's decision-making to this proposal (e.g., *Korematsu v. United States*).[142] Thus, the Court may have been more supportive of civil liberties claims than it had been in previous times of war.

Moreover, the enactment of the Judges' Bill is positively associated with the Court's policy preferences in judicial power decisions. Hence, in addition to the effects associated with a change in membership, the Court's aggregate policy preferences are associated with the occurrence of several external events within the institution's political environment.

CHAPTER SUMMARY

During the last one hundred years or so, the Supreme Court's docket has been dominated by economics and civil liberties–civil rights decisions as the nation worked its way through the Panic of 1893, Progressivism, the Great Depression, the Spanish-American War, and two world wars. Judicial power decisions have come to represent a quantitatively significant portion of the Court's agenda as well. During this period, the Court's decision-making is shown to be largely stable, even amid these turbulent times. I examine the relationship among the justices' political values and their policy views, as expressed in the Court's rulings in those three policy domains. This study reports several important findings.

First, this study demonstrates that the aggregate measures of liberalism and several of the proxies of the justices' political values are fractionally or near-integrated. The policy views measures are most clearly fractionally integrated, while the attitudinal proxies are most probably near-integrated.[143] This is an important finding in that it suggests that scholars may need to carefully consider the fractional order of integration of their series, especially when a series is an aggregate of individual behavior, as most data on Supreme Court behavior are, rather than simply opting to wholly difference data that may not in fact be characterized by unit roots. They then can choose the most appropriate measure of stationarity to conduct and, in turn, fractionally difference the data accordingly. By vigilantly examining the structure and the genesis of their data, scholars may come to more satisfying results, both empirically and theoretically.

Second, I find that the Court's policy views in the three domains and the political values of its members are, in fact, related in the long run. That is, they are long-memoried processes. Indeed, one would expect that the three concepts would be associated across time because justices do come to the bench with well-formed ideological views that affect their voting behavior, thus bolstering the attitudinal influences on the Court.[144] These views arise, in part, from their respective social backgrounds.[145] This is an important finding because prior studies have been limited largely to the post-1945 period, when the Court has become arguably more involved in the political actions of the coordinate branches of government.[146] Indeed, the Court's economic rulings become more liberal after the Great Depression. The findings also show that the Judges' Bill is associated with an increase in the Court's liberalism rate in its judicial power rulings, thereby extending the findings of other studies of the effect of external events to include an expansion of the Court's discretionary jurisdiction. Having found that even pre-1945 Courts' rulings are associated with the justices' political values demonstrates that the attitudinal component of the Court's behavior extends further back in time than scholars have as yet demonstrated. Also, it demonstrates an element of the stability that the Court as an institution has enjoyed, despite dramatic, large-scale events in the Court's exogenous political environment.

Third, although the Court's political values do serve as a long-run equilibrium for its decision-making, the strength of that relationship is not monolithic but rather dynamic and much less strong than expected, both critical findings. For all three policy domains, exogenous shocks to the system tend to affect the Court for several periods after the shocks occur, much longer than prior literature has suggested. These results imply that the Court's policy preferences, as expressed in their voting behavior, do return to the preshock level, but only very slowly as the effects of the interventions decay. This view, while somewhat contrary to previous findings, does provide a picture of the Court that is consistent with what we know about the Court: its members attend to and consider carefully the expected behavior of other relevant actors so as to strategically attain their respective goals.[147] To do otherwise would be ill-advised. Hence, the results suggest that the behavior of the Court is not simply a function of the members' unmediated policy views, but also dependent on events outside the Court building that may impact the relative utility of favoring one policy view over another. Thus, the Court's decision-making is less insulated than we may have otherwise believed from the "profane hand of politics."[148]

7

The Continuity of Change:
The Supreme Court across Time

THIS CHAPTER SUMMARIZES THE FINDINGS DISCUSSED IN THE PRIOR CHAPTERS and discusses the implications of the study. It also offers suggestions for future research in the field of judicial politics.

OVERVIEW OF THE BOOK'S FINDINGS

This study examines the agenda-setting and decision-making behavior of the United States Supreme Court from 1888 to 1997. Its primary analytical focus, however, is on the period prior to 1945, since the bulk of the existing research investigates the behavior of the Court in the post–World War II period.

Importance of the Dataset

One important aspect of this study is to explore a newly created dataset that contains original data on the Court's agenda-setting and voting behavior across more than a century of jurisprudence. Prior studies have been primarily limited to investigating the Court's behavior in the post-1945 period. The dataset employed in the present study enables more long-term analyses than have heretofore been completed, during a period that contained many important historic events, such as World Wars I and II, the Panic of 1893, the Great Depression, the New Deal, and Franklin Roosevelt's attack on the Court. Accordingly, these results obtained from such studies may be more generalizable than findings of those studies limited to the post-1945 period.

Workload and Agenda Dynamics

During the period of analysis, the present study finds that the Court's workload has declined. The Court issues an historic high of 292 decisions in 1913, but the number of cases on its docket during each term year steadily decreases. The high number of rulings that the Court announces during the early part of the series may be due to the uncertainty that then characterized the law, as Casper and Posner suggest.[1] Due to the unprecedented expansion of industrialism and economic activity surrounding the turn-of-the-century, the Court was then faced with novel questions regarding the constitutional guarantees afforded businesses against regulatory efforts.

However, the number of decisions that the Court announced does decline, beginning in the 1920s. This decline may be due to the promulgation of the Judges' Bill. After the act was passed, the Court consistently decides fewer than two hundred cases in a term year until the early 1970s, but the 1990s witness a return to the days of about one hundred opinions per term. There are moderate increases in the size of the Court's caseload during the 1960s perhaps due, in part, to the increase in expanded rights recognized by the Court's decision-making, particularly in its civil liberties–civil rights jurisprudence. Near the end of the period analyzed, however, the series begins to decline. From 1989 to 1997, the Court issues only about 136 decisions on average per term.

The substance of the Court's decisions is also quite dynamic during the period the study examines. From 1888 to 1950, economics cases constitute the largest portion of the Court's agenda. In 1891, the Court issues 199 economic decisions alone. This finding is expected because of the prevailing concern within the political system at that time of the limits of governmental regulation of business activity. Economics cases comprise around 60 percent of the decisions that the Court announced through the 1930s, when they began to decline in number. This decline continues even through the period of the Great Depression when one might expect that the Court to be overwhelmed with requests to resolve economic issues. For the period from 1933 to 1937, Pacelle reports similar findings.[2] In more recent times, Pacelle's study and the present investigation find that economic cases comprise only about one-fifth of the cases on average that the Court hears in a term year.

The second issue area analyzed in this study of the Court's agenda is judicial power. The Court issues a relatively large share of these cases during the entire period of analysis. Its historic high occurs in 1888 (27 percent); its historic low in 1930 (3.9 percent). From 1888 to 1930, the proportion of judicial power decisions on the Court's docket declines. After 1930, the series is relatively volatile, moving sharply upward from one term year to the next. It increases through 1968, when it turns gently downward once again.

The third issue series examined in this chapter is the proportion of federal taxation decisions. Since 1926, the series increases, reaching its historic high in 1930 (27.5 percent). This is a theoretically consistent finding, since the Sixteenth Amendment (authorizing a federal income tax) was adopted in 1913. The series after 1930 declines and rarely exceeds 10 percent. In the later years of the series, it rarely exceeds 5 percent. There are some discrepancies between the findings of the present study and those of Pacelle. However, these differences may be due to the different methodologies of the two studies: Pacelle reports five-year averages, which may be less precise than the single-year figures employed in this investigation.[3]

The Court's agenda also includes criminal procedure decisions. The series overall increases during the period analyzed. However, the series does not become well established until 1939, before which it most often comprises 5 to 10 percent of the Court's agenda on average. The series historic high is observed in 1967 (33.9 percent), perhaps due to the expansive rulings of the Warren Court. Although there are differences with the findings of Pacelle in terms of the magnitude of the series in specific term years, the present study's findings agree with the existence of a trend in the series and its direction across the period from 1933 to 1989.

Civil rights cases are relatively small portions of the Court's agenda through 1945. Prior to that year, the series exceeds 5 percent only twice (1903 and 1944). In many term years, the Court issues no such decisions, the first year being 1925. After 1945, however, these decisions become a consistent part of the Court's rulings. The historic high occurs in 1978 (25.0 percent), with three term years (1963: 24.6 percent; 1969: 24.8; and, 1976: 24.0) nearly matching that mark. This upward movement in the proportion of civil rights cases supports McCloskey's observation that the Court's priorities were changing to begin to support civil rights cases.[4] This is an expected finding since the Court, as the nation's ultimate forum of conflict resolution, would consider the issues that the larger political system was debating. This increasing trend in the proportion of civil rights cases demonstrates a fundamental change in the Court's agenda: from one dominated by concerns of economic regulation to one more closely concerned with issues of civil rights.

First Amendment cases also comprise a very modest proportion of the Court's agenda from 1888 to 1997. These cases do not appear on the docket until 1935. Even then, they do not comprise a significant portion of the rulings announced until the 1950s, and do not consistently consume more than 10 percent of the docket until 1965. The series high is observed in 1970 (16.7 percent). The growth and decline of the series parallel the proportion of the Court's decisions that civil rights rulings represent.

Similarly, privacy cases do not comprise a significant part of the Court's docket. In many of the term years examined, the Court issues no such decisions, largely because Supreme Court precedent did not explicitly recognize privacy rights until the 1960s. The series increases, although modestly, in 1970 but then begins to decline in 1979. The historic high is observed in 1996 (6.4 percent).

Due process cases do not show a consistent trend during the period of analysis. The series maximum occurs in 1906 (8.7 percent), and there are several term years in which the Court announced no due process rulings. However, their number increases in the 1960s. At the end of the series, due process decisions account for only 3.6 percent of the Court's agenda.

Federalism cases are an erratic component of the Court's docket from 1888 to 1989. There are several large increases during the 1920s and the 1930s. The series stabilizes in 1954, declines in 1963 and then trends upward once again in 1971. The historic high for the series occurs in 1927 (14.9 percent). Like many other series examined in this study, federalism cases comprise zero percent of the Court's agenda in many of the term years investigated.

Interstate relations and separation of powers cases do not individually comprise more than five percent of the Court's agenda. Interstate relations cases increase during the period surrounding World War II, but thereafter they began to decline. Through 1997, they comprise less than 2 percent of the Court's decisions on average. Separation of powers cases attain their historic high in 1929 (4.6 percent). Pacelle finds that the series increases from 1933 to 1982.[5] Between 1983 and 1987, these cases comprise 1.1 percent of the Court's agenda.

Attorney and union cases are found to be very small portions of the Court's decisions during the period of analysis. Until 1936, union cases are nearly nonexistent. After 1936, they fluctuate from about 2 percent to about 10 percent in 1960. This growth is an expected finding, since the Court was then beginning to turn its attention to the interests of economic "underdogs." Thereafter, the series subsides to a consistent 2 to 5 percent. The series high is observed in 1959 (10.3 percent).

Attorney cases are similarly a very modest portion of the Court's decisions. Only after the end of the Second World War do they represent even a very small proportion of the Court's docket. It increases slightly from 1952 to 1956. By 1979, the series becomes more consistent and, by 1984, it reaches 4.2 percent of the Court's agenda, its historic high.

In addition to examining the proportion of these individual issue areas, this study reports the relative share of the Court's agenda that four aggregated issue dimensions captured from 1888 to 1989. As the analysis of individual issue areas reflects, economics decisions comprise the largest part of the Court's agenda across time. From 1888 to 1948, the series hovers around 65 percent. During the Great Depression, the series increases to over 70 percent. These are findings are theoretically consistent in that the Court's docket theoretically should have been dominated by these types of cases because the nation was in the throes of perhaps the most significant macroeconomic event it has experienced during its existence. In addition, the Progressive movement sought to implement increased regulation of business activity, which was sure to be challenged and brought to the Court for resolution. In the late 1940s, economics decisions begin to consume less of the Court's agenda. Beginning in the late 1970s and continuing through 1997, they on average comprise 25.4 percent of the Court's rulings.

Civil liberties–civil rights cases are relatively infrequent until 1937. Because of the dominance of economics cases and the structural constraints on the Court, this is an expected finding. Prior to that time, the series attains 20 percent or more only four times (1895, 1909, 1912, and 1926). Its average from 1888 to 1936 is roughly 12 percent. In 1937, the Court begins to include more of these decisions, perhaps due to new justices who more strongly supported the rights of the criminally accused and civil liberties claimants than prior justices generally had. The series attains its historic high in 1967 (64.4 percent) and then stabilizes thereafter at slightly more than 50 percent. Thus, in recent years, civil liberties–civil rights cases nearly match the level that economics decisions reach during the early part of the period analyzed.

These findings confirm the observations of McCloskey, who suggests that the Court's priorities early in the century focused on questions of economic regulation. However, McCloskey also suggests that, by the 1950s, the Court began to turn away from such issues and refocused its priorities on questions of civil liberties–civil rights because the nation as a whole was then beginning to consider these questions in depth.[6] Moreover, the findings redocument Schubert's description that reports that the Court's docket after World War II was primarily composed of economics and civil liberties–civil rights decisions.[7]

The third aggregated issue area that is analyzed in the present study is that of judicial power. From 1888 to 1907, the series hovers around 20 percent, after which it begins to decline until 1939. Thereafter, the series begins to increase gently until the 1970s, when it stabilizes. Between 1925 and the early 1960s, the series remains below 20 percent, and often below

15 percent. Thereafter until 1997, the series is on average between 15 and 20 percent, and exceeds 20 percent several times. The historic high occurs in 1888 (27.1 percent); the historic low in 1930 (3.9 percent).

The final aggregated issue dimension, "other," is quite volatile. The historic high is observed in 1927 (16.1 percent). Typically, however, these decisions account for less than 6 percent of the Court's agenda throughout the 110 terms years analyzed in the present study.

Unanimity of Decisions

The study finds that the Court's decisions have become much less unanimous over time, particularly since the 1930s. Before 1937, approximately 75 percent of the Court's decisions are unanimous. The series declines thereafter until it reaches its historic low in 1952 of 21.7 percent. It stabilizes after 1952 around 35 percent.

Prior to Chief Justice Hughes's tenure (1930–40), strong norms of consensus prevailed due to the social and task leadership of Chief Justices Melville Fuller and William Howard Taft, both of whom sought to unite the Court behind a single opinion. While Hughes is found in prior literature to have begun to unravel these norms, this study finds that the White Court may have represented an earlier erosion of unanimity on the Court. The rate of concurring votes increases from nearly zero to approximately 10 percent across the last five years of the White Court (1916–20). However, it increases even further when Hughes becomes chief justice and jumps dramatically under Harlan Fiske Stone.

The rate of dissenting votes also changes considerably during the period of analysis. The rate jumps to 19.3 percent during the last five years of the White Court from the rate seen during the Fuller Court (about 16.7 percent). This increase may be due to the Court's consideration of Progressive reforms, which may have increased the level of conflict on the Court. Justices such as Louis Brandeis and Charles Evans Hughes joined Oliver Wendell Holmes on the Court, all of whom were generally liberal in their policy orientations.

However, when Taft joined the Court in 1921, the series declines to about 13 percent. During Taft's tenure, the final two members of the conservative voting coalition known as the "Four Horsemen" (George Sutherland and Pierce Butler) joined the Court. Although the promulgation of the Judges' Bill has been linked with an increase in the dissent rate, this study finds that the series does not appreciably increase after it was enacted.

During the Hughes Court, the dissent rate increases, just as the rate of concurring opinions does. Approximately 21 percent of the Court's decisions have at least one dissenting vote filed with them. The dissent rate increases even further during the tenure of Harlan Fiske Stone, reaching an average of 48.26 percent. After Stone left the Court, the dissent rate remains high. From 1948 to 1997, the average is 60.29 percent.

The study also finds an increase in the rate of decisions with two or more dissenting votes. Mirroring the changes in the rates of dissenting votes and concurring opinions, the rate of multiple dissents is relatively flat through 1937 when the series begins to trend upward. The Fuller Court, however, has a higher rate of 5-4 decisions than does the White Court or Taft Court. This is a surprising finding given the strong norms of consensus that allegedly prevailed during Fuller's tenure. During Stone's tenure, the rate of multiple dissents increases dramatically. The historic high is observed in 1948 (65.3 percent). Although the series declines somewhat, it stabilizes thereafter around 50 percent through 1989, but then declines to about 47 percent in 1997. Hence, the changes that occurred in the norms of consensus during the Hughes and Stone Courts (and to some extent the White Court) affect the rate of multiple dissents through 1997.

Thus, this study's findings support the results of Haynie, who finds that the unanimity rate declines during Hughes's tenure and continued to do so during the Stone Court.[8] However, this study finds that the dissent rate during the last five years of the White Court is also elevated, perhaps initiating the erosion of the consensual norms that had prevailed since the Court began deciding cases with a single majority opinion in the early 1800s. Also, this study lends less support to the results that Walker, Epstein, and Dixon report.[9] They attribute the rise of nonunanimity to Harlan Fiske Stone's peculiar social and task leadership. Although the dissent rate dramatically increases during Stone's tenure, the rate begins to increase during Edward White's time at the helm, returns to its average level under Taft, but then increases once again under Hughes and then greatly increases during the Stone Court.

However, the study's findings do support the previous studies' findings of a rise of dissenting opinions during the last several years of the Hughes Court. Up to 1937, dissenting opinions are relatively infrequent. During the Hughes Court, the rate jumps to 14.74 percent (up from 8.29 percent during the Taft Court). The series continues to increase during the Stone Court: it rises to 43.18 percent. Hence, the results that Haynie, and Walker, Epstein, and Dixon report of an increase in the rate of dissenting opinions are supported by the findings of the present study.[10]

Liberalism of the Court's Decisions

The level of the liberalism of the Court's decisions changes dramatically during the period of the study. The results are in some respects surprising based upon the findings reported in prior studies of the Court's policy preferences. First, the rates of liberal economic dimension decisions during the Fuller, White and Taft Courts are higher than previous studies have suggested.[11] The present study finds that these Courts issued liberal rulings in slightly more than 50 percent of their economics decisions. One would have predicted, based on existing literature, that the figure would have been much less than this rate. Thus, the Fuller, White and Taft Courts' economic policy preferences are relatively liberal.

Second, the study finds that the rate of liberal economic decisions increases during the Hughes Court, perhaps due to the much-publicized conflict with President Roosevelt over the Court consistently striking down New Deal legislation. The rate is around 70 percent on average during Hughes's tenure. This high level of liberalism is an expected finding given the policy preferences of the justices who composed the Hughes Court and the environmental demands put on the Court by the Great Depression and the New Deal, in addition to Roosevelt's attack on the Court's legitimacy. The liberalism rate during the Stone Court declines somewhat, but it still approximated 60 percent liberal. After the Stone Court, the level of the series declines, but then rebounds sharply in 1953. The average liberalism rate during the Warren Court is 73.83. Thereafter the series declines, particularly during the Burger and Rehnquist Courts. These latter results are expected given the purported conservatism of the justices who served on those Courts. The findings of Pritchett and Haynie and Tate are quite similar to those of this study.[12]

The second major issue dimension analyzed in the present study is civil liberties–civil rights. The findings for this issue area conform to the expectations arising from prior studies. The Court's policy preferences for this aggregated issue area are generally conservative from 1888 to 1930. During the Hughes Court, the series increases dramatically to over 50 percent liberal. It remains near that level during the Stone Court. These findings support the results that prior studies report[13] and the suggestions of historical analyses.[14]

The liberalism rate of judicial power decisions hovers around 20 percent from 1888 to the early 1920s. Thereafter, the series fluctuates wildly, but on average it is about 35 percent. This finding is consistent with theoretical expectations given the Court's demonstrated liberalism in reviewing economics cases. Since the courts are part of the governmental structure, it follows that the Court would be likely to uphold claims for greater judicial power. The series stabilizes in the mid-1930s through the mid-1960s at approximately 45 percent, at which time it declines. In 1970, however, the series rebounds and begins to increase. In 1997, the series exceeds 38 percent liberal.

The series describing the rate of liberalism of decisions in the "other" aggregated issue area shows no consistent trend. The series becomes less dynamic from 1917 to 1945, although it is mostly noise due to the small number of cases on which the series is based. The averages during the four chief justice courts increase slightly from Fuller (59.01 percent) to Hughes (66.71 percent), but then decline during the Stone Court (57.70 percent).

Explaining the Supreme Court's Liberalism

Models of the Court's policy preferences are specified for economics, civil liberties–civil rights, and judicial power decisions so as to determine if they are related in the long-run to proxies of the justices' attitudes and to historical events. I first find that these measure of policy preferences are fractionally integrated, having the characteristics of long-memoried series and some of stationary series. Hence, in future works, scholars may choose to assess the level of fractional integration in this series. The model of economic liberalism, in particular, demonstrates that the justices' decision-making in this aggregated dimension is related in the long run to the justices' personal attributes, the effect of that relationship decaying quite slowly, thus implying that the Court's voting behavior is sensitive to changes in its decision-making environment.

In addition, the Court's level of economic liberalism is shown to be associated with certain events within the Court's political environment, even while controlling for changes in membership. First, the Great Depression is shown to be associated with higher levels of economic liberalism following its occurrence, supporting Haynie and Tate's finding of a similar association.[15] This is an expected finding, since the Depression was arguably the most significant macroeconomic event to occur in United States history. However, Franklin Roosevelt's proposal of a Court-packing plan in February of 1937 is not found to be associated with an increase in the Court's economic liberalism. This finding supports the observations of Schwartz, among others, that the Supreme Court had already brought its policy preferences more in line with those of the President and Congress prior to the announcement of FDR's plan.[16] Third, the effects of the Panic of 1893 and the rise of Progressivism are examined. They, however, are not shown to be significantly related to the Court's level of economic liberalism. Hence, the Court's economic voting is to some extent insulated from external political events, but yet it is not entirely unaware of political forces beyond the Court building.

However, attributes that have been shown in other contexts to be related to the Court's decision-making are found to be insignificant in the short-term in these analyses. For example, the justices' party identification and their Southern regional origins are found not be significantly related to the level of the Court's economic rulings, which is contrary to the results that Haynie and Tate report.[17] Moreover, Tate and Handberg's finding of the significance of presidential policy intentions is not supported by the present analyses.[18]

The dynamics in the level of the Court's civil liberties–civil rights liberalism are also explored in this study. As this study finds in the economic analysis, the justices' personal attributes as proxies for their attitudes are associated in the long run with their expressed policy preferences in this second aggregated issue dimension. However, shocks to the system tend to dissipate at a slower rate (18 percent decay per period) than they do for the Court's economic policy preferences (27 percent decay per period). Perhaps the Court at this time viewed changes in civil liberties–civil rights rulings to be more critical to the political system and, thus, was more sensitive to the dynamics of that policy context than it was in other areas.

As this study finds in the analyses of the Court's economic liberalism, the justices' party identifications are not significantly related to the Court's liberalism in the short term, although this variable is found to be negatively signed with respect to the Court's decision-making, suggesting that Democrats are less supportive of claims of civil liberties and civil rights than are Republicans during the bulk of the period. However, presidential intentions are closely and positively related to the Court's policy views, implying that the president's nomination strategy can illuminate to some extent the justice's political views. The remainder of the personal attributes was shown not to be associated with their voting behavior in the short run. These results comport with the findings of Segal, Epstein, Cameron, and Spaeth, who find that the scores of the justices' ideologies are less robust for justices who served during the Roosevelt era than they are for justices who served during more contemporary periods.[19]

There are three environmental shocks whose effect on the Court's civil liberties–civil rights liberalism are examined in the study: World War I, World War II, and the Spanish-American War. Only World War II's impact is negatively related to the liberalism of the Court's decisions. This finding implies that the Court's decisions became less liberal during the war. This is an expected finding since historical analyses have suggested that the Court's decisions became more conservative during times of war due to concerns of national security.[20] However, the impacts of the other two wars are found not to be statistically significant. Perhaps the Spanish-American War simply did not represent as significant a national threat as the more large-scale conflict of World War I did. The finding of the nonsignificance of World War I is contrary to Pritchett, who suggests that the Court was less concerned about issues of national security during the World War II than had the Court been during World War I.[21]

The third aggregated issue area examined in this study is judicial power. The error correction term, capturing the long-run relationship between the justices' attributes and their voting behavior, is significant, implying that the two constructs were related over time. But none of the justices' attributes are related to the level of the dependent variable in the short term. This finding indicates that the Court's policy preferences in this aggregated issue dimension are resilient to membership changes in the short term.

The study also examines the impact of the promulgation of the Judiciary Act of 1925 on the Court's liberalism in judicial power decisions. It finds that the act is associated with an increase in the level of the series. The series, thus, attains a new, higher level of liberalism due to the passage of the act, suggesting that jurisdictional changes can influence the Court's policy output in this context.

IMPORTANCE OF THE BOOK'S FINDINGS

The findings of the study are important to research in the subfield of judicial politics and the discipline of political science generally in several respects. First, the study provides systematic analysis of the Court's agenda across more than a century of Supreme Court history, as opposed to prior studies of the Court that have focused on one chief justice court or a limited period of the Court's history. While McCloskey and Schwartz suggest that the Court's docket was composed primarily of economics decisions up until the 1940s,[22] this study is the first to demonstrate the empirical validity of those observations across the twentieth century. The study also finds that when economics rulings became less frequent, civil liberties–civil rights decisions began to increase, signaling a change in the Court's priorities. This result, too, confirms the suggestions of McCloskey, Schwartz, and other scholars.[23]

Second, the study demonstrates the large decline in unanimity that has occurred in Supreme Court decision-making. This finding underlines the rise of dissents and concurrences that prior studies find during the Hughes and Stone Courts. However, the present study's findings do suggest that there is a modest increase in the proportion of concurring and dissenting votes during the last five years of the White Court (1916–20). Perhaps this decline of unanimity led to the permanent erosion of the norms of consensus under which the Court operated in the later years of the Hughes Court.

Third, this study's findings are important because they demonstrate that the Court's economic policy preferences during the Fuller, White, and Taft Courts were not as conservative as many prior studies suggest.[24] During these years (and throughout the period of analysis), the Court's liberalism rate is on average about 50 percent, hardly reaching the level of entrenched conservatism that prior studies had suggested described the Court's decision-making in this aggregated issue dimension. Moreover, the Court's liberalism in civil liberties–civil rights rulings is, as prior studies implied, consistently conservative prior to the 1950s.

Fourth, the study demonstrates, through the time serial analyses, that several of the justices' personal attributes are associated with the Court's institutional policy preferences in economics, civil liberties–civil rights and judicial power rulings in the long run. This finding demonstrates that the justices have for over one hundred years been influenced, in part, by their political values. Their decision-making is also shown to be sensitive to changes in the macropolitical environment of the Court. The justices, thus, consider institutional and environmental constraints in forming their policy preferences. Hence, they are strategic actors.

Fifth, many of the hypotheses generated in studies examining the Court's behavior in the post-1945 period are not supported in these longer analyses. This is an important finding, too. Perhaps these results suggest that the Court has undergone a structural change in its relation to the larger political environment of which it is a part. Franklin Roosevelt's attack on the Court in 1937, the unprecedented demands placed on it as a result of the Great Depression and the New Deal, and the rise of civil liberties–civil rights issues may have contributed to the development of a more political perspective among the justices. As a result of these tremendously important historic events, the Court may have been permanently transformed as a result, moving away from its cloistered posture to a position more integrated into the political dynamics of the American political system.

SUGGESTIONS FOR FURTHER RESEARCH

This study's findings are in some respects unexpected based on the results reported in prior research. Accordingly, the results reported in the present investigation suggest that further work should be done to explore more completely the agenda-setting and decision-making of the United States Supreme Court.

First, the analyses of the unanimity of the Court's decisions provide some surprising findings. It is found that the proportion of unanimous decisions declines during the period of the study, confirming the results reported

in several prior studies. An unexpected finding is that the decline in unanimity begins with the White Court. The Court experiences an increased,
albeit modest, rate of dissenting votes, perhaps due to the change in membership on the Court and the novel issues of economic and political reform
that it was considering. Although this study finds that the rate of concurrences and dissents also increases during the Hughes and Stone Courts, the
norms of consensus that long held the Court together begin to erode during the White Court.[25] Indeed, even during the very congenial and cohesive Fuller Court, there is a very high number of 5-4 decisions. Thus, these
rather unexpected findings suggest that further investigation should be done
to determine if Courts prior to 1888 experienced any decline in unanimity.
Perhaps the conclusions that prior research has drawn may be overdrawn
because of the limited time period that such studies examined.

Additionally, scholars should endeavor to collect decisional data on the
Court prior to the 1880s. This process, while certainly expensive and time-
consuming, will yield a rich resource in which many further studies can be
completed, including case studies of particular Courts or comparative analyses with more contemporary Courts. Each of these potential investigations
would provide scholars a greater understanding of the dynamics underlying the Court's agenda-setting and decision-making processes.

This study, which was largely based on newly collected data, yields some
surprises with regard to the liberalism of some of the chief justice courts
examined here. The Fuller and White Courts' economic liberalism are found
to be more liberal than prior analyses implied. This is an intriguing finding.
Perhaps scholars' impressions of the policy preferences of prior Courts were
guided too strongly by decisions in particular cases. While the Fuller Court
did strike down several regulatory laws as being unconstitutional, its jurisprudence cannot be accurately assessed without examining the entire body
of rulings that it issued. While McCloskey, Schwartz, and others have suggested that the White Court became somewhat more liberal in its economic
voting behavior,[26] the White Court is consistently more liberal than even
these studies had found. Hence, as with the analyses of unanimity, scholars
should endeavor to explore the policy preferences of prior Courts. Perhaps
they too are more liberal than prior research has suggested.

The study also examines the composition of the Court's agenda over
time. It confirms the observations of McCloskey and Schubert, most notably, that economics cases dominated the Court's docket during the pre-
1945 period.[27] Although the study suggests possible explanations for growth
and decline in the various issues areas examined, further research may attempt to model formally the changes in the Court's agenda. More systematic analysis would lead to greater theory building about the relationship
between the Court's priorities (expressed in the cases that it considers) and

the structural and environmental demands placed on it. Scholars would, thus, gain a greater and more comprehensive understanding of the Court's place within the institutional structure of the American government.

The study develops fractionally cointegrating models of the level of the Court's liberalism in three aggregated issue areas. The results demonstrate that the justices' personal attributes are related to the Court's policy preferences in the long run. However, the Segal and Cover methodology of scoring the justices' ideologies has been shown to be less robust in the era of Franklin Roosevelt.[28] These scores may be even weaker indicators of the justices' attitudes in earlier periods. Moreover, a prior study suggests that replication of the Segal and Cover protocol is simply impossible.[29] Thus, although the study does not find very strong associations between the justices' personal attributes and the Court's policy-making, this kind of data is readily available for all of the Supreme Court justices. For the moment, it is perhaps the best indicator scholars can use to indirectly measure the attitudes of the justices in periods prior to 1945. Hence, scholars should endeavor to develop personal attribute models of Supreme Court decision-making prior to the 1880s. Perhaps the influence of attributes will decline, which will provide even more grist for the theoretical mill of judicial politics.

Moreover, scholars may seek to add a comparative perspective to their analyses. The American judiciary is unique among the court systems of the world because of its power of judicial review. Perhaps this structural power has affected the relationship between the justices' attributes, historical events, and their voting behavior. Indeed, this could affect the rate of their dissents and concurrences and even the kinds of cases that the Court agrees to hear.

Overall, this study suggests that much further work is needed to understand the dynamics underlying the Court's agenda-setting and decisional processes. However, the study has provided a key link between the studies that have most frequently examined the Court in the post-1945 era and those yet to be done.

Coding Sheet for Agenda and Decisional Data for the United States Supreme Court, 1888–1937

DATA ENTRY 1888

FulName: _____

v

_____

Party1 (8 letters) _____ v Party 2 _____

US Reports _____ US _____   Solicitor General _____

SCT _____ SCT _____   Dir Lower Court _____

Docket _____   Decision Type _____

Date Oral _____   Vote _____

Decision Date _____   Vote Questionable _____

Source _____   Majority Author _____

Issue _____   Assigned By _____

Direction _____

#	Justice	Majority	Wrote	A1	A2
51	Fuller				
62	Miller				
57	Field				
60	Bradley				
49	Harlan				
63	Matthews				
56	Gray				
59	Blatchford				
61	Lamar				

Coding Protocol for Agenda and Decisional Data for the United States Supreme Court, 1888–1937

Number: unique number identifying each decision.

FulName: names of the two parties.

Party 1 and 2: eight-letter identification of each party.

US Reports: U.S. Reports citation following volume-page format.

SCT: Supreme Court Reporter citation following volume-page format.

Docket: the docket number the Clerk of the Court assigned the case.

Date Oral: the day on which oral argument was heard. It follows the standard month-day-year format. If oral argument continued more than one day, only the first day was noted.

Decision Date: the day on which the Court announced the decision. It follows the standard month-day-year format.

Source: indicates the court from which the case was appealed. Federal Circuit courts are identified with the number or set of letters associated with them (e.g., "8C" for Eighth Circuit, or "DCC" for the D.C. Circuit). Federal District Courts are noted by their geographic place. For example, the North District Court of Texas is coded "NDTX." State Courts are identified with the United States Postal abbreviation for their state (e.g., "TX" for the Texas Supreme Court). Trial courts carry the abbreviation "TR." State appellate courts carry the abbreviation "AP."

Issue: identifies one of the fourteen issue areas into which cases are categorized. Most often, only one issue area was identified for each decision. In some cases, two issue areas were identified. The issues, and their respective codes, are:

1 = Criminal Procedure	8 = Economics
2 = Civil Rights	9 = Judicial Power
3 = First Amendment	10 = Federalism
4 = Due Process	11 = Interstate Relations
5 = Privacy	12 = Federal Taxation
6 = Attorneys	13 = Miscellaneous
7 = Unions	14 = Separation of Powers

Direction: indicates the liberalism of the decision. Those decisions that were liberal were scored "1"; those conservative scored "0."

Solicitor General: indicates the participation of the solicitor general's and the attorney general's office, and the filing of amicus curiae briefs.

0 = No participation
1 = Solicitor General's Office
2 = Attorney General's Office
4 = Amicus Briefs Filed

Dir Lower Court: notes the disposition of the Court relative to the lower court's ruling. If the decision was affirmed, then this variable is scored "1"; if it was reversed, then it is scored "0."

Decision Type: indicates the form of the decision. The decision types are:

1 = The Court heard oral argument and it issues a signed opinion indicating a particular justice as the author of the majority opinion.
2 = Decisions that received a full opinion but the Court did not hear oral argument. These are known as "per curiam" opinions.
3 = These are brief decisions that involve certiorari petitions, individuals' various requests, and many other motions, orders, and rulings that the Court has issued. These are known as "memorandum" opinions.
4 = Decrees. This type of decision most often involves the Court's original jurisdiction. These decisions are labeled "decree" at the top of the decision, to distinguish it from the other types of decisions.
5 = Judgment of the Court. These are decisions in which there is an equally divided vote. The lower court's ruling in this context is affirmed.

6 = No signed opinion. This decision is similar to the formally, signed opinion, but this type ruling does not bear any justice's name as the opinion's author. Although they are orally argued (and, hence, different than type 2 decisions), they receive the label "per curiam."

Vote: indicates the number of votes in the majority and in the minority. If there are eight votes in the majority and one in the minority, then this variable would be coded "81." If there are only eight justices participating, then the code would be "80."

Vote Questionable: notes whether the decision was "affirmed in part, and reversed in part." If so, then the variable is coded "1"; otherwise, it is coded "0."

Majority Author: indicates the unique number assigned to the author of the majority opinion. Each of the justices who were on the Court during the period of analysis were assigned such a number.

Assigned By: indicates the unique number of the justice who assigned the writing of the majority opinion.

#: justices' unique identifying number.

Justice: the justice's name.

Majority: whether a justice joined the majority opinion, wrote a concurring or a dissenting opinion, or did not participate.

  1 = voted with the majority
  2 = dissented
  3 = regular concurrence (agreed with both the opinion and the disposition of the case)
  4 = special concurrence (agreed with the disposition of the case, but not with the Court's opinion)
  5 = nonparticipation
  6 = judgment of the Court
  7 = dissent from denial of certiorari
  8 = jurisdictional dissent

Wrote: indicates if the justice wrote any kind of opinion (majority, concurring, or dissenting) or not. If so, then the variable is scored "1"; "0" otherwise.

A1 and A2: indicates the opinion of another justice that the justice joined. For example, refer to Appendix A. If Taft (#40) wrote a concurring opinion, which Holmes (#39) joined, then "39" would appear in Taft's A1 column. The same would hold true if another justice joined Taft's opinion too. The second justice's identifying number would appear in the A2 column.

Notes

CHAPTER 1. THE DECISION-MAKING AND AGENDA-SETTING OF THE UNITED STATES SUPREME COURT, 1888–1997

1. Richard L. Pacelle, Jr., *The Tranformation of the Supreme Court's Agenda: From Roosevelt to Reagan* (Boulder, CO: Westview Press, 1991); Gerhard Casper and Richard A. Posner, *The Workload of the Supreme Court* (Chicago: American Bar Foundation, 1976).

2. C. Herman Pritchett, *The Roosevelt Court: A Study in Judicial Politics and Values, 1937–1947* (New York: Macmillan, 1948).

3. Glendon Schubert, *The Judicial Mind: Attitudes and Ideologies of Supreme Court Justices, 1946–1963* (Evanston, IL: Northwestern University Press, 1965); Glendon Schubert, *The Judicial Mind Revisited: Psychometric Analysis of Supreme Court Ideology* (New York: Oxford University Press, 1974).

4. E.g., Jeffrey A. Segal and Harold J. Spaeth, *The Supreme Court and the Attitudinal Model* (New York: Cambridge University Press, 1993).

5. Pacelle, *Supreme Court's Agenda*.

6. Charles R. Epp, *The Rights Revolution: Lawyers, Activists, and Supreme Courts in Comparative Perspective* (Chicago: University of Chicago Press, 1998), 27.

7. E.g., Alexander Bickel, *The Least Dangerous Branch: The Supreme Court at the Bar of Politics*, 2d ed. (New Haven: Yale University Press, 1968); William Mishler and Reginald S. Sheehan, "The Supreme Court as a Countermajoritarian Institution: The Impact of Public Opinion on Supreme Court Decisions," *American Political Science Review* 87 (1993): 87–101.

8. Casper and Posner, *Workload*.

9. Paul A. Freund, *Federal Judicial Center Report of the Study Group on the Case Load of the Supreme Court* (Washington, DC: Administrative Office, U.S. Courts for Federal Judicial Center, 1972).

10. Casper and Posner, *Workload*, 27.

11. Ibid., 28–29.

12. Ibid.

13. Ibid.

14. Ibid.

15. Ibid., 17.

16. Ibid.

17. Ibid., 18.

18. 26 Stat. 826 (1891).

19. Casper and Posner, *Workload*, 18.

20. Ibid.

21. Ibid., 19–21.
22. Ibid., 20.
23. Ibid., 35.
24. Ibid., 38.
25. Ibid., 41.
26. Ibid., 43–44.
27. Ibid., 46.
28. Ibid., 49.
29. Ibid., 50–51.
30. Ibid., 54–55.
31. Ibid., 55–56.
32. Pacelle, *Supreme Court's Agenda*.
33. Ibid., 23–24.
34. See James L. Gibson, "Judges' Role Orientations, Attitudes and Decisions: An Interactive Model," *American Political Science Review* 71 (1978): 911–24.
35. Pacelle, *Supreme Court's Agenda*, 23–24.
36. Ibid., 140.
37. Ibid.
38. Ibid., 28.
39. Ibid.
40. Ibid., 28–29.
41. See Walter F. Murphy, *Elements of Judicial Strategy* (Chicago: University of Chicago Press, 1964), 21–22.
42. Pacelle, *Supreme Court's Agenda*, 29.
43. Ibid., 29–30.
44. Gregory A. Caldeira and John R. Wright, "Organized Interests and Agenda Setting in the U.S. Supreme Court," *American Political Science Review* 82 (1988): 1109–27.
45. Pacelle, *Supreme Court's Agenda*, 24–30.
46. Ibid., 32.
47. *Gideon v. Wainwright*, 372 US 335 (1963); Pacelle, *Supreme Court's Agenda*, 32–33.
48. Pacelle, *Supreme Court's Agenda*, 40.
49. Ibid.
50. Ibid., 114–15.
51. Ibid., 120–21.
52. Ibid., 41–42.
53. Ibid., 34–35.
54. Ibid., 33.
55. Ibid., 35–36.
56. Ibid., 63–65.
57. Ibid., 65.
58. Ibid., 128–29.
59. Ibid., 190–92.
60. Robert G. McCloskey, *The American Supreme Court*, 2d ed. (Chicago: University of Chicago Press, 1994).
61. Schubert, *Judicial Mind*.
62. Ibid., 44.
63. Harold Laswell, *Power and Personality* (New York: W. W. Norton, 1948).
64. Schubert, *Judicial Mind*, 12.
65. Ibid., 20–21.
66. Ibid., 27.
67. Ibid.

68. Schubert, *Judicial Mind Revisited*, 18.

69. Ibid.

70. Schubert, *Judicial Mind*, 38–39.

71. Ibid., 102–3.

72. Ibid., 101.

73. Ibid., 127–28.

74. Ibid., 99–103.

75. Ibid., 233–35.

76. Ibid., 144.

77. Ibid., 173.

78. C. Neal Tate, "The Methodology of Judicial Behavior Research: A Review and Critique," *Political Behavior* 5 (1983): 51–82.

79. Segal and Spaeth, *Attitudinal Model*.

80. Ibid., 62–65; Morton J. Horwitz, *The Transformation of American Law, 1870–1960* (New York: Oxford University Press, 1992).

81. Jeffrey A. Segal and Albert D. Cover, "Ideological Values and the Votes of U.S. Supreme Court Justices," *American Political Science Review* 83 (1989): 557–65.

82. Ibid.

83. Segal and Spaeth, *Attitudinal Model*, 228.

84. Ibid., 230.

85. Ibid., 252.

86. Jeffrey A. Segal, Lee Epstein, Charles M. Cameron, and Harold J. Spaeth, "Ideological Values and the Votes of U.S. Supreme Court Justices Revisited," *The Journal of Politics* 57 (1995): 812–23.

87. Lee Epstein and Carol Mershon, "Measuring Political Preferences," *American Journal of Political Science* 40 (1996): 261–94.

88. C. Neal Tate, "Personal Attribute Models of the Voting Behavior of U.S. Supreme Court Justices: Liberalism in Civil Liberties and Economics Decisions, 1946–1978," *American Political Science Review* 75 (1981): 355–67; C. Neal Tate and Roger Handberg, "Time Binding and Theory Building in Personal Attribute Models of Supreme Court Voting Behavior, 1916–1988," *American Journal of Political Science* 35 (1991): 460–80.

89. Henry Glick, *Courts, Politics, and Justice*, 3d ed. (New York: McGraw-Hill, 1993), 313–14.

90. Tate, "Personal Attribute Models," 361.

91. Ibid., 358–59.

92. Ibid., 361.

93. S. Sidney Ulmer, "Are Social Background Models Timebound?," *American Political Science Review* 80 (1986): 957–67.

94. Tate and Handberg, "Time Binding," 464–71. Tate and Handberg thus provide systematic data covering Supreme Court behavior back to 1916, but a gap remains prior to that year.

95. Ibid., 474.

96. Stacia L. Haynie and C. Neal Tate, "Institutional Liberalism in the United States Supreme Court, 1916–1988: An Explanation of Economics and Civil Rights and Liberties Cases" (paper presented at the annual meeting of the American Political Science Association, San Francisco, CA, August–September 1990), 2.

97. Ibid., 6–7.

98. Ibid., 7.

99. Ibid., 16.

100. Ibid.

101. Roger Handberg, Jr., "Decision-Making in a Natural Court, 1916–1921," *American Politics Quarterly* 4 (1976): 357–78.

102. Ibid., 363–75.

103. Donald C. Leavitt, "Attitudes and Ideology on the White Supreme Court, 1910–1920" (Ph.D. diss., Michigan State University, 1970).

104. Handberg, "Natural Court."

105. Mary R. Mattingly, "The Hughes Court, 1931–36" (Ph.D. diss., Michigan State University, 1969).

106. Peter George Renstrom, "The Dimensionality of Decision-Making of the 1941–45 Stone Court: A Computer Dependent Analysis of Supreme Court Behavior" (Ph.D. diss., Michigan State University, 1972).

107. Pritchett, *The Roosevelt Court.*

108. Casper and Posner, *Workload.*

109. Pacelle, *Supreme Court's Agenda.*

110. McCloskey, *American Supreme Court.*

111. Pritchett, *The Roosevelt Court.*

112. Schubert, *Judicial Mind*; Schubert, *Judicial Mind Revisited.*

113. Segal and Spaeth, *Attitudinal Model.*

114. Segal, Epstein, Cameron, and Spaeth, "Ideological Values Revisited."

115. Tate, "Personal Attributes"; Tate and Handberg, "Time Binding."

CHAPTER 2. HISTORICAL SETTING OF THE UNITED STATES SUPREME COURT, 1888–1946

1. David M. O'Brien, *Storm Center: The Supreme Court in American Politics,* 5th ed. (New York: W. W. Norton, 2000), 104.

2. Lee Epstein, Jeffrey A. Segal, Harold J. Spaeth, and Thomas G. Walker, *The Supreme Court Compendium: Data, Decisions and Developments* (Washington, DC: Congressional Quarterly Press, 1993).

3. Bernard Schwartz, *A History of the Supreme Court* (New York: Oxford University Press, 1993).

4. William F. Swindler, *Court and Constitution in the 20th Century: The Old Legality, 1889–1932* (Indianapolis: Bobbs-Merrill, 1969), 1–2.

5. Howard B. Furer, *The Fuller Court, 1888–1910,* vol. 5 of *The Supreme Court in American Life* (New York: Associated Faculty Press, 1986), 218.

6. Ibid.

7. Henry J. Abraham, *Justices and Presidents: A Political History of Appointments to the Supreme Court,* 3d ed. (New York: Oxford University Press, 1993), 118.

8. Furer, *Fuller Court,* 221.

9. Abraham, *Justices and Presidents,* 119.

10. Furer, *Fuller Court,* 221.

11. Furer, *Fuller Court,* 222; *Slaughterhouse Cases,* 83 US 36 (1873).

12. Furer, *Fuller Court,* 223.

13. Ibid., 224.

14. Ibid., 226.

15. Ibid., 227.

16. Ibid., 227–28.

17. Leavitt, "Attitudes and Ideology," 335.

18. Furer, *Fuller Court,* 229.

19. Ibid., 230.

20. Ibid., 231.

21. Ibid., 232.

22. Ibid., 233.

23. Ibid., 235.

24. Ibid., 236.

25. Ibid., 238.

26. Ibid., 239.

27. Ibid., 241.

28. Ibid., 242.

29. Ibid., 243.

30. Joan Biskupic and Elder Witt, *The Supreme Court at Work*, 2d ed. (Washington, DC: Congressional Quarterly Press, 1997), 230.

31. Furer, *Fuller Court*, 244.

32. Ibid.

33. Ibid., 246.

34. Ibid., 247.

35. Abraham, *Justices and Presidents*, 150.

36. Furer, *Fuller Court*, 248.

37. Abraham, *Justices and Presidents*, 150; *Plessy v. Ferguson*, 163 US 537 (1896).

38. Furer, *Fuller Court*, 286.

39. Ibid., 250–51.

40. Ibid., 251.

41. Abraham, *Justices and Presidents*, 151

42. Furer, *Fuller Court*, 253

43. Ibid.

44. Abraham, *Justices and Presidents*, 154; Furer, *Fuller Court*, 254.

45. Furer, *Fuller Court*, 254; *Pollock v. Farmers' Loan and Trust Co.*, 158 US 601 (1895).

46. Epstein, Segal, Spaeth, and Walker, *Supreme Court Compendium*, 307–8.

47. Furer, *Fuller Court*, 286.

48. Ibid., 287.

49. Abraham, *Justices and Presidents*, 145; Furer, *Fuller Court*, 257.

50. Schwartz, *History*, 178.

51. Furer, *Fuller Court*, 260.

52. Ibid.

53. Abraham, *Justices and Presidents*, 146.

54. Furer, *Fuller Court*, 261.

55. Abraham, *Justices and Presidents*, 146.

56. For further information on this development with the law of contracts, see Horwitz, *Transformation of American Law*.

57. Schwartz, *History*, 174.

58. Furer, *Fuller Court*, 263.

59. Leavitt, "Attitudes and Ideologies," 435.

60. Furer, *Fuller Court*, 264.

61. Ibid., 264–65.

62. Ibid., 266.

63. Ibid., 267.

64. Leavitt, "Attitudes and Ideologies," 233.

65. Furer, *Fulller Court*, 267.

66. Schwartz, *History*, 219.

67. Furer, *Fuller Court*, 267–68.

68. Furer, *Fuller Court*, 270.

69. Ibid.

70. Ibid., 272.

71. Ibid., 273.

72. Ibid., 273–74.

73. Ibid., 275.

74. Ibid., 276.

75. Ibid., 276–77.

76. Paul Kens, *Judicial Power and Reform Politics: The Anatomy of* Lochner v. New York (Lawrence: University Press of Kansas, 1990), 4.

77. McCloskey, *American Supreme Court*, 89.

78. See *Chicago, Milwaukee & St. Paul Railway Co. v. Minnesota*, 134 US 418 (1890).

79. McCloskey, *American Supreme Court*, 88–89.

80. Biskupic and Witt, *Supreme Court at Work*, 29.

81. Schwartz, *History*, 180–82.

82. *United States v. E.C. Knight Co.*, 156 US 1 (1895).

83. Biskupic and Witt, *Supreme Court at Work*, 30.

84. *Pollock v. Farmers' Loan and Trust Co.*.

85. Schwartz, *History*, 184.

86. *Lochner v. New York*, 198 US 45 (1905); Schwartz, *History*, 173.

87. For a detailed discussion of the history and politics leading up to and surrounding the Court's decision, see Kens, *Judicial Power*.

88. Schwartz, *History*, 190; *Scott v. Sanford*, 60 US 393 (1857).

89. *In Re Debs*, 158 US 564 (1895).

90. Biskupic and Witt, *Supreme Court at Work*, 30.

91. Ibid., 33.

92. *Muller v. Oregon*, 208 US 412 (1908).

93. Biskupic and Witt, *Supreme Court at Work*, 32.

94. McCloskey, *American Supreme Court*, 113.

95. Schwartz, *History*, 188; *Plessy v. Ferguson*.

96. Ibid., 189.

97. Biskupic and Witt, *Supreme Court at Work*, 30.

98. Ibid., 29–30.

99. Schwartz, *History*, 209–12.

100. Leavitt, "Ideologies and Values."

101. Ibid., 98; Epstein, Segal, Spaeth, and Walker, *Supreme Court Compendium*, 344.

102. Epstein, Segal, Spaeth, and Walker, *Supreme Court Compendium*, 309.

103. Leavitt, "Ideologies and Values," 334–35.

104. Ibid., 334.

105. Abraham, *Justices and Presidents*, 169.

106. Elder Witt, *Congressional Quarterly's Guide to the U.S. Supreme Court*, 2d ed. (Washington, DC: Congressional Quarterly Press, 1990), 849; Leavitt, "Ideologies and Values," 414.

107. Leavitt, "Ideologies and Values," 415.

108. Abraham, *Justices and Presidents*, 172–73.

109. Ibid., 173.

110. Leavitt, "Ideologies and Values," 410.

111. Ibid.

112. Ibid., 411.

113. Ibid., 421–23.

114. Ibid., 335.
115. Abraham, *Justices and Presidents*, 177.
116. Handberg, "Natural Court."
117. Ibid., 178.
118. Leavitt, "Ideologies and Values," 477.
119. Ibid., 334.
120. Abraham, *Justices and Presidents*, 181.
121. Leavitt, "Ideologies and Values," 466.
122. Ibid., 467.
123. Ibid., 468–69.
124. Ibid., 151.
125. Ibid., 334.
126. Ibid., 458.
127. Ibid., 459–60.
128. Ibid., 460–61.
129. Ibid., 277.
130. Ibid., 288.
131. Ibid., 98.
132. Ibid., 99.
133. Ibid., 253.
134. Ibid., 151.
135. Ibid., 151–52.
136. Ibid., 223.
137. *Hammer v. Dagenhart*, 247 US 251 (1918).
138. Schwartz, *History*, 212.
139. Biskupic and Witt, *Supreme Court at Work*, 33.
140. Ibid., 34.
141. Ibid., 35.
142. Ibid., 34.
143. *Schenck v. United States*, 249 US 47 (1919).
144. Biskupic and Witt, *Supreme Court at Work*, 35.
145. Epstein, Segal, Spaeth, and Walker, *Supreme Court Compendium*, 309–10.
146. Alpheus T. Mason, *The Supreme Court from Taft to Warren* (Baton Rouge: Louisiana State University Press, 1958), 41.
147. Ibid., 42–43.
148. Abraham, *Justices and Presidents*, 188.
149. Ibid., 189.
150. Ibid., 189–90.
151. Witt, *Supreme Court Guide*, 156.
152. Abraham, *Justices and Presidents*, 190–91.
153. Ibid., 190.
154. Witt, *Supreme Court Guide*, 857.
155. Ibid., 857–58.
156. Abraham, *Justices and Presidents*, 195.
157. Ibid., 197; Renstrom, "Stone Court," 66.
158. Drew Noble Lanier and Sandra L. Wood, "Moving on Up: Institutional Position, Politics, and the Chief Justice," *The American Review of Politics* 22 (2001): 93–127.
159. Mason, *Taft to Warren*, 39.
160. Schwartz, *History*, 216.
161. *Adkins v. Children's Hospital*, 261 US 525 (1923).

162. Schwartz, *History*, 218.
163. Biskupic and Witt, *Supreme Court at Work*, 37.
164. *Gitlow v. New York*, 268 US 652 (1925).
165. Biskupic and Witt, *Supreme Court at Work*, 37.
166. *Corrigan v. Buckley*, 271 US 323 (1926).
167. Biskupic and Witt, *Supreme Court at Work*, 38.
168. *Myers v. United States*, 272 US 52 (1926).
169. Biksupic and Witt, *Supreme Court at Work*, 38.
170. Mattingly, "The Hughes Court," 37.
171. Witt, *Supreme Court Guide*, 858.
172. Abraham, *Justices and Presidents*, 202; Witt, *Supreme Court Guide*, 859.
173. Witt, *Supreme Court Guide*, 859.
174. Abraham, *Justices and Presidents*, 203.
175. Ibid., 203–4.
176. Witt, *Supreme Court Guide*, 859.
177. Benjamin N. Cardozo, *The Nature of the Judicial Process* (1921; New Haven: Yale University Press, 1967).
178. Abraham, *Justices and Presidents*, 206; Witt, *Supreme Court Guide*, 859.
179. Abraham, *Justices and Presidents*, 214; Witt, *Supreme Court Guide*, 860.
180. Witt, *Supreme Court Guide*, 860.
181. Pritchett, *The Roosevelt Court*, 131, 258.
182. *Gideon v. Wainwright*.
183. Abraham, *Justices and Presidents*, 215–16; Pritchett, *The Roosevelt Court*, 89, 258.
184. Witt, *Supreme Court Guide*, 860–61.
185. Ibid., 861.
186. Abraham, *Justices and Presidents*, 219; Witt, *Supreme Court Guide*, 860–61.
187. Abraham, *Justices and Presidents*, 219; Pritchett, *The Roosevelt Court*, 131, 260.
188. Renstrom, "Stone Court," 69.
189. Witt, *Supreme Court Guide*, 861.
190. Ibid., 861–62.
191. Pritchett, *The Roosevelt Court*, 131, 260.
192. Ibid., 89, 260.
193. Renstrom, "Stone Court," 270.
194. Witt, *Supreme Court Guide*, 862.
195. Ibid., 862–63.
196. Pritchett, *The Roosevelt Court*, 131, 257.
197. Witt, *Supreme Court Guide*, 862.
198. Ibid.; Renstrom, "Stone Court," 71.
199. Pritchett, *The Roosevelt Court*, 259.
200. *Korematsu v. United States*, 323 US 214 (1944).
201. Renstrom, "Stone Court," 71.
202. Schwartz, *History*, 228.
203. Ibid., 229.
204. Ibid., 230.
205. Pritchett, *The Roosevelt Court*, 258–60.
206. Ibid., 249.
207. Stacia L. Haynie, "Leadership and Consensus on the U.S. Supreme Court," *The Journal of Politics* 54 (1992): 1158–69.
208. Schwartz, *History*, 232.
209. Robert H. Jackson, *The Struggle for Judicial Supremacy* (New York: Alfred A. Knopf, 1941), 315.

210. *Nebbia v. New York*, 291 US 502 (1934).
211. Biskupic and Witt, *Supreme Court at Work*, 40.
212. Ibid.
213. *West Coast Hotel Co. v. Parrish*, 300 US 379 (1937).
214. Biskupic and Witt, *Supreme Court at Work*, 41.
215. *West Coast Hotel*, 391.
216. *National Labor Relations Board v. Jones & Laughlin Steel Corp.*, 301 US 1 (1937).
217. Biskupic and Witt, *Supreme Court at Work*, 41–42.
218. Schwartz, *History*, 234.
219. Ibid., 235.
220. Biskupic and Witt, *Supreme Court at Work*, 38.
221. Ibid., 39.
222. Ibid., 42.
223. Schwartz, *History*, 238–40.
224. Biskupic and Witt, *Supreme Court at Work*, 42.
225. Schwartz, *History*, 244.
226. *United States v. Darby Lumber Co.*, 312 US 100 (1941).
227. Biskupic and Witt, *Supreme Court at Work*, 43.
228. *United States v. Carolene Products*, 304 US 144 (1938).
229. Biskupic and Witt, *Supreme Court at Work*, 42.
230. *Lovell v. Griffin*, 303 US 444 (1938).
231. Biskupic and Witt, *Supreme Court at Work*, 43.
232. *Brown v. Board of Education*, 347 US 483 (1954).
233. Biskupic and Witt, *Supreme Court at Work*, 44.
234. *Hague v. CIO*, 307 US 496 (1939).
235. Biskupic and Witt, *Supreme Court at Work*, 43.
236. Schwartz, *History*, 245.
237. Renstrom, "Stone Court," 19.
238. Ibid., 64.
239. Ibid., 72.
240. Witt, *Supreme Court Guide*, 864.
241. Renstrom, "Stone Court," 72–73.
242. Ibid., 73.
243. Pritchett, *The Roosevelt Court*, 89, 261.
244. Witt, *Supreme Court Guide*, 865–66.
245. Renstrom, "Stone Court," 73.
246. Pritchett, *The Roosevelt Court*, 259–60.
247. Ibid., 89.
248. Renstrom, "Stone Court," 74.
249. Ibid.; Pritchett, *The Roosevelt Court*, 89.
250. Renstrom, "Stone Court," 154.
251. *NLRB v. Jones-Laughlin*.
252. Renstrom, "Stone Court," 18.
253. Ibid., 18–19.
254. *Korematsu v. United States*.
255. Schwartz, *History*, 250.
256. *Murdock v. Pennsylvania*, 319 US 105 (1943).
257. Biskupic and Witt, *Supreme Court at Work*, 44–45.
258. Ibid., 45.
259. Schwartz, *History*, 252; see also *Yakus v. United States*, 321 US 414 (1944).

CHAPTER 3. CONTOURS OF JUDICIAL ATTENTION: COMPOSITION
AND DYNAMICS OF THE WORKLOAD AND THE AGENDA OF THE
UNITED STATES SUPREME COURT, 1888–1997

1. McCloskey, *American Supreme Court*; Pacelle, *Supreme Court's Agenda*.

2. E.g., Segal and Spaeth, *The Attitudinal Model*.

3. Harold J. Spaeth, United States Supreme Court Judicial Data Base, 1953–1997 Terms Computer File, 9th ICPSR Version (East Lansing: Michigan State University, Dept. of Political Science producer; Ann Arbor, MI: Inter-University Consortium for Political and Social Research Distributor, 1999).

4. Sandra L. Wood, "In the Shadow of the Chief: The Role of the Senior Associate Justice on the United States Supreme Court" (Ph.D. diss., University of Minnesota, 1994).

5. In Spaeth's original dataset, he specifies a category for miscellaneous cases. These cases cannot be meaningfully analyzed here. Hence, they are excluded and the analysis is completed on the remaining thirteen issue areas. Spaeth, Supreme Court Data Base.

6. Lee Epstein, Jeffrey A. Segal, Harold J. Spaeth, and Thomas G. Walker, *The Supreme Court Compendium: Data, Decisions and Developments*, 2d ed. (Washington, DC: Congressional Quarterly Press, 1996), 194.

7. Casper and Posner, *Workload*, 56.

8. Stephen G. Halpern and Kenneth N. Vines, "Institutional Disunity, The Judges' Bill, and the Role of the U.S. Supreme Court," *Western Political Quarterly* 30 (1977): 471–83.

9. Spaeth, Supreme Court Data Base.

10. Pacelle, *Supreme Court's Agenda*, 207–9.

11. Ibid., 57.

12. Ibid., 208.

13. Another slight difference between this analysis and that of Pacelle is that he codes only those cases that covered one page or more in the United States Reports, so to exclude "relatively trivial cases." The present analysis covers all decisions that the Court announced during the time period at hand. Pacelle, *Supreme Court's Agenda*, 207.

14. Ibid., 57.

15. The figures for the present analysis aggregate "economic," "attorney," and "union" cases so as to provide a closer comparison to Pacelle's protocol and results.

16. Ibid.

17. Pacelle does not have a distinct category of cases that correspond to the conceptualization of judicial power cases as discussed in this analysis.

18. Ibid.

19. Ibid.

20. Ibid., 207.

21. Ibid., 56.

22. Ibid.

23. McCloskey, *American Supreme Court*.

24. Pacelle, *Supreme Court's Agenda*, 208.

25. Ibid., 56.

26. Ibid.

27. Ibid.

28. For a discussion of First Amendment cases that the Court considered earlier in its history, see David M. Rabban, "The First Amendment in its Forgotten Years," *The Yale Law Journal* 90 (1981): 514–95; David M. Rabban, "The Free Speech League, the ACLU, and Changing Conceptions of Free Speech in American History," *Stanford Law Review* 45 (1992): 47–114.

29. Ibid., 56, 158–59; McCloskey, *American Supreme Court,* 113.

30. In deciding the case in favor of the individual, the Court looked to the "penumbras" of the Bill of Rights, "formed by emanations of those guarantees that help give them life and substance." *Griswold v. Connecticut,* 381 US 479 (1965).

31. Pacelle, *Supreme Court's Agenda,* 207.

32. Ibid., 56.

33. Ibid.

34. Ibid., 56–57.

35. Schwartz, *History,* 242–43.

36. The operationalizations of these cases of the two studies are equivalent.

37. Pacelle, *Supreme Court's Agenda,* 57.

38. Ibid., 207.

39. Ibid., 208 (emphasis added).

40. Ibid., 56.

41. Spaeth, Supreme Court Data Base.

42. Pacelle, *Supreme Court's Agenda,* 56; Schwartz, *History,* 236–38.

43. Schwartz, *History,* 244–45.

44. Pacelle, *Supreme Court's Agenda,* 209.

45. Schubert, *Judicial Mind,* 101.

46. Ibid.

47. Ibid., 127.

48. Schubert, *Judicial Mind Revisited.*

49. Schubert, *Judicial Mind,* 150–57.

50. Carl N. Degler, Thomas C. Cochran, Vincent P. De Santis, Holman Hamilton, William H. Harbaugh, James M. McPherson, Russel B. Nye, and Clarence L. Ver Steeg, *The Democratic Experience: An American History* (Dallas, TX: Scott, Foresman, 1981), 424.

51. McCloskey, *American Supreme Court;* Schwartz, *History;* Kens, *Judicial Power.*

52. Pacelle, *Supreme Court's Agenda;* McCloskey, *American Supreme Court.*

53. See Figures 3-7 and 3-9.

54. Pacelle, *Supreme Court's Agenda,* 56–57.

55. Ibid.

56. E.g., *Schenck v. United States,* holding that distributing antidraft leaflets represented a "clear and present danger" to the security of the United States. 249 US 47 (1919).

57. *Palko v. Connecticut,* 302 US 319 (1937).

58. *Duncan v. Louisiana,* holding that the right to a jury trial is a fundamental guarantee protected by the Fourteenth Amendment. 391 US 145 (1968).

59. Pacelle, *Supreme Court's Agenda,* 56, 138.

60. Ibid.

61. McCloskey, *American Supreme Court.*

CHAPTER 4. GOING THEIR OWN WAY: UNANIMITY OF UNITED STATES SUPREME COURT DECISION-MAKING, 1888–1997

1. Epstein, Segal, Spaeth, and Walker, *Supreme Court Compendium* 2d, 195–204.

2. Haynie, "Leadership and Consensus"; Thomas G. Walker, Lee Epstein, and William J. Dixon, "On the Mysterious Demise of Consensual Norms in the United States Supreme Court," *The Journal of Politics* 50 (1988): 361–89.

3. Pritchett, *The Roosevelt Court,* xii–xiii.

4. Learned Hand, *The Bill of Rights* (Cambridge: Harvard University Press, 1958),

72–73. For further support of the institutional benefits of consensus, see Fred M. Vinson, "The Role of Dissent," in *The Judiciary*, ed. John Roche and Leonard Levy (New York: Harcourt Brace, 1964).

5. David J. Danelski, "The Influence of the Chief Justice in the Decisional Process of the Supreme Court," in *American Court Systems: Readings in Judicial Process and Behavior*, ed. Sheldon Goldman and Austin Sarat, 2d ed. (San Francisco: W. H. Freeman, 1989), 496.

6. Ibid.

7. Ibid.

8. Ibid., 497–98.

9. Pritchett, *The Roosevelt Court*, 49.

10. Arthur M. Schlesinger, "The Supreme Court: 1947," *Fortune* 35 (1947): 78.

11. Abraham, *Justices and Presidents*, 152; Kermit Hall, ed., *The Oxford Companion to the Supreme Court* (New York: Oxford University Press, 1992), 442.

12. Henry J. Abraham, *The Judicial Process*, 6th ed. (New York: Oxford University Press, 1993), 199; Stephen L. Wasby, *The Supreme Court in the Federal System* (Chicago: Nelson-Hall, 1993), 237.

13. Abraham, *Justices and Presidents*, 256; Robert J. Steamer, *Chief Justice: Leadership and the Supreme Court* (Columbia: University of South Carolina Press, 1986), 294.

14. Schubert, *Judicial Mind*, 65; Schubert, *Judicial Mind Revisited*.

15. Epstein, Segal, Spaeth, and Walker, *Supreme Court Compendium* 2d, 193–94.

16. Walker, Epstein, and Dixon, "Mysterious Demise," 384–85.

17. Ibid., 379.

18. See O'Brien, *Storm Center*, 270.

19. Walker, Epstein, and Dixon, "Mysterious Demise," 379.

20. Danelski, "The Influence of the Chief Justice," 489.

21. Ibid.

22. Walker, Epstein, and Dixon, "Mysterious Demise," 379.

23. David J. Danelski, "Causes and Consequences of Conflict and Its Resolution in the Supreme Court," in *Judicial Conflict and Consensus: Behavioral Studies of American Appellate Courts*, ed. Sheldon Goldman and Charles M. Lamb (Lexington: University Press of Kentucky, 1986), 33.

24. Danelski, "The Influence of the Chief Justice," 492.

25. Danelski, "Causes and Consequences," 32.

26. Haynie, "Leadership and Consensus," 1160.

27. Ibid., 1167.

28. Walker, Epstein, and Dixon, "Mysterious Demise," 382; Danelski, "The Influence of the Chief Justice," 491.

29. Haynie, "Leadership and Consensus," 1167.

30. Charles Evans Hughes, *The Supreme Court of the United States* (New York: Columbia University Press, 1928), 68.

31. Haynie, "Leadership and Consensus," 1167; Walker, Epstein, and Dixon, "Mysterious Demise," 384.

32. Haynie, "Leadership and Consensus"; Walker, Epstein, and Dixon, "Mysterious Demise."

33. Spaeth, Supreme Court Data Base.

34. See Epstein, Segal, Spaeth, and Walker, *Supreme Court Compendium* 2d, 561.

35. Ibid.

36. O'Brien, *Storm Center*, 114, 270; Schwartz, *History*, 175–76. For example, Fuller was an able social and task leader due in part to his sharp wit and sense of humor. "There is also the story of Holmes's interrupting one of the senior John Harlan's discourses, violating the

unwritten rule against interruptions. 'But that won't wash,' he said, outraging Harlan. Thereupon Chief Justice Melville Fuller quickly started a washboard motion with his hands and said, 'But I just keep scrubbing away, scrubbing away.'" O'Brien, *Storm Center*, 270. Also, Chief Justice Fuller began the custom of the justices shaking hands before they go on to the bench or before beginning conferences. O'Brien, *Storm Center*, 114.

37. Trend is defined as movement in a specific upward or downward direction or, more particularly, "any systematic change in the level of a time series process." David McDowell, Richard McClearly, Errol E. Meidinger, and Richard A. Hay, Jr., *Interrupted Time Series* (Beverly Hills, CA: Sage Publications, 1980), 19–20.

38. Pritchett, *The Roosevelt Court*, 52.

39. Pritchett, *The Roosevelt Court*, 48. For an analysis of the occurrence of divided opinions from 1939 to 1941, see also C. Herman Pritchett, "Division of Opinion Among Justices of the U.S. Supreme Court, 1939–1941," *American Political Science Review* 35 (1941): 890–98.

40. Walker, Epstein, and Dixon, and Haynie find no significant increase in the number of concurring opinions during this term year. Walker, Epstein, and Dixon, "Mysterious Demise," 363; Haynie, "Leadership and Consensus," 1159.

41. Epstein, Segal, Spaeth, and Walker, *Supreme Court Compendium* 2d, 201–4; see also Albert P. Blaustein and Roy M. Mersky, *The First One Hundred Justices: Statistical Studies on the Supreme Court of the United States* (New York: Archon Books, 1978), 127–36.

42. Epstein, Segal, Spaeth, and Walker, *Supreme Court Compendium* 2d, 204.

43. Haynie, "Leadership and Consensus," 1163.

44. Ibid., 1166. For a dissenting opinion on the influence of Chief Justice Hughes in contributing to the decline of norms of consensus on the Court, see Walker, Epstein, and Dixon, "Mysterious Demise."

45. Walker, Epstein, and Dixon, "Mysterious Demise," 382.

46. Haynie, "Leadership and Consensus," 1167.

47. Ibid., 1163.

48. Ibid., 1164.

49. Walker, Epstein, and Dixon, "Mysterious Demise"; Haynie, "Leadership and Consensus."

50. Haynie, "Leadership and Consensus."

51. Pritchett, *The Roosevelt Court*, xii–xiii.

52. Ibid., xii.

53. Ibid.; see also Schubert, *Judicial Mind*, 14.

54. For example, dissents have only recently been allowed in Germany's Constitutional Court. They are, however, not allowed in the courts of Italy or France. Walter F. Murphy and C. Herman Pritchett, *Courts, Judges, and Politics: An Introduction to the Judicial Process*, 4th ed. (New York: McGraw-Hill, 1986), 555.

55. Pritchett, *The Roosevelt Court*, 24.

56. Ibid.

57. For an analysis of the dissent rate during the last five years of the White Court, see Handberg, "Natural Court."

58. Ibid., 364.

59. Ibid.

60. Biskupic and Witt, *Supreme Court at Work*, 33–34; McCloskey, *American Supreme Court*, 104–5; Schwartz, *History*, 210–12.

61. *Wilson v. New*, 243 US 332 (1917).

62. Abraham, *Justices and Presidents*, 418–19.

63. Haynie, "Leadership and Consensus"; Walker, Epstein, and Dixon, "Mysterious Demise."

64. McCloskey, *American Supreme Court*, 106–8.

65. Abraham, *Justices and Presidents*, 418–19.
66. Halpern and Vines, "Institutional Disunity," 478; Blaustein and Mersky, *First One Hundred Justices*, 130–36.
67. Pritchett, *The Roosevelt Court*, 24–25.
68. Ibid., 25; see also Robert E. Cushman, "The Constitutional Decisions of the Supreme Court of the United States in the October Term, 1944," *American Political Science Review* 40 (1946): 231–55.
69. Pritchett's findings are as follows:

Term Yerm	Nonunanimous Opinions	Term Year	Nonunanimous Opinions
1930	11	1939	30
1931	17	1940	28
1932	16	1941	36
1933	16	1942	44
1934	13	1943	58
1935	16	1944	58
1936	19	1945	56
1937	27	1946	64
1938	34		

Pritchett, *The Roosevelt Court*, 25.
70. Ibid.
71. Ibid., 49.
72. Ibid., 50.
73. Halpern and Vines, "Institutional Disunity," 480.
74. Ibid., 475–76.
75. Ibid., 481.
76. Ibid.
77. Walker, Epstein, and Dixon, "Mysterious Demise," 365.
78. Haynie, "Leadership and Consensus," 1165.
79. Gregory A. Caldeira and Christopher J. W. Zorn, "Of Time and Consensual Norms in the Supreme Court," *American Journal of Political Science* 42 (1998): 874–902; Walker, Epstein, and Dixon, "Mysterious Demise."
80. See Schwartz, *History*, 179–84.
81. Pritchett, *The Roosevelt Court*, 25.
82. Ibid.
83. Halpern and Vines, "Institutional Disunity," 476–77.
84. For example, Taft retired in February 1930. Epstein, Segal, Spaeth, and Walker, *Supreme Court Compendium* 2d, 345. Because he served as chief justice for the majority of the 1929 term year, he is scored as chief for that year. Similar decisions are made for the calculation of the averages for the other chief justices.
85. Halpern and Vines, "Institutional Disunity," 473.
86. Walker, Epstein, and Dixon, "Mysterious Demise," 384.
87. See Pritchett, *The Roosevelt Court*, 40.
88. Walker, Epstein, and Dixon, "Mysterious Demise," 361.
89. Caldeira and Zorn, "Judicial Consensus."
90. Haynie, "Leadership and Consensus."
91. Walker, Epstein, and Dixon, "Mysterious Demise," 381–83.

92. Epstein, Segal, Spaeth, and Walker, *Supreme Court Compendium* 2d, 196–99; Blaustein and Merksy, *First One Hundred Justices*, 130–36.

93. Haynie, "Leadership and Consensus," 167.

94. Alpheus T. Mason, *Harlan Fiske Stone: Pillar of the Law* (New York: Viking Press, 1956), 629.

95. Ibid., 591.

96. Pritchett, *The Roosevelt Court*, 52–53.

97. Haynie, "Leadership and Consensus."

98. Walker, Epstein, and Dixon, "Mysterious Demise."

CHAPTER 5. WHO WINS AND WHO LOSES ACROSS TIME: LIBERALISM OF UNITED STATES SUPREME COURT DECISION-MAKING, 1888–1997

1. "For the last couple of years Charles E. Merriam has been predicting gleefully that I would wind up before the bar of the Supreme Court on a contempt charge. I hope it will be obvious to anyone who reads this book that I am *amicus curiae*, with a deep respect for the judicial process and a great sympathy for the present Court. The attempts made here to examine into the personal foundations of judicial decisions may be wide of the mark, but in any event they are honest attempts and not intended to suggest that the present justices are motivated by their own preferences to any greater extent or are more politically minded than their predecessors. It is my view that the Supreme Court inevitably acts in a political context, and that the greatest danger to the Court and from the Court comes when that fact is inadequately realized." Pritchett, *The Roosevelt Court*, xiii; see also Horwitz, *Transformation*, 4–7.

2. Pritchett, *The Roosevelt Court*, 14.

3. Ibid., 15.

4. Ibid., 16.

5. Max Lerner, *Ideas for the Ice Age* (New York: Viking Press, 1941), 259.

6. U.S. Constitution, art. 3; see also Murphy, *Elements of Judicial Strategy*.

7. Lawrence Baum, "Measuring Policy Change in the U.S. Supreme Court," *American Political Science Review* 82 (1988): 905–12; Lawrence Baum, "Comparing the Policy Periods of Supreme Court Justices from Different Periods," *Western Political Quarterly* 42 (1989): 509–21.

8. Baum, "Measuring Policy Change," 907.

9. James Q. Wilson and John J. DiIulio, Jr., *American Government: Institutions and Policies*, 8th ed. (Boston: Houghton Mifflin Co., 2001), 118–19.

10. S. Sidney Ulmer, "Selecting Cases for Supreme Court Review: An Underdog Model," *American Political Science Review* 72 (1978): 902–10.

11. Pamela Johnson Conover and Stanley Feldman, "The Origins and Meaning of Liberal/Conservative Self-Identification," in *Controversies in Voting Behavior*, ed. Richard G. Niemi and Herbert F. Weisberg, 2d ed. (Washington, DC: Congressional Quarterly Press, 1984), 374.

12. Spaeth, Supreme Court Data Base.

13. Ibid.

14. Schwartz, *History*, 174, 209.

15. Cf. Melvin I. Urofsky, "Myth and Reality: The Supreme Court and Protective Legislation in the Progressive Era," *Yearbook of the Supreme Court Historical Society* (Washington,

DC: Supreme Court Historical Society, 1983) with Charles Warren, "The Progressiveness of the United States Supreme Court," *Columbia Law Review* 13 (1913): 294–313.

16. McCloskey, *American Supreme Court*, 117–20; Schwartz, *History*, 233–36.

17. Pritchett, *The Roosevelt Court*, 89.

18. Ibid., 262.

19. Segal and Spaeth, *Attitudinal Model*, 244.

20. See McCloskey, *American Supreme Court*, 96–108; Schwartz, *History*, 96–108.

21. *Pollock v. Farmers' Loan and Trust Co.*

22. However, Walker, Epstein, and Dixon discount this influence ("Mysterious Demise," 370).

23. Pritchett, *The Roosevelt Court*, 141.

24. Lee Epstein, Thomas G. Walker, and William J. Dixon, "The Supreme Court and Criminal Justice Disputes: A Neo-Institutional Perspective," *American Journal of Political Science* 33 (1989): 825–41.

25. Ibid., 834.

26. Ibid.

27. *Plessy v. Ferguson.*

28. *Brown v. Board of Education.*

29. Schwartz, *History*, 221–23.

30. McCloskey, *American Supreme Court*, 115–16.

31. Biskupic and Witt, *Supreme Court at Work*, 37.

32. Pritchett, *The Roosevelt Court*, 131.

33. Epstein, Walker, and Dixon, "Supreme Court and Criminal Disputes."

34. McCloskey, *American Supreme Court*, 115–16.

35. Pritchett, *The Roosevelt Court*.

36. *West Virginia State Board of Education v. Barnette*, 319 US 624 (1943); Pritchett, *The Roosevelt Court*, 98–99.

37. Pacelle, *Supreme Court's Agenda*.

38. *Olmstead v. United States*, 277 US 438 (1928).

39. Ulmer, "Selecting Cases," 902–10.

40. Pacelle, *Supreme Court's Agenda*, 120–21.

41. Pritchett, *The Roosevelt Court*, 208, 257.

42. Ibid.; Schubert, *Judicial Mind*; Schubert, *Judicial Mind Revisited*.

43. McCloskey, *American Supreme Court*; Schwartz, *History*.

44. McCloskey, *American Supreme Court*; Schwartz, *History*.

45. Urofsky, "Myth and Reality"; Warren, "Progressiveness."

46. Handberg, "Natural Court," 360.

47. Ibid.

48. Ibid.

49. Abraham, *Justices and Presidents*, 212.

50. Pritchett, *The Roosevelt Court*, 257.

51. Haynie and Tate, "Institutional Liberalism," 18, Figure 2a.

52. Segal and Spaeth, *Attitudinal Model*, 244–55.

53. Haynie and Tate, "Institutional Liberalism," 19, Figure 2b.

54. Ibid.

55. Epstein, Walker, and Dixon, "Supreme Court and Criminal Disputes."

56. Haynie and Tate, "Institutional Liberalism."

57. Schwartz, *History*.

58. McCloskey, *American Supreme Court*.

59. Haynie and Tate, "Institutional Liberalism," 19, Figure 2b.

60. Pritchett, *The Roosevelt Court*, 254.

61. Segal and Spaeth, *Attitudinal Model*, 244; Haynie and Tate, "Institutional Liberalism," 19.

62. Segal and Spaeth, *Attitudinal Model*, 244–55.

63. See also the discussion of the liberalism of judicial power in the section of this chapter analyzing the individual issue areas.

64. Haynie and Tate, "Institutional Liberalism"; McCloskey, *American Supreme Court*; Schwartz, *History*.

65. Pacelle, *Supreme Court's Agenda*.

Chapter 6. The Long-Run Relationship between the Supreme Court's Decision-Making Environment and Its Liberalism, 1888–1997

1. Pritchett, *The Roosevelt Court*, 14.

2. See the analyses presented in chapter 5.

3. David W. Rohde and Kenneth A. Shepsle, "Thinking About Legislative Reform," in *Legislative Reform: The Policy Impact*, ed. Leroy N. Rieselbach (Lexington, MA: Lexington Books, 1978); John A. Aldrich, "Rational Choice Theory and the Study of American Politics," in *The Dynamics of American Politics: Approaches and Interpretations*, ed. Lawrence C. Dodd and Calvin Jillson (Boulder, CO: Westview Press, 1994).

4. Murphy, *Elements of Judicial Strategy*.

5. See, e.g., Robert Lowry Clinton, "Game Theory, Legal History, and the Origins of Judicial Review: A Revisionist Analysis of *Marbury v. Madison*," *American Journal of Political Science* 38 (1994): 285–302; Forrest Maltzman and Paul J. Wahlbeck, "May It Please the Chief? Opinion Assignments in the Rehnquist Court," *American Journal of Political Science* 40 (1996): 421–43; Peter C. Ordeshook, *A Political Theory Primer* (New York: Routledge, 1992); Jeffrey A. Segal, "Separation-of-Powers Games in the Positive Theory of Congress and Courts," *American Political Science Review* 91 (1997): 28–44.

6. Lee Epstein and Jack Knight, *The Choices Justices Make* (Washington, DC: Congressional Quarterly Press, 1998).

7. Ibid.

8. Segal and Spaeth, *Attitudinal Model*.

9. See Murphy, *Elements of Judicial Strategy*.

10. See Bickel, *Least Dangerous Branch*.

11. *Scott v. Sanford*.

12. McCloskey, *American Supreme Court*; Schwartz, *History*.

13. Epstein and Knight, *Choices*; Murphy, *Elements of Judicial Strategy*.

14. For example, Congress may pass a constitutional amendment so as to nullify one of the Court's decisions. It did so following the Civil War when it proposed the Thirteenth Amendment following the Court's decision in *Scott v. Sanford*. Epstein and Knight, *Choices*; Murphy, *Elements of Judicial Strategy*.

15. William Howard Taft did so from 1909–1913. Wilson and DiIulio, *American Government*, A31; see also Epstein, Segal, Spaeth, and Walker, *Supreme Court Compendium* 2d.

16. Abraham, *Justices and Presidents*.

17. Epstein and Knight point out that John Marshall's opinion in *Marbury v. Madison* is illustrative of this concept in that Marshall crafted an opinion in which he acted in a strategic manner in that he did not vote his sincere policy preferences (i.e., order President Jefferson

to deliver Marbury's commission) for fear that the President's refusal to obey the Court's order would drastically injure the Court's fledgling legitimacy. Epstein and Knight, *Choices*.

18. Caldeira and Zorn, "Of Time and Consensual Norms," 871; see also Jack Knight, *Institutions and Social Conflict* (New York: Cambridge University Press, 1992); Jack Knight and Itai Sened, *Explaining Social Institutions* (Ann Arbor: University of Michigan Press, 1995).

19. Paul Brace and Melinda Gann Hall, "Integrated Models of Judicial Dissent," *The Journal of Politics* 55 (1993): 914–31.

20. Epstein and Knight, *Choices*; see also Caldeira and Zorn, "Of Time and Consensual Norms"; Edward P. Schwartz, "The Proliferation of Concurring Opinions on the U.S. Supreme Court: Politics Killed the Norm" (paper presented at the annual meeting of the American Law and Economics Association, Toronto, ON, 1997).

21. Lawrence Baum, *The Supreme Court*, 7th ed. (Washington, DC: Congressional Quarterly Press, 2001).

22. Aldrich, "Rational Choice Theory," 227.

23. For exceptions, see, e.g., Haynie and Tate, "Institutional Liberalism"; Epstein, Walker, and Dixon, "Criminal Justice Disputes."

24. See chapter 5.

25. See Table 3-1.

26. Pacelle, *Supreme Court's Agenda*.

27. Spaeth, Supreme Court Data Base.

28. Baum, *The Supreme Court*.

29. E.g., Segal and Spaeth, *The Attitudinal Model*.

30. Baum, *The Supreme Court*; Roger Handberg and C. Neal Tate, "Length of Service and Behavior of the U.S. Supreme Court Justices, 1916–1989" (paper presented at the annual meeting of the Midwest Political Science Association, Chicago, IL, April 1990); Schubert, *Judicial Mind Revisited*; but see Lee Epstein, Valerie Hoekstra, Jeffrey Segal, and Harold J. Spaeth, "Do Political Preferences Change? A Longitudinal Study of U.S. Supreme Court Justices," *The Journal of Politics* 60 (1998): 801–18.

31. Segal and Cover, "Ideological Values"; see chapter 1.

32. Jeffrey A. Segal, Lee Epstein, Charles M. Cameron, and Harold J. Spaeth, "Ideological Values and the Votes of U.S. Supreme Court Justices Revisited," *The Journal of Politics* 57 (1995): 812–23.

33. Lee Epstein and Carol Mershon, "Measuring Political Preferences," *American Journal of Political Science* 40 (1996): 261–94.

34. Baum, "Measuring Policy Change"; Baum, "Comparing Policy Periods."

35. Baum, *The Supreme Court*.

36. Tate, "Personal Attribute Models"; Tate and Handberg, "Time Binding"; Haynie and Tate, "Institutional Liberalism." Although most justices identify with either the Democratic or Republican parties, Felix Frankfurter has been, to this point, the lone nominal independent on the Court, although he was linked with Democratic politics prior to and after his nomination. Epstein, Segal, Spaeth, and Walker, *Supreme Court Compendium* 2d, 319.

37. Haynie and Tate, "Institutional Liberalism," 16.

38. Epstein, Walker, and Dixon, "Criminal Justice Disputes."

39. Epstein, Segal, Spaeth, and Walker, *Supreme Court Compendium* 2d, 315–21.

40. Haynie and Tate, "Institutional Liberalism," 3.

41. Abraham, *Justices and Presidents*; Baum, *The Supreme Court*; Robert Scigliano, *The Supreme Court and the Presidency* (New York: Free Press, 1971).

42. Tate and Handberg, "Time Binding," 466.

43. Abraham, *Justices and Presidents*.

44. Tate and Handberg, "Time Binding," 466–67.

45. Seymour M. Lipset and Stein Rokkan, "Cleavage Structures, Party Systems, and Voting Alignments," in *Party Systems and Voter Alignments*, ed. Seymour M. Lipset and Stein Rokkan (New York: Free Press, 1967).

46. Tate, "Personal Attribute Models"; Tate and Handberg, "Time Binding."

47. Sheldon Goldman, "Voting Behavior on the United States Courts of Appeals Revisited," *American Political Science Review* 69 (1975): 461–506; S. Sidney Ulmer, "Social Background as an Indicator to the Votes of Supreme Court Justices in Criminal Cases," *Midwest Journal of Political Science* 17 (1973): 622–30.

48. Epstein, Segal, Spaeth, and Walker, *Supreme Court Compendium* 2d, 239–51.

49. Tate and Handberg, "Time Binding," 468.

50. Epstein, Segal, Spaeth, and Walker, *Supreme Court Compendium* 2d, 239–51.

51. Although the West and the Midwest certainly are regionally important, no clear theory can be proposed about their effect on political attitudes. For example, many people who reside in the West (primarily California, Oregon, and Washington) tend to have liberal political attitudes. Many others in these same states tend to hold conservative attitudes. Furthermore, the Western region more generally is difficult to clearly operationalize, for it includes the Big Sky states of Montana, Wyoming, Idaho, and Utah, all of which tend to be generally associated with a conservative ideology. This confounds construction of measures of the likely effect on political attitudes. Moreover, contemporary literature in the judicial politics subfield does not disaggregate regional origins beyond the traditional South/Non-South dichotomy.

52. Epstein, Segal, Spaeth, and Walker, *Supreme Court Compendium* 2d, 305–21.

53. V. O. Key, Jr., *Southern Politics in State and Nation* (Knoxville: University of Tennessee Press, 1949).

54. Richard E. Johnston, "Supreme Court Voting Behavior: A Comparison of the Warren and Burger Courts," in *Cases in American Politics*, ed. Robert L. Peabody (New York: Praeger, 1976), 83; John Schmidhauser, *Constitutional Law in the Political Process* (Chicago: Rand McNally, 1963).

55. Walker, Epstein, and Dixon, "Mysterious Demise," 385.

56. Ibid.

57. Tate and Handberg, "Time Binding," 474.

58. Johnston, "Supreme Court Voting Behavior."

59. Haynie and Tate, "Institutional Liberalism"; Tate and Handberg, "Theory Building."

60. Tate and Handberg, "Time Binding," 470–71.

61. Epstein, Segal, Spaeth, and Walker, *Supreme Court Compendium* 2d, 296–303.

62. O'Brien, *Storm Center*, 104.

63. Mary Frances Berry, *Stability, Security, and Continuity: Mr. Justice Burton and Decision-Making in the Supreme Court, 1945–1958* (Westport, CT: Greenwood Press, 1978), 27.

64. Degler et al., *Democratic Experience*, 411.

65. Ibid.

66. See Haynie and Tate, "Institutional Liberalism."

67. John B. Gates, *The Supreme Court and Partisan Realignment: A Macro- and Microlevel Perspective* (Boulder, CO: Westview Press, 1992), 8.

68. Degler et al., *Democratic Experience*, 456–57.

69. Handberg, "Natural Court"; Degler et al., *Democratic Experience*, 456–57.

70. McCloskey, *American Supreme Court*, 109.

71. Ibid.

72. Ibid., 117–20.

73. Haynie and Tate, "Institutional Liberalism."

74. E.g., McCloskey, *American Supreme Court*; Schwartz, *History*.

75. See chapter 3.

76. McCloskey, *American Supreme Court*, 117.

77. Ibid.

78. Ibid., 113.

79. Scigliano, *Supreme Court and the Presidency*, 44.

80. McCloskey, *American Supreme Court*, 113; Scigliano, *Supreme Court and the Presidency*, 44. The justices who caused Roosevelt the most consternation were the vaunted "Four Horsemen of the Apocalypse": George Sutherland, Willis Van Devanter, James C. McReynolds, and Pierce Butler. Schwartz, *History*, 279. Prior to 1936, Owen Roberts and Charles Evans Hughes would occasionally vote with the conservative bloc. In reality, however, the justices about whom Roosevelt was particularly concerned were the very ones who were the staunchest opponents of his New Deal programs. Scigliano, *Supreme Court and the Presidency*, 45.

81. McCloskey, *American Supreme Court*, 113.

82. Ibid., 117.

83. Glendon A. Schubert, *Quantitative Analysis of Judicial Behavior* (Glencoe, IL: Free Press, 1959). However, see Gregory A. Caldeira ("Public Opinion and the U.S. Supreme Court: FDR's Court-Packing Plan," *American Political Science Review* 81 [1987]: 1139–53), who investigates the effect of public opinion on FDR's plan.

84. Schubert, *Quantitative Analysis*, 193.

85. Ibid., 193–94.

86. Ibid., 198–99.

87. Ibid., 206–10.

88. See chapter 3.

89. Spaeth, Supreme Court Data Base.

90. For ease of usage, "civil liberties" is used to refer to the aggregated issue dimension of civil liberties–civil rights, discussed in more detail in chapter 5.

91. Pritchett, *The Roosevelt Court*, 273.

92. Tate and Handberg, "Time Binding," 471.

93. Ibid.; Tate, "Personal Attribute Models," 481.

94. Tate and Handberg, "Theory Building," 471.

95. Ibid., 474–75, note 21.

96. Haynie and Tate, "Institutional Liberalism," 16.

97. McCloskey, *American Supreme Court*, 170.

98. The present analysis is limited to formally declared wars because I expect that they represent long-term and substantively greater threats to the nation than undeclared military actions.

99. See chapter 3.

100. Tate and Handberg, "Time Binding," 471.

101. Tate, "Personal Attribute Models, 361.

102. Johnston, "Supreme Court Voting Behavior," 83.

103. Baum, *Supreme Court*; Pritchett, *Elements of Judicial Strategy*.

104. Halpern and Vines, "Institutional Disunity," 483.

105. The Judiciary Act of 1925 is not theorized to become influential until the 1927 term year so as to allow the Court to dispose of the cases that were on its docket prior to the passage of that act. See Halpern and Vines, "Institutional Disunity."

106. Robert Engle and Clive W. J. Granger, "Co-Integration and Error Correction: Representation, Estimation, and Testing," *Econometrica* 55 (1987): 251–76.

107. Clive W. J. Granger and Roselyne Joyeux, "An Introduction to Long-Memory Time Series Models and Fractional Differencing," *Journal of Time Series* 1 (1980): 15–29.

Differencing, while common, may not always be a benign transformation of the data. Overdifferencing the data may upset the inferential process that is at the heart of empirical research. Suzanne DeBoef and Jim Granato discuss the consequences of differencing time series data and the use of near-integrated data in political science literature. Suzanne DeBoef and Jim Granato, "Near-Integrated Data and the Analysis of Political Relationships," *American Journal of Political Science* 41 (1997): 619–40. Issues of the noninteger, or fractional, integration of the data are also of concern in this context.

108. David A. Dickey and Wayne A. Fuller, "Likelihood Ratio Statistics for Autoregressive Time Series With a Unit Root," *Econometrica* 49 (1981): 1057–72; Engle and Granger, "Co-Integration and Error Correction."

109. Janet Box-Steffensmeier and Renee Smith, "Investigating Political Dynamics Using Fractional Integration Methods," *American Journal of Political Science* 42 (1998): 661–89; Clive W. J. Granger, "Long Memory Relationships and the Aggregation of Dynamic Models," *Journal of Econometrics* 14 (1980): 227–38; Granger and Joyeux, "Long-Memory Time Series"; J. R. M. Hosking, "Fractional Differencing," *Biometrika* 68 (1981): 165–76.

John T. Barkoulas and Christopher F. Baum describe fractionally integrated series as having a long memory. "Long memory, or long term dependence, describes the correlation structure of a series at long lags. If a series exhibits long memory, there is persistent temporal dependence even between distant observations." John T. Barkoulas, and Christopher F. Baum, "Long Term Dependence in Stock Returns," *Economic Letters* 52 (1997): 253–60. To model such long-term relationships among the data, researchers can describe the data generating process as,

$$\Phi(L)(1-L)^d x_t = \theta(L)\hat{\epsilon}_t$$

The parameter $\Phi(L)$ represents stationary autoregressive processes and the parameter $\theta(L)$ represents moving average components. The fractional differencing parameter, d, can take noninteger values, and $\hat{\epsilon}_t$ has an unconditional distribution $(N(0,\sigma^2))$. See Box-Steffensmeier and Smith, "Investigating Political Dynamics." If d in Equation (1) is 0, then x_t is characterized by mean reversion, and finite variance and covariance. Then, the data generating process for the stationary series can be modeled using theoretically interesting combinations of autoregressive and/or moving-average components, so-called ARMA (p, 0, q) models. See Bruce L. Bowerman and Richard T. O'Connell, *Forecasting and Time Series: An Applied Approach*, 3d ed. (Belmont, CA: Duxbury Press, 1993). On the other hand, if d is 1, then x_t is nonstationary, characterized by mean, variance, and covariance nonstationarity. This ARIMA (p, 1, q) model is referred to as "integrated because the effects of a shock persist at full force in each period and accumulate over time. Integrated processes have theoretically infinite variances, exhibit long stochastic swings up or down, and do not return to a constant mean level." Box-Steffensmeier and Smith, "Investigating Political Dynamics," 664.

Fractionally integrated series present unique time serial dependencies, as compared to those of stationary ($d=0$) and fully integrated, or unit root, series ($d=1$). These fractionally integrated series are long-memoried, mean-reverting, and either have finite variance if d is less than 0.5 or infinite variance if d is greater than 0.5. Such series differ from a stationary, autoregressive (AR) series in that the fractionally integrated series decays very slowly, while the AR process decays exponentially. Thus, while shocks to a stationary series quickly dissipate, or are forgotten, a fractionally integrated series exhibits long memory but not the perfect memory that is characteristic of a random walk; that is, the series' value during each period is equal to its value in the previous period plus any shock that the system incurred since the previous period. Matthew J. Lebo and Robert W. Walker, "Long Memory and Fractional Cointegration in Models of British Politics" (paper presented at the annual meeting of the Midwest Political Science Association, Chicago, IL, April 1999); Matthew J. Lebo,

Robert W. Walker, and Harold D. Clarke, "You Must Remember This: Dealing With Long Memory in Political Analyses" (paper presented at the Annual Meeting of the American Political Science Association, Boston, MA, September 1998).

110. Box-Steffensmeier and Smith, "Investigating Political Dynamics"; Lebo and Walker, "Long Memory."

111. See Lebo and Walker, "Long Memory."

112. See DeBoef and Granato, "Near-Integrated Data," for a discussion of the perils of overdifferencing.

113. Janet Box-Steffensmeier and Andrew R. Tomlinson, "Fractional Integration Methods in Political Science," *Electoral Studies* 19 (2000): 63–76; Lebo and Walker, "Long Memory."

114. Granger, "Long-Memory Relationships."

115. Granger, "Long-Memory Relationships"; Caldeira and Zorn, "Of Time and Consensual Norms."

116. Gibson, "Judges' Role Orientations."

117. The code necessary to implement Robinson's procedure to estimate the degree of fractional integration of a series can be downloaded from the RATS website (http://www.estima.com). For further technical information, see Peter M. Robinson, "Gaussian Semi-Parametric Estimation of Long Range Dependence," *Annals of Statistics* 23 (1995): 1630–61.

118. Richard T. Baille, "Long Memory Processes and Fractional Integration in Econometrics," *Journal of Econometrics* 73 (1996): 5–59, 39.

119. See Lebo, Walker, and Clarke, "You Must Remember This"; Box-Steffensmeier and Smith, "Investigating Political Dynamics."

120. DeBoef and Granato, "Near-Integrated Data."

121. David A. Dickey and Wayne A. Fuller, "Distribution of the Estimators for Autoregressive Time Series With a Unit Root," *Journal of the American Statistical Association* 74 (1979): 427–31. The Dickey-Fuller tests the null hypothesis of a random walk against the hypothesis of a series containing a unit root and thus being stationary. The Augmented Dickey-Fuller test involves the addition of lagged values of the differenced series so that the residuals from the regression are white-noise so that inferences about the degree of stationarity of the series can validly be determined. Damodar N. Gujarati, *Basic Econometrics*, 3d ed. (New York: McGraw-Hill, 1995).

122. Denis Kwiatkowski, Peter C. B. Phillips, Peter Schmidt, and Yongcheol Shin, "Testing the Null Hypothesis of Stationarity Against the Alternative of a Unit Root," *Journal of Econometrics* 54 (1992): 159–78. See also Lebo, Walker, and Clarke, "You Must Remember This."

123. Francis X. Diebold and Glenn D. Rudebusch, "Long Memory and Persistence in Aggregate Output," *Journal of Monetary Economics* 24 (1989): 189–209. For space considerations, the results of the variance ratio tests are not reported. They are, however, available from the author on request.

124. Engle and Granger, "Co-Integration and Error Correction"; see also Granger and Joyeux, "Long-Memory Time Series," for the deleterious implications of differencing operations.

125. See Caldeira and Zorn, "Of Time and Consensual Norms."

126. If the series are stationary in their level form, then the analyst can proceed to complete traditional methods of statistical analysis since the potential of spurious regression is not present.

127. Engle and Granger, "Co-Integration and Error Correction"; see also Robert S. Pindyck and Daniel L. Rubinfeld, *Econometric Models and Economic Forecasts*, 3d ed. (New York: McGraw-Hill, 1991).

128. See also Pindyck and Rubinfeld, *Econometric Models*.

129. The residuals from the KPSS test for the civil liberties–civil rights model, including a constant and no trend term (η_μ), demonstrate stationarity at high levels of statistical significance. The results including a constant and a trend term (η_τ) also demonstrate stationarity at conventional levels of significance.

130. Yin-Wong Cheung and Kon S. Lai, "A Fractional Cointegration Analysis of Purchasing Power Parity," *Journal of Business and Economic Statistics* 11 (1993): 103–12; Michael Dueker and Richard Startz, "Maximum-Likelihood Estimation of Fractional Cointegration With an Application to U.S. and Canadian Bond Rates," *The Review of Economics and Statistics* 80 (1998): 420–26; Matthew J. Lebo, "Fractional Integration and Political Modeling" (Ph.D. diss., University of North Texas, 1999); Drew Noble Lanier and Mark S. Hurwitz, "Traversing the Bounds of Consensus: The Long-Run Relationship Between Concurring and Dissenting Opinions in the U.S. Supreme Court, 1888–1997" (paper presented at the annual meeting of the American Political Science Association, Atlanta, GA, September 1999).

131. Box-Steffensmeier and Tomlinson, "Fractional Integration Methods," 11.

132. Ibid.; Lebo, "Fractional Integration"; Lanier and Hurwitz, "Traversing the Bounds of Consensus."

133. Robinson, "Gaussian Semi-Parametric Estimation."

134. See Lebo, "Fractional Integration."

135. Engle and Granger, "Co-Integration and Error Correction."

136. Caldeira and Zorn, "Of Time and Consensual Norms," 894.

137. Ibid.

138. Schwartz, *History*.

139. Biskupic and Witt, *Supreme Court at Work*; McCloskey, *American Supreme Court*.

140. Haynie and Tate, "Institutional Liberalism," 16, table 1.

141. Pritchett, *The Roosevelt Court*, 177.

142. *Korematsu v. United States*.

143. See DeBoef and Granato, "Near-Integrated Data."

144. Segal and Spaeth, *Attitudinal Model*.

145. Tate, "Personal Attribute Models"; Tate and Handberg, "Time Binding."

146. Pacelle, *Supreme Court's Agenda*.

147. Maltzman and Wahlbeck, "May It Please the Chief?"; Forrest Maltzman, James F. Spriggs, and Paul J. Wahlbeck, "Strategy and Judicial Choice: New Institutionalist Approaches to Supreme Court Decision-Making," in *Supreme Court Decision-Making*, ed. Cornell W. Clayton and Howard Gillman (Chicago: University of Chicago Press, 1999).

148. Pritchett, *The Roosevelt Court*, 14.

CHAPTER 7. THE CONTINUITY OF CHANGE:
THE SUPREME COURT ACROSS TIME

1. Casper and Posner, *Workload*.

2. Pacelle, *Supreme Court's Agenda*, 57.

3. Ibid.

4. McCloskey, *American Supreme Court*.

5. Pacelle, *Supreme Court's Agenda*.

6. McCloskey, *American Supreme Court*.

7. Schubert, *Judicial Mind*; Schubert, *Judicial Mind Revisited*.

8. Haynie, "Leadership and Consensus."

9. Walker, Epstein, and Dixon, "Mysterious Demise."

10. Haynie, "Leadership and Consensus"; Walker, Epstein, and Dixon, "Mysterious Demise."

11. McCloskey, *American Supreme Court*; Schwartz, *History*.

12. Pritchett, *The Roosevelt Court*; Haynie and Tate, "Institutional Liberalism."

13. Epstein, Walker, and Dixon, "Criminal Justice Disputes"; Haynie and Tate, "Institutional Liberalism"; Pritchett, *The Roosevelt Court*; Segal and Spaeth, *Attitudinal Model*.

14. McCloskey, *American Supreme Court*; Schwartz, *History*.

15. Haynie and Tate, "Institutional Liberalism."

16. Schwartz, *History*.

17. Haynie and Tate, "Institutional Liberalism."

18. Tate and Handberg, "Time Binding."

19. Segal, Epstein, Cameron, and Spaeth, "Ideological Values Revisited."

20. McCloskey, *American Supreme Court*; Schwartz, *History*.

21. Pritchett, *The Roosevelt Court*.

22. McCloskey, *American Supreme Court*; Schwartz, *History*.

23. McCloskey, *American Supreme Court*; Schwartz, *History*.

24. However, Warren, and Urofsky argue that the Court's economic decision-making was not as conservative as commonly believed. Urofsky, "Myth and Reality"; Warren, "Progressiveness."

25. Caldeira and Zorn, "Of Time and Consensual Norms"; Lanier and Hurwitz, "Traversing the Bounds of Consensus."

26. McCloskey, *American Supreme Court*; Schwartz, *History*.

27. McCloskey, *American Supreme Court*; Schubert, *Judicial Mind*; Schubert, *Judicial Mind Revisited*.

28. Segal and Cover, "Ideological Values"; Segal, Epstein, Cameron, and Spaeth, "Ideological Values Revisited."

29. Sandra L. Wood, Linda Camp Keith, Drew Noble Lanier, and Ayo Ogundele, "Is the Attitudinal Model of Supreme Court Decision Making Time-Bound?" (paper presented at the annual meeting of the Southern Political Science Association, Tampa, FL, November 1995).

References

Abraham, Henry J. *The Judicial Process*. 6th ed. New York: Oxford University Press, 1993.

————. *Justices and Presidents: A Political History of Appointments to the Supreme Court*. 3d ed. New York: Oxford University Press, 1993.

Adkins v. Children's Hospital. 261 US 525 (1923).

Aldrich, John A. "Rational Choice Theory and the Study of American Politics." In *The Dynamics of American Politics: Approaches and Interpretations*, edited by Lawrence C. Dodd and Calvin Jillson. Boulder, CO: Westview Press, 1994.

Baille, Richard T. "Long Memory Processes and Fractional Integration in Econometrics." *Journal of Econometrics* 73 (1996): 5–59.

Barkoulas, John T., and Christopher F. Baum. "Long Term Dependence in Stock Returns." *Economic Letters* 52 (1997): 253–60.

Baum, Lawrence. "Measuring Policy Change in the U.S. Supreme Court." *American Political Science Review* 82 (1988): 905–12.

————. "Comparing the Policy Periods of Supreme Court Justices from Different Periods." *Western Political Quarterly* 42 (1989): 509–21.

————. *The Supreme Court*. 7th ed. Washington, DC: Congressional Quarterly Press, 2001.

Berry, Mary Frances. *Stability, Security, and Continuity: Mr. Justice Burton and Decision-Making in the Supreme Court, 1945–1958*. Westport, CT: Greenwood Press, 1978.

Bickel, Alexander. *The Least Dangerous Branch: The Supreme Court at the Bar of Politics*. 2d ed. New Haven: Yale University Press, 1968.

Biskupic, Joan, and Elder Witt. *The Supreme Court at Work*. 2d ed. Washington, DC: Congressional Quarterly Press, 1997.

Blaustein, Albert P., and Roy M. Mersky. *The First One Hundred Justices: Statistical Studies on the Supreme Court of the United States*. New York: Archon Books, 1978.

Bowerman, Bruce L., and Richard T. O'Connell. *Forecasting and Time Series: An Applied Approach*. 3d ed. Belmont, CA: Duxbury Press, 1993.

Box-Steffensmeier, Janet, and Renée Smith. "Investigating Political Dynamics Using Fractional Integration Methods." *American Journal of Political Science* 42 (1998): 661–89.

Box-Steffensmeier, Janet, and Andrew R. Tomlinson. "Fractional Integration Methods in Political Science." *Electoral Studies* 19 (2000): 63–76.

Brace, Paul, and Melinda Gann Hall. "Integrated Models of Judicial Dissent." *The Journal of Politics* 55 (1993): 914–31.

Brown v. Board of Education. 347 US 483 (1954).

Caldeira, Gregory A. "Public Opinion and the U.S. Supreme Court: FDR's Court-Packing Plan." *American Political Science Review* 81 (1987): 1139–53.

Caldeira, Gregory A., and John R. Wright. "Organized Interests and Agenda Setting in the U.S. Supreme Court." *American Political Science Review* 82 (1988): 1109–27.

Caldeira, Gregory A., and Christopher J. W. Zorn. "Of Time and Consensual Norms in the Supreme Court." *American Journal of Political Science* 42 (1998): 874–902.

Cardozo, Benjamin N. *The Nature of the Judicial Process.* 1921; New Haven: Yale University Press, 1967.

Casper, Gerhard, and Richard A. Posner. *The Workload of the Supreme Court.* Chicago: American Bar Foundation, 1976.

Cheung, Yin-Wong, and Kon S. Lai. "A Fractional Cointegration Analysis of Purchasing Power Parity." *Journal of Business and Economic Statistics* 11 (1993): 103–12.

Chicago, Milwaukee & St. Paul Railway Co. v. Minnesota. 134 US 418 (1890).

Clinton, Robert Lowry. "Game Theory, Legal History, and the Origins of Judicial Review: A Revisionist Analysis of *Marbury v. Madison.*" *American Journal of Political Science* 38 (1994): 285–302.

Conover, Pamela Johnston, and Stanley Feldman. "The Origins and Meaning of Liberal/Conservative Self-Identification." In *Controversies in Voting Behavior*, edited by Richard G. Niemi and Herbert F. Weisberg. 2d ed. Washington, DC: Congressional Quarterly Press, 1984.

Corrigan v. Buckley. 271 US 323 (1926).

Cushman, Robert E. "The Constitutional Decisions of the Supreme Court of the United States in the October Term, 1944." *American Political Science Review* 40 (1946): 231–55.

Danelski, David J. "Causes and Consequences of Conflict and Its Resolution in the Supreme Court." In *Judicial Conflict and Consensus: Behavioral Studies of American Appellate Courts*, edited by Sheldon Goldman and Charles M. Lamb. Lexington: University Press of Kentucky, 1986.

———. "The Influence of the Chief Justice in the Decisional Process of the Supreme Court." In *American Court Systems: Readings in Judicial Process and Behavior*, edited by Sheldon Goldman and Austin Sarat. 2d ed. San Francisco: W. H. Freeman, 1989.

DeBoef, Suzanna, and Jim Granato. "Near-Integrated Data and the Analysis of Political Relationships." *American Journal of Political Science* 41 (1997): 619–40.

Degler, Carl N., Thomas C. Cochran, Vincent P. De Santis, Holman Hamilton, William H. Harbaugh, James M. McPherson, Russel B. Nye, and Clarence L. Ver Steeg. *The Democratic Experience: An American History.* Dallas, TX: Scott, Foresman, 1981.

Dickey, David A., and Wayne A. Fuller. "Distribution of the Estimators for Autoregressive Time Series with a Unit Root." *Journal of the American Statistical Association* 74 (1979): 427–31.

———. "Likelihood Ratio Statistics for Autoregressive Time Series With a Unit Root." *Econometrica* 49 (1981): 1057–72.

Diebold, Francis X., and Glenn D. Rudebusch. "Long Memory and Persistence in Aggregate Output." *Journal of Monetary Economics* 24 (1989): 189–209.

Dueker, Michael, and Richard Startz. "Maximum-Likelihood Estimation of Fractional Cointegration with an Application to U.S. and Canadian Bond Rates." *The Review of Economics and Statistics* 80 (1998): 420–26.

Duncan v. Louisiana. 391 US 145 (1968).

Engle, Robert, and Clive W. J. Granger. "Co-Integration and Error Correction: Representation, Estimation, and Testing." *Econometrica* 55 (1987): 251–76.

Epp, Charles R. *The Rights Revolution: Lawyers, Activists, and Supreme Courts in Comparative Perspective.* Chicago: University of Chicago Press, 1998.

Epstein, Lee, Valerie Hoekstra, Jeffrey Segal, and Harold J. Spaeth. "Do Political Preferences Change? A Longitudinal Study of U.S. Supreme Court Justices." *The Journal of Politics* 60 (1998): 801–18.

Epstein, Lee, and Jack Knight. *The Choices Justices Make.* Washington, DC: Congressional Quarterly Press, 1998.

Epstein, Lee, and Carol Mershon. "Measuring Political Preferences." *American Journal of Political Science* 40 (1996): 261–94.

Epstein, Lee, Jeffrey A. Segal, Harold J. Spaeth, and Thomas G. Walker. *The Supreme Court Compendium: Data, Decisions and Developments.* Washington, DC: Congressional Quarterly Press, 1993.

———. *The Supreme Court Compendium: Data, Decisions and Developments.* 2d ed. Washington, DC: Congressional Quarterly Press, 1996.

Epstein, Lee, Thomas G. Walker, and William J. Dixon. "The Supreme Court and Criminal Justice Disputes: A Neo-Institutional Perspective." *American Journal of Political Science* 33 (1989): 825–41.

Freund, Paul A. *Federal Judicial Center Report of the Study Group on the Case Load of the Supreme Court.* Washington, DC: Administrative Office, U.S. Courts for Federal Judicial Center, 1972.

Furer, Howard B. *The Fuller Court, 1888–1910.* Vol. 5 of *The Supreme Court in American Life.* New York: Associated Faculty Press, 1986.

Gates, John B. *The Supreme Court and Partisan Realignment: A Macro- and Microlevel Perspective.* Boulder, CO: Westview Press, 1992.

Gibson, James L. "Judges' Role Orientations, Attitudes and Decisions: An Interactive Model." *American Political Science Review* 71 (1978): 911–24.

Gideon v. Wainwright. 372 US 335 (1963).

Gitlow v. New York. 268 US 652 (1925).

Glick, Henry. *Courts, Politics, and Justice.* 3d ed. New York: McGraw-Hill, 1993.

Goldman, Sheldon. "Voting Behavior on the United States Courts of Appeals Revisited." *American Political Science Review* 69 (1975): 461–506.

Granger, Clive W. J. "Long Memory Relationships and the Aggregation of Dynamic Models." *Journal of Econometrics* 14 (1980): 227–38.

Granger, Clive W. J., and Roselyne Joyeux. "An Introduction to Long-Memory Time Series Models and Fractional Differencing." *Journal of Time Series* 1 (1980): 15–29.

Griswold v. Connecticut. 381 US 479 (1965).

Gujarati, Damodar N. *Basic Econometrics.* 3d ed. New York: McGraw-Hill, 1995.

Hague v. CIO. 307 US 496 (1939).

Hall, Kermit, ed. *The Oxford Companion to the Supreme Court.* New York: Oxford University Press, 1992.

Halpern, Stephen G., and Kenneth N. Vines. "Institutional Disunity, The Judges' Bill, and the Role of the U.S. Supreme Court." *Western Political Quarterly* 30 (1977): 471–83.

Hammer v. Dagenhart. 247 US 251 (1918).

Hand, Learned. *The Bill of Rights.* Cambridge: Harvard University Press, 1958.

Handberg, Roger, Jr. "Decision-Making in a Natural Court, 1916–1921." *American Politics Quarterly* 4 (1976): 357–78.

Handberg, Roger, and C. Neal Tate. "Length of Service and the Behavior of U.S. Supreme Court Justices, 1916–1989." Paper presented at the annual meeting of the Midwest Political Science Association, Chicago, IL, April 1990.

Haynie, Stacia L. "Leadership and Consensus on the U.S. Supreme Court." *The Journal of Politics* 54 (1992): 1158–69.

Haynie, Stacia L., and C. Neal Tate. "Institutional Liberalism in the United States Supreme Court, 1916–1988: An Explanation of Economics and Civil Rights and Liberties Cases." Paper presented at the annual meeting of the American Political Science Association, San Francisco, CA, August–September 1990.

Horwitz, Morton J. *The Transformation of American Law, 1870–1960.* New York: Oxford University Press, 1992.

Hosking, J. R. M. "Fractional Differencing." *Biometrika* 68 (1981): 165–76.

Hughes, Charles Evans. *The Supreme Court of the United States.* New York: Columbia University Press, 1928.

In Re Debs. 158 US 564 (1895).

Jackson, Robert H. *The Struggle for Judicial Supremacy.* New York: Alfred A. Knopf, 1941.

Johnston, Richard E. "Supreme Court Voting Behavior: A Comparison of the Warren and Burger Courts." In *Cases in American Politics,* edited by Robert L. Peabody. New York: Praeger, 1976.

Kens, Paul. *Judicial Power and Reform Politics: The Anatomy of* Lochner v. New York. Lawrence: University Press of Kansas, 1990.

Key, V. O., Jr. *Southern Politics in State and Nation.* Knoxville: University of Tennessee Press, 1949.

Knight, Jack. *Institutions and Social Conflict.* New York: Cambridge University Press, 1992.

Knight, Jack, and Itai Sened. *Explaining Social Institutions.* Ann Arbor: University of Michigan Press, 1995.

Korematsu v. United States. 323 US 214 (1944).

Kwiatkowski, Denis, Peter C. B. Phillips, Peter Schmidt, and Yongcheol Shin. "Testing the Null Hypothesis of Stationarity against the Alternative of a Unit Root." *Journal of Econometrics* 54 (1992): 159–78.

Lanier, Drew Noble, and Mark S. Hurwitz. "Traversing the Bounds of Consensus: The Long-Run Relationship between Concurring and Dissenting Opinions in the U.S. Supreme Court, 1888–1997." Paper presented at the annual meeting of the American Political Science Association, Atlanta, GA, September 1999.

Lanier, Drew Noble, and Sandra L. Wood. "Moving on Up: Institutional Position, Politics, and the Chief Justice." *The American Review of Politics* 22 (2001): 93–127.

Laswell, Harold. *Power and Personality.* New York: W. W. Norton, 1948.

Leavitt, Donald C. "Attitudes and Ideology on the White Supreme Court, 1910–1920." Ph.D. diss., Michigan State University, 1970.

Lebo, Matthew J. "Fractional Integration and Political Modeling." Ph.D. diss., University of North Texas, 1999.

Lebo, Matthew J., and Robert W. Walker. "Long Memory and Fractional Cointegration in Models of British Politics." Paper presented at the annual meeting of the Midwest Political Science Association, Chicago, IL, April 1999.

Lebo, Matthew J., Robert W. Walker, and Harold D. Clarke. "You Must Remember This: Dealing with Long Memory in Political Analyses." Paper presented at the annual meeting of the American Political Science Association, Boston, MA, September 1998.

Lerner, Max. *Ideas for the Ice Age*. New York: Viking Press, 1941.

Lipset, Seymour M., and Stein Rokkan. "Cleavage Structures, Party Systems, and Voting Alignments." In *Party Systems and Voter Alignments*, edited by Seymour M. Lipset and Stein Rokkan. New York: Free Press, 1967.

Lochner v. New York. 198 US 45 (1905).

Lovell v. Griffin. 303 US 444 (1938).

MacKinnon, James C. "Critical Values for Cointegration Tests." In *Long-Run Economic Relationships: Readings in Cointegration*, edited by Robert F. Engle and Clive W. J. Granger. New York: Oxford University Press, 1991.

Maltzman, Forrest, and Paul J. Wahlbeck. "May It Please the Chief? Opinion Assignments in the Rehnquist Court." *American Journal of Political Science* 40 (1996): 421–43.

Maltzman, Forrest, James F. Spriggs, and Paul J. Wahlbeck. "Strategy and Judicial Choice: New Institutionalist Approaches to Supreme Court Decision-Making." In *Supreme Court Decision-Making*, edited by Cornell W. Clayton and Howard Gillman. Chicago: University of Chicago Press, 1999.

Mason, Alpheus T. *Harlan Fiske Stone: Pillar of the Law*. New York: Viking Press, 1956.

———. *The Supreme Court from Taft to Warren*. Baton Rouge: Louisiana State University Press, 1958.

Mattingly, Mary R. "The Hughes Court, 1931–36." Ph.D. diss., Michigan State University, 1969.

McCloskey, Robert G. *The American Supreme Court*. 2d ed. Chicago: University of Chicago Press, 1994.

McDowell, David, Richard McClearly, Errol E. Meidinger, and Richard A. Hay, Jr. *Interrupted Time Series*. Beverly Hills, CA: Sage Publications, 1980.

Mishler, William, and Reginald S. Sheehan. "The Supreme Court as a Countermajoritarian Institution: The Impact of Public Opinion on Supreme Court Decisions." *American Political Science Review* 87 (1993): 87–101.

Muller v. Oregon. 208 US 412 (1908).

Murdock v. Pennsylvania. 319 US 105 (1943).

Murphy, Walter F. *Elements of Judicial Strategy*. Chicago: University of Chicago Press, 1964.

Murphy, Walter F., and C. Herman Pritchett. *Courts, Judges, and Politics: An Introduction to the Judicial Process*. 4th ed. New York: McGraw-Hill, 1986.

Myers v. United States. 272 US 52 (1926).

National Labor Relations Board v. Jones & Laughlin Steel Corp. 301 US 1 (1937).

Near v. Minnesota. 283 US 697 (1931).

Nebbia v. New York. 291 US 502 (1934).

O'Brien, David M. *Storm Center: The Supreme Court in American Politics*. 5th ed. New York: W. W. Norton, 2000.

Olmstead v. United States. 277 US 438 (1928).

Ordeshook, Peter C. *A Political Theory Primer*. New York: Routledge, 1992.

Pacelle, Richard L., Jr. *The Transformation of the Supreme Court's Agenda: From the New Deal to the Reagan Administration*. Boulder, CO: Westview Press, 1991.

Palko v. Connecticut. 302 US 319 (1937).

Pindyck, Robert S., and Daniel L. Rubinfeld. *Econometric Models and Economic Forecasts.* 3d ed. New York: McGraw-Hill, 1991.

Plessy v. Ferguson. 163 US 537 (1896).

Pollock v. Farmers' Loan and Trust Co. 158 US 601 (1895).

Pritchett, C. Herman. "Division of Opinion Among Justices of the U.S. Supreme Court, 1939–1941." *American Political Science Review* 35 (1941): 890–98.

———. *The Roosevelt Court: A Study in Judicial Politics and Values, 1937–1947.* New York: Macmillan, 1948.

Rabban, David M. "The First Amendment in its Forgotten Years." *The Yale Law Journal* 90 (1981): 514–95.

———. "The Free Speech League, the ACLU, and Changing Conceptions of Free Speech in American History." *Stanford Law Review* 45 (1992): 47–114.

Renstrom, Peter George. "The Dimensionality of Decision-Making of the 1941–1945 Stone Court: A Computer Dependent Analysis of Supreme Court Behavior." Ph.D. diss., Michigan State University, 1972.

Robinson, Peter M. "Gaussian Semi-Parametric Estimation of Long Range Dependence." *Annals of Statistics* 23 (1995): 1630–61.

Rohde, David W., and Kenneth A. Shepsle. "Thinking about Legislative Reform." In *Legislative Reform: The Policy Impact,* edited by Leroy N. Rieselbach. Lexington, MA: Lexington Books, 1978.

Schenck v. United States. 249 US 47 (1919).

Schlesinger, Arthur M. "The Supreme Court: 1947." *Fortune* 35 (1947): 78.

Schmidhauser, John. *Constitutional Law in the Political Process.* Chicago: Rand McNally, 1963.

Schubert, Glendon A. *Quantitative Analysis of Judicial Behavior.* Glencoe, IL: Free Press, 1959.

———. *The Judicial Mind: Attitudes and Ideologies of Supreme Court Justices, 1946–1963.* Evanston, IL: Northwestern University Press, 1965.

———. *The Judicial Mind Revisited: Psychometric Analysis of Supreme Court Ideology.* New York: Oxford University Press, 1974.

Schwartz, Bernard. *A History of the Supreme Court.* New York: Oxford University Press, 1993.

Schwartz, Edward P. "The Proliferation of Concurring Opinions on the U.S. Supreme Court: Politics Killed the Norm." Paper presented at the annual meeting of the American Law and Economics Association, Toronto, ON, 1997.

Scigliano, Robert. *The Supreme Court and the Presidency.* New York: Free Press, 1971.

Scott v. Sanford. 60 US 393 (1857).

Segal, Jeffrey A. "Separation-of-Powers Games in the Positive Theory of Congress and Courts." *American Political Science Review* 91 (1997): 28–44.

Segal, Jeffrey A., and Albert D. Cover. "Ideological Values and the Votes of U.S. Supreme Court Justices." *American Political Science Review* 83 (1989): 557–65.

Segal, Jeffrey A., Lee Epstein, Charles M. Cameron, and Harold J. Spaeth. "Ideological Values and the Votes of U.S. Supreme Court Justices Revisited." *The Journal of Politics* 57 (1995): 812–23.

Segal, Jeffrey A., and Harold J. Spaeth. *The Supreme Court and the Attitudinal Model.* New York: Cambridge University Press, 1993.

Slaughterhouse Cases. 83 US 36 (1873).

Spaeth, Harold J. United States Supreme Court Judicial Data Base, 1953–1997 Terms Computer File. 9th ICPSR Version. East Lansing: Michigan State University, Dept. of Political Science producer. Ann Arbor: Inter-University Consortium for Political and Social Research Distributor, 1999.

Steamer, Robert J. *Chief Justice: Leadership and the Supreme Court*. Columbia: University of South Carolina Press, 1986.

Swindler, William F. *Court and Constitution in the 20th Century: The Old Legality, 1889–1932*. Indianapolis, IN: Bobbs-Merrill, 1969.

Tate, C. Neal. "Personal Attribute Models of the Voting Behavior of U.S. Supreme Court Justices: Liberalism in Civil Liberties and Economics Decisions, 1946–1978." *American Political Science Review* 75 (1981): 355–67.

———. "The Methodology of Judicial Behavior Research: A Review and Critique." *Political Behavior* 5 (1983): 51–82.

Tate, C. Neal, and Roger Handberg. "Time Binding and Theory Building in Personal Attribute Models of Supreme Court Voting Behavior, 1916–1988." *American Journal of Political Science* 35 (1991): 460–80.

Ulmer, S. Sidney. "Social Background as an Indicator to the Votes of Supreme Court Justices in Criminal Cases." *Midwest Journal of Political Science* 17 (1973): 622–30.

———. "Selecting Cases for Supreme Court Review: An Underdog Model." *American Political Science Review* 72 (1978): 902–10.

———. "Are Social Background Models Timebound?" *American Political Science Review* 80 (1986): 957–67.

United States v. Carolene Products. 304 US 144 (1938).

United States v. Darby Lumber Co. 312 US 100 (1941).

United States v. E. C. Knight Co. 156 US 1 (1895).

Urofsky, Melvin I. "Myth and Reality: The Supreme Court and Protective Legislation in the Progressive Era." In *Yearbook of the Supreme Court Historical Society*. Washington, DC: Supreme Court Historical Society, 1983.

Vinson, Fred M. "The Role of Dissent." In *The Judiciary*, edited by John Roche and Leonard Levy. New York: Harcourt, Brace, 1964.

Walker, Thomas G., Lee Epstein, and William J. Dixon. "On the Mysterious Demise of Consensual Norms in the United States Supreme Court." *The Journal of Politics* 50 (1988): 361–89.

Warren, Charles. "The Progressiveness of the United States Supreme Court." *Columbia Law Review* 13 (1913): 294–313.

Wasby, Stephen L. *The Supreme Court in the Federal System*. Chicago: Nelson-Hall Publishers, 1993.

West Coast Hotel Co. v. Parrish. 300 US 379 (1937).

West Virginia State Board of Education v. Barnette. 319 US 624 (1943).

Wilson, James Q., and John J. DiIulio, Jr. *American Government: Institutions and Policies*. 8th ed. Boston: Houghton Mifflin, 2001.

Wilson v. New. 243 US 332 (1917).

Witt, Elder. *Congressional Quarterly's Guide to the U.S. Supreme Court*. 2d ed. Washington, DC: Congressional Quarterly Press, 1990.

Wood, Sandra L. "In the Shadow of the Chief: The Role of the Senior Associate Justice on the United States Supreme Court." Ph.D. diss., University of Minnesota, 1994.

Wood, Sandra L., Linda Camp Keith, Drew Noble Lanier, and Ayo Ogundele. "Is the Attitudinal Model of Supreme Court Decision Making Time-Bound?" Paper presented at the annual meeting of the Southern Political Science Association, Tampa, Fl., November 1995.

Yakus v. United States. 321 US 414 (1944).

Index

Italicized page numbers relate to illustrations. Bold page numbers refer to tables.

Court, 167, 170; comparison to
Warren Court, 170; and concurring
opinions, 110, 111; criminal procedure
decision-making, 146; and decline of
consensual norms, 124, 127, 219;
dissenting opinions' rate in, 125; due
process decision-making, 151, 153;
economic decisions and, 132, 139;
economics dimension decision-making,
167, 169, 215; federalism decision-
making of, 55, 155, 157; First
Amendment decision-making, 150; as
forerunner of White Court, 119; and
Franklin D. Roosevelt's Court-packing
plan, 49; Franklin D. Roosevelt's
influence on, 54; Haynie's findings on,
110, 214; and Holmes's influence, 54;
initial opposition to New Deal, 52–53;
judicial power decision-making, 142,
171; later economic rulings, 53, 54;
multiple dissent rate, 123, 124, 214;
and *Nebbia v. New York*, 53; pre- and
post-1937 voting coalitions, 52–53;
political context's influence on, 49;
post-1937 membership changes, 54;
response to Great Depression, 53; shift
in decision-making, 53–54, 54, 55;
unanimity and, 105–6, 110–11, 213,
218, 219; uniqueness, 49; union
decision-making, 55, 161; voting
coalitions, 189; and *West Coast Hotel Co.
Parish*, 53. *See also individual justices'
names*

In Re Debs: Fuller Court decision in, 51
Income Tax Act of 1894: Fuller Court's
invalidation, 40
Interstate Commerce Act, 33

Jackson, Howell E., 35; educational and
familial background, 36; illness of, and
Court service, 36, 98; judicial and
political experience, 36; nomination by
Cleveland to appellate court, 36;
nomination by Benjamin Harrison to
Supreme Court, 36; and *Pollack v.
Farmers' Loan and Trust Co.*, 36; service
in Confederate government, 36; views
of, 36
Jackson, Robert H.: educational and
familial background of, 56; govern-

mental service of, 56; on judiciary's
check on elective branches, 53; and
lack of support for civil liberties, 21; as
member of Stone Court, 56, 57; as
New Deal proponent, 56; nomination
of, by Franklin D. Roosevelt, 56; and
Nuremburg Trials, 56; private practice
of, 56; views of, in economic and civil
liberties questions, 56–57
Jefferson, Thomas, 244–45n. 17
Johnson, Lyndon Baines: policy intentions
in nominations, 183
Johnston, Richard E.: on link between
judicial experience and decision-
making, 184, 185
Joyeux, Roselyene, 247n. 107
Judges' Bill. *See* Judiciary Act of 1925
Judicial Mind, The, 18; as extension of
Pritchett, 24
Judicial Mind Revisited, The, 18
Judiciary Act of 1925: association with
Court's docket, 20, 63, 120–21;
influence on judicial-power decision-
making, 142, **205**, 206, 218, 247n.
105; multiple dissents and, 123–24;
Taft's influence on, 46; and unanimity,
121, 213

Keith, Linda Camp, 61
Kennedy, Anthony, 28
Key, V. O., Jr.: definition of the South, 184
Knight, Jack: on rational choice decision-
making, 177, 244–45n. 17
Korematsu v. United States, 52, 58, 206
Kwiatkowski, Denis: stationarity test of,
197, **199**, **201**, 250n. 129

Lamar, Joseph R.: as anti-Progressive, 44;
effect of Civil War on views, 43;
familial background, 43; as member of
White Court, 42; nomination by Taft,
43; political experience, 43; and
private practice, 43; views on economic and civil liberties–civil rights
questions, 43
Lamar, Lucius Q. C., 32: as author of
Mississippi secession ordinance, 34;
educational and familial background,
34; nomination by Cleveland, 35;
private practice and political involvement, 34–35; views on economic and

economic decision-making, 132, 139; economics dimension decision-making, 167, 169, 215; federal taxation decision-making and, 142; federalism decision-making, 155, 157; First Amendment decision-making, 150; as forerunner to Warren Court, 151; judicial power decision-making, 144, 171; as progeny of White Court, 119; multiple dissent rate of, 123, 124, 214; preparation to meet World War II's challenges, 57–58; Pritchett on decision-making of, 146; unanimity rate of, 106, 124, 213–14, 218, 219; union decision-making, 161; and views on civil liberties, 21; views in civil rights questions, 58; voting blocs, 57; World War II and, 57–58, 174. *See also individual justices' names*

Supreme Court Compendium, The, 182, 183, 184, 185

Sutherland, George: death, 51; friendship with Harding, 47; legal and political background, 47; as member of Four Horsemen of the Apocalypse, 47, 52, 119, 167, 213; as member of Hughes Court, 49; as member of Taft Court, 46, 47; replacement by Reed, 51; views, 47, 189, 247n. 80

Swindler, William F.: on sociological changes in the late 1880s to 1930s, 31

Taft, William Howard, 31; as chief justice, 46, 84; comparison of Hughes's nomination (as chief justice) with that of Warren, 42; comparison to Wilson as Progressive, 45; and coveting of chief justice position, 46; as friend of Lurton, 39; policy intentions of in nominations, 183; judicial and political experience, 46; and Judiciary Act of 1925, 46; and nomination of Hughes (as associate justice), 42; nomination of Joseph Lamar, 43; nomination of Van Devanter, 43; nomination of Harding, 46; policy intentions of in nominations, 183; presidential service, 46, 244n. 15; and service of McReynolds, 43; social context of tenure as chief justice, 48; on unanimity's importance, 98, 213; views on Court, 46, 119, 167

Taft Court, 46–49; attorneys' decision-making of, 159; Brandeis's influence on, 48; civil liberties–civil rights decision-making, 48, 170; civil rights cases on agenda, 146; civil rights decision-making, 148; comparison to Fuller Court, 167; comparison to Hughes Court, 119, 170; comparison to Rehnquist Court, 144; comparison to White Court, 167; and concurring opinions, 110, 111; and concurring votes, 107; criminal procedure decision-making, 146; and dissenting opinions, 125; and dissenting votes, 117, 119; due process decision-making, 151, 153; economic decision-making, 48, 132, 139; economics dimension decision-making, 167, 215, 219; federal taxation decision-making and, 141–42; federalism decision-making, 155; First Amendment decision-making of, 148, 150; and judicial power decision-making, 142, 171; membership of, 46; membership change and, 167; multiple dissent rate of, 123, 124, 214; response to Great Depression, 48; separation of powers decision-making, 48; as spark for due process revolution, 48; and sociological context of decision-making, 48; unanimity rate of, 106, 213; union decision-making, 161; views, 146, 167

Tate, C. Neal: on agricultural origins' effect on policy views, 183; and civil liberties and economic decision-making, 27; on career experience and decision-making, 185, 191–92; comparison with present study, 168, 217; on economics dimension decision-making, 169; on Great Depression's and decision-making, 187, 216; judicial experience index of, 185; and pre-1945 civil liberties–civil rights dimension findings, 28, 170; on pre-1945 economic decision-making, 28, 181; and use of personal attribute models in pre-1945 period, 28; on utility of personal attribute models, 27; on World War II and decision-making, 204

Teapot Dome scandal, 49